THE BARCELONA PROCESS
Building a Euro-Mediterranean Regional Community

Of Related Interest

PERSPECTIVES ON DEVELOPMENT
The Euro-Mediterranean Partnership
edited by George Joffé

THE EURO-MEDITERRANEAN PARTNERSHIP
Political and Economic Perspectives
edited by Richard Gillespie

SOUTHERN EUROPEAN WELFARE STATES
Between Crisis and Reform
edited by Martin Rhodes

FEDERALISM, UNIFICATION AND EUROPEAN INTEGRATION
edited by Charlie Jeffery and Roland Sturm

THE CRISIS OF REPRESENTATION IN EUROPE
edited by Jack Hayward

'EUROPEANISATION' AND THE SOUTHERN PERIPHERY
edited by Kevin Featherstone and George Kazamias

THE REGIONAL DIMENSION OF THE EUROPEAN UNION
Towards a Third Level in Europe?
edited by Charlie Jeffery

THE BARCELONA PROCESS

Building a Euro-Mediterranean
Regional Community

Edited by

ÁLVARO VASCONCELOS

and

GEORGE JOFFÉ

FRANK CASS
LONDON • PORTLAND, OR

First published in 2000 in Great Britain by
FRANK CASS PUBLISHERS
Newbury House, 900 Eastern Avenue
London IG2 7HH, England

and in the United States of America by
FRANK CASS PUBLISHERS
c/o ISBS
5804 N.E. Hassalo Street
Portland, Oregon 97213–3644

Website: www.frankcass.com

British Library Cataloguing in Publication Data

The Barcelona Process : building a Euro-Mediterranean regional community
  1. European Union – Mediterranean Region 2. Free trade –
  Mediterranean Region 3. National security – Mediterranean
  Region 4. Mediterranean Region – Economic policy
  5. Mediterranean Region – Foreign economic relations – European
  Union Countries 6. European Union Countries – Foreign economic
  relations – Mediterranean Region
  I. Vasconcelos, Alvaro II. Joffe, E.G.H. (E George H)
  337.4'01822

  ISBN 0 7146 5109 5 (cloth)
  ISBN 0 7146 8147 4 (paper)

Library of Congress Cataloging-in-Publication Data

The Barcelona process : building a Euro-Mediterranean regional community
/ edited by Alvaro Vasconcelos and George Joffe.
      p. cm.
    Special issue of the journal 'Mediterranean politics', vol. 5/1, Spring 2000.
    Includes bibliographical references and index.
    ISBN 0-7146-5109-5 (cloth) – ISBN 0-7146-8147-4 (pbk.)
      1. Europe–Foreign relations – Mediterranean Region. 2. Mediterranean
  Region – Foreign Relations – Europe. 3. Europe – Economic integration.
  4. Mediterranean Region – Economic integration. I. Vasconcelos, Alvaro.
  II. Joffâe, E. G. H. (E. George H.) III. Mediterranean politics (Frank Cass & Co.)
  D1065.M628 B37 2000
  327.40182'2–dc21

                                                          00-034647

This group of studies first appeared in a Special Issue on 'The Barcelona Process: Building a
Euro-Mediterranean Regional Community' of *Mediterranean Politics* (ISSN 1362-9395)
5/1 (Spring 2000) published by Frank Cass.

Contents

List of Abbreviations   vii

INTRODUCTION
1. Towards Euro-Mediterranean Regional Integration
   Álvaro Vasconcelos and George Joffé   3

ECONOMIC CHANGE
2. The Euro-Mediterranean Free Trade Zone: Economic Challenges
   and Social Impacts on the Countries of the South and East
   Mediterranean
   Hafedh Zaafrane and Azzem Mahjoub   9

3. Foreign Investment and the Rule of Law
   George Joffé   33

THE POLITICAL PROCESS
4. Political Transition in the Middle East
   May Chartouni-Dubarry   53

5. Democratization in the Mashreq: The Role of External Factors
   Mustafa Hamarneh   77

6. Political Reform and Social Change in the Maghreb
   Gema Martin-Muñoz   96

SECURITY ISSUES IN THE MEDITERRANEAN
7. Towards a New WMD Agenda in the Euro-Mediterranean
   Partnership: An Arab Perspective
   Mohammed El-Sayed Selim   133

8. Weapons of Mass Destruction and Euro-Mediterranean Policies
   of Arms Control: An Israeli Perspective
   Mark A. Heller   158

9. Arms Control in the Mediterranean Area: A European
   Perspective
   Pascal Boniface   167

10. The Euro-Mediterranean Security Partnership: Prospects for
    Arms Limitation and Confidence-Building
    Fred Tanner   189

CONCLUSION
11. Challenges and Prospects
    Roberto Aliboni and Abdel Monem Said Aly   209

Notes on Contributors   225

Index   227

List of Abbreviations

AC	Arms Control
ACDA	Arms Control and Disarmament Agency
ACRS	[Working Group on] Arms Control and Regional Security
APMs	Anti-Personnel Mines
ASMP	Air-sol moyenne porté (Medium-range air-to-ground) [missiles]
BWC	Biological Weapon Convention
CBMs	Confidence-Building Measures
CCW	Convention on Prohibition or Restriction of the Use for Conventional Weapons Deemed to be Excessively Injurious or to have Indiscriminate Effects
CFSP	Common Foreign and Security Policy
CIA	Central Intelligence Agency
CSBMs	Confidence- and Security-Building Measures
CTBT	Comprehensive Test Ban Treaty
CWC	Chemical Weapons Convention
CSCE	Conference on Security and Co-operation in Europe
CSCME	Conference on Security and Co-operation in the Middle East
DPKO	UN Department of Peace-keeping Operations
ECU	European Currency Unit - Euro
EMP	Euro-Mediterranean Partnership
ESDI	European Security and Defence Identity
EU	European Union
IAEA	International Atomic Energy Agency
IDF	Israel Defence Force
INCSEAS	Prevention of Incidents at Sea Agreement
INF	Intermediate-range Nuclear Force
IISS	International Institute of Strategic Studies
IRIS	Institut de Relations Internationales et Stratégiques
ISIS	International Security Information System
MEADS	Medium Extended Air Defence System
MENA	Middle East and North Africa
MTCR	Missile Technology Control Regime
NATO	North Atlantic Treaty Organization

NBC	Nuclear-Biological-Chemical [Weapons]
NGOs	Non-Governmental Organizations
NPT	Non-Proliferation Treaty
OAS	Organization of American States
OAU	Organization of African Unity
OSCE	Organization for Security and Co-operation in Europe
PLO	Palestine Liberation Organisation
REDWG	Regional Economic Development Working Group
SALT	Strategic Arms Limitation Talks
SAR	Search and rescue operations
SIPRI	Stockholm International Peace Research Institute
START	Strategic Arms Reduction Talks
TNP	*see* NPT
UK	United Kingdom
UEO	*see* WEU
UN	United Nations
UNIDIR	United Nations Institute for Disarmament Research
UNSCOM	United Nations Special Commission on Iraq
US/USA	United States of America
USSR	Union of the Soviet Socialist Republics
WEU	Western European Union
WMD	Weapons of Mass Destruction
WMDFZ	Weapons of Mass Destruction Free Zone
WTO	World Trade Organisation

Introduction

1

Towards Euro-Mediterranean Regional Integration

ÁLVARO VASCONCELOS and GEORGE JOFFÉ

The Euro-Mediterranean Partnership, which was launched in Barcelona in November 1995, is the first real initiative designed to expand European economic integration towards the South. The objective is to apply in North Africa and the Middle East the model developed successfully in Europe, even though the conditions in this new region are different and the means available for doing so are more limited. In other words, the objective is to create a zone of economic development, democracy and peace through a process of integration, even though this is a strategy that can only yield its results in the long term.

One of the major reasons for this is that such an approach to regional security – and in seeking to create a zone of peace and stability, the Barcelona Process is acutely concerned with security – requires a far more complex approach than was the case in the past. It is not merely a question of conflict resolution but of building mutual confidence and trust within a context of political change and economic success. It is evident that peace and security cannot be established simply by resolving inter-state conflicts such as the Arab–Israeli conflict, for political, economic and social considerations, such as economic under-development, unemployment and illiteracy, also play a role, not to mention other issues including abuses of human rights, lack of the rule-of-law and democratic deficits. Dealing with such problems in ways that produce long-term and equitable effects is a slow and incremental process in which the mechanisms involved will require constant attention and modification as problems emerge.

The key and proximate objective is to establish a Euro-Mediterranean regional grouping which will be based on the construction of a common free trade area by the year 2010. The Barcelona Process, however, sought to reach beyond this economic horizon by intensifying cross-Mediterranean co-operation in political and social spheres as well, although in more tentative ways than those proposed for economic change. Inevitably, however, the difficulties which confront the Process are, perhaps, as great as its potential for success, as the various contributions to this book make clear. Its contents have resulted from the academic activities of the group of institutes of international relations brought together in the EuroMeSCo network, a network created in response to the Barcelona Process with the encouragement of the European Commission as a confidence-building measure and involving the 27 countries within the Euro-Mediterranean Partnership.

The creation of an integrated free trade area in the Mediterranean has been hampered by the lack of South–South co-operation and has, to date, been limited to association agreements between the European Union and individual countries in the South, on a bilateral basis. Furthermore, agricultural trade issues, which are vital concerns for the Southern economies, have not been included in the association agreements. In addition – and perhaps even more important – the social consequences of trade liberalisation without substantive support measures is unlikely to be positive. The South Mediterranean is a region which, after all, has already undergone extensive and painful economic restructuring but still fails to attract significant amounts of foreign private investment which might, otherwise, ease the pain of further transition and restructuring. The MEDA (Mesures d'Adjustement) Programmes, which are European Commission five-year aid programmes offering private sector and regional funding to help ease the process of transition in the South Mediterranean partner countries is a positive initiative but insufficient to compensate for the social disruption that the transition process will cause.

Yet, without increased funds, the social and economic – and even the political – impact of the free trade area now under construction will have to depend on increased inflows of private investments, attracted by terms and conditions that the countries of North Africa and the Middle East will be able to offer. Unless there is a radical change in the nature of these flows, the outlook is grim, for investment, particularly from Europe, is not directed towards the southern shores of the Mediterranean. Amongst the reasons for this, alongside questions of competitive rates-of-return and comparative advantage, are the lack of attractive investment codes and inadequacies in judicial systems and the rule-of-law, as well as the market restrictions implicit in the lack of sub-regional economic integration, as Azzam Mahzoub, Hafedh Zaafrane and George Joffé point out. In short, increased investment flows towards the states of the South Mediterranean will depend primarily on the success of political reform there, particularly in the context of 'good governance'.

Indeed, this is the key question that is considered in the second section of this volume. May Chartouni-Dubarry, Gema Martin Muñoz and Mustafa Hamarneh all discuss the difficulties facing a successful outcome of political transition in the South Mediterranean region, a process which has been rendered both more delicate and more necessary by the social crisis which these countries face. The strengthening of democracy and the respect for human rights which forms a key element of the Barcelona Declaration is essential for the success of the Partnership.

Yet progress in these fields has been hesitant and limited, even though the creation of a Euro-Mediterranean regional grouping must involve the intensified participation of civil society on both sides of the Mediterranean in the process. Within the context of the Euro-Mediterranean Partnership, the global cross-Mediterranean, as well as the South Mediterranean and European sub-regional, dialogues on democracy and human rights must be overtly and expressly linked with a parallel debate on rights to religious and cultural diversity. Indeed, particular attention should be given to such issues of cultural and religious rights, as well as to the rights of migrants and to the right of free movement amongst the members of the Partnership. This is a process which should also evolve outside the confines of formal government, as civil societies on both the Northern and Southern shores of the Mediterranean reinforce their common bonds and interests.

These issues are often linked in Europe to wider security concerns. Yet, in this field, the Partnership has made little progress, as the contributions by Pascal Boniface, Mark Heller, Mohamed Selim and Fred Tanner demonstrate. At the same time, the Partnership has managed to maintain an open dialogue between the European Union and its twelve Southern partners, despite the blockages in the peace process, thus providing an important contribution to building mutual North–South confidence. In reality, however, most of the major security concerns do not reflect North–South concerns but involve sub-regional issues within the South itself – a domain which the Partnership does not cover. The free trade zone must, therefore, be complemented by cooperation in conflict prevention and arms control at the sub-regional and regional levels.

One of the most striking aspects of the current Partnership is the asymmetry that exists between the two regions – North and South – in institutional terms. The European Union is a clearly defined actor but the Maghreb and the Middle East are notable for the lack of institutionalized regional groupings. Interestingly enough, the free trade zone system should be able to contribute to a change in this situation. Membership of it should necessarily imply improvement in diplomatic relations between neighbour-states, as well as meaningful co-operation between the two sub-regions of the Maghreb and the Mashreq.

If this is to be achieved, association agreements between states in the South are essential as the first stage in constructing the integrated Southern region that the Union has proposed after 2010, which itself is an essential step towards a genuinely integrated multilateral cooperative free trade region equally involvinmg all 27 states in the Partnership. Such sub-regional co-operation would be a vital tool for achieving the Partnership's objectives successfully and for creating a more balanced relationship across and within the Mediterranean region. Its success would ensure sub-regional integration which is key to the interests of the Partnership itself, whose members must use their best efforts to achieve peaceful solutions to the problems that they confront and which themselves prevent regional integration.

Acknowledgements

The editors of this volume and the member institutes of the EuroMeSCo network would like to acknowledge the financial support of the European Commission without which the research leading to this study could not have been undertaken.

The editors would also like to thank the Western European Union Institute for Security Studies in Paris for its generosity in covering the production costs of this volume.

Economic Change

2

The Euro-Mediterranean Free Trade Zone: Economic Challenges and Social Impacts on the Countries of the South and East Mediterranean

HAFEDH ZAAFRANE and AZZEM MAHJOUB

The Barcelona Process, when it was first introduced in 1995 in the Barcelona Declaration, was a holistic initiative designed to address the issue of creating a shared zone of peace, prosperity and stability in the Mediterranean basin. It drew, of course, on earlier, bilateral initiatives undertaken by the European Union towards the states of the South and East Mediterranean (CSEM) which had been largely economic in nature and, given its overall objectives, it is not surprising that the Barcelona Process itself also highlights the future economic relationship. However, this is not all that it does and, alongside proposals for bilateral free trade areas designed to stimulate industrial activity and trade, there are specific recommendations for multilateral progress in political, security, cultural and social fields. At the same time, the economic dimension of the Process will have quite clear social consequences and it is towards these issues that this discussion is directed.

Linking the Economic Partnership with Other Partnerships

The general objective set by the signatories of the Barcelona Declaration during the Euro-Mediterranean conference of 27–28 November 1995 stated that: 'Turning the Mediterranean region into an area of dialogue, exchange and co-operation guaranteeing peace, stability and prosperity requires a strengthening of democracy and respect for human rights, sustainable and balanced economic and social development, measures to combat poverty and the promotion of greater understanding between cultures, which are all essential aspects of the Partnership.'

This vision can be articulated diagrammatically in the following manner:

Dialogue		Peace		Democracy
Exchange	**➡**	Stability	**⬅**	Economic development
	guarantee		imply	
Co-operation		Shared prosperity		Social, human and cultural development

A threefold proposition which can be derived from this diagram provides the foundations for a global Euro-Mediterranean Partnership, as envisaged in the Barcelona Declaration:

- political and security partnership, to define an arena of peace and stability;
- economic and financial partnership, to build an area of shared prosperity;
- social, cultural and human partnership, to develop human resources, promote greater inter-cultural understanding and exchanges between civil societies.

On this basis, the Barcelona Process can now be systematised according to the following diagram:

Outcomes	Means	Mechanisms
Peace	Democracy	Dialogue
Stability	Economic development	Exchanges
Shared prosperity	Social, human and cultural development	Co-operation

The diagram immediately provokes one question, concerning the nature of this approach to the problems of the region – is it intended to be an integrated approach and do the three types of partnership described, although presented separately, provide the foundations of a comprehensive and integrated partnership? In other words, to what extent is the Euro-Mediterranean project coherent and cohesive? This, in essence, is the problem we wish to address.

The Objectives: Are Peace, Stability and Shared Prosperity Separable?

Is the establishment of an area of peace and stability – essentially through political dialogue and with a view to consolidating the rule-of-law, democracy, respect for human rights and fundamental freedoms – separable from the creation of an area of shared prosperity based on free trade and economic and financial co-operation in order to encourage balanced economic and social development? Similarly, are peace, stability and shared prosperity conceivable without social, human and cultural development being accompanied by economic development, itself based on the rule-of-law where fundamental social rights are respected, including the right to development?

The answer to both these questions has to be in the negative and the object of this paper is to demonstrate that economic and financial development, which are seen in the Process to depend on the establishment of a Euro-Mediterranean free trade zone, are inseparable from the other partnerships to be established in the political, security, social, human and cultural fields. In reality, there are links and dialectical interactions between the various forms of partnership and between the outcomes, means and mechanisms set out in the Barcelona Declaration. What is new in the Euro-Mediterranean approach initiated in Barcelona is that, perhaps correctly, it reveals an integrated and comprehensive joint vision of what must be done. It is, indeed, a statement which is devoid of ambiguity, misunderstanding or inaccuracies, as will be shown later.

The Economic and Financial Partnership

The key to the economic and financial partnership is the creation of bilateral free trade zones in industrial goods, together with five-year protocols providing financial aid to the private sector, under the *Mésures d'Adjustement* (MEDA) programmes, alongside equivalent amounts of soft loan facilities from the European Investment Bank. The key difference between these arrangements and their predecessors is that now South and East Mediterranean countries must abandon their own tariff barriers to European industrial goods and their industrial sectors must now accept unfettered competition with European producers. Turkey and Israel have slightly different arrangements from the remaining South and East Mediterranean countries but the effect is virtually the same.

Creating an Area of Shared Prosperity Based on Free Trade

Beyond a timid reference in the Barcelona Declaration to the debt question, which is of key concern to Mediterranean non-partner states and which will eventually require further dialogue and progress, Euro-Mediterranean partners have agreed on three long-term objectives, together with three different means of establishing a zone of shared prosperity. The agreed objectives and means can be summed up in the table on page 12.

The progressive implementation of the free trade zone is therefore one of the essential, although not exclusive, means of achieving the three declared objectives of:

Objectives	Means
To increase the pace of sustainable economic and social development	Establishment of a free trade zone
To improve living conditions, increase the level of employment and reduce the development gap in the Euro-Mediterranean region	Fostering appropriate economic co-operation and dialogue in the domains concerned
To promote regional co-operation and integration	Substantial increase in EU financial aid to its partners

- speeding up development;
- reducing the development gap in the region; and
- promoting regional co-operation and integration.

By a process of convergence, these three objectives are expected to lay the foundations of an 'area of shared prosperity' (ASP).

In fact, the establishment of free trade in the Euro-Mediterranean region, which is accompanied by diversified and widespread economic co-operation and intensified financial aid, should be the decisive lever enabling the construction of the ASP, according to the Barcelona Declaration. Indeed, it should be stressed that the free trade zone (FTZ) concept, *stricto sensu*, commits its partners to specific means in addition to the progressive principles implicit in its implementation, namely, they must:

(1) pursue policies based on the principles of market economy;
(2) initiate economic adjustment by:
    (a) modernizing economic structures,
    (b) promoting the private sector,
    (c) upgrading the production sector;
(3) initiate social adjustment by:
    (a) modernizing social structures
    (b) mitigating negative effects through
    (c) programmes aimed at the neediest population;
(4) initiate institutional adjustment by:
    (a) setting up an institutional regulating framework favourable to market economy.

Thus, the Barcelona Declaration contains clear statements on free trade adjustment (FTA) which have three different dimensions – economic, social and institutional in nature. Furthermore, there is a specific reference to the social cost of the FTA and to the necessity to minimise it, particularly for the most deprived populations.

As far as economic and financial co-operation is concerned, two points must be stressed because of their direct linkage with the Free Trade Zone (FTZ):

- economic development must be supported both by domestic savings and by direct foreign investment (DFI); this confirms the importance of promoting an environment favourable to the removal of obstacles to such investments;

- reforms of the political-institutional environment and the removal of extra-economic obstacles appear to be implicit conditions for the success of the FTZ. Indeed, as far as financial co-operation is concerned and quite apart from the promise of substantial increases in financial aid, the Barcelona Declaration specifies that: 'sound macro-economic management is of fundamental importance and to this end the partners agree to promote dialogue on their respective economic policies and on the methods of optimising financial co-operation'. It is legitimate to pose the question that sound management, dialogue and the optimization of financial aid could diplomatic references to the dual conditionality inherent in financial, economic and political assistance.

DFI: The Decisive Variable in the FTZ and Politico-institutional Adjustment

The question of DFI is essential in understanding the politico-institutional dimension of the FTA. Indeed, every study of the degree to which the impact of the FTZ over the CSEM area can be predicted shows that an increase in foreign capital flows is often used to highlight the positive aspects of such a zone. The argument is based on the predicted impact that the actual announcement of the creation of a FTZ may have on foreign investors – a phenomenon which has already been observed during the implementation of other FTZs. The significance of this phenomenon must be reduced, however, by the specific nature of the Euro-Mediterranean FTZ since it offers new investors no new economic opportunity when compared to the previous cooperation agreements. Indeed, as far as European and other capital in search of offshore investment are concerned, it does not offer new markets, new fiscal terms or new financial opportunities. The only new element in the FTZ that may have relevance to investors is the political aspect of the increased openness of the Mediterranean economies, as they engage in greater integration within the European economic arena.

As far as these states themselves are concerned, the creation of a FTZ can only be beneficial to the CSEM if three interlinked conditions are fulfilled:

- The official implementation of active macro-economic support measures to upgrade domestic companies and attract foreign investment;
- The success of the upgrading programmes in transforming domestic companies, in order to signal that competitive economic conversion has been achieved; and
- A significant increase of foreign investment, particularly in the form of DFI, directed towards creating the appropriate conditions for the achievement of the desired competitive conversion of the CSEM economies.

In fact, although adjustment will incur costs, the potential gains associated with the FTZ remain largely dependent on foreign investment which will create new activities in competitive areas, thereby compensating for fiscal and social losses inherent in the creation of the FTZ and initiating measures which will upgrade production systems. A recent study based on a quantifiable general equilibrium model, designed specifically to take into account the role of direct foreign investment,[1] clearly showed that a significant decline in the risk premium linked to the inflow of private capital should stimulate a substantial rise in living standards and thus allow for a measurable reduction of migration flows as a result as domestic employment should increase. The calculated fall in the risk premium reflects several factors. It stems, first, from the national commitment implicit in the irreversible character of the FTZ agreement. In addition, positive expectations are associated with integration within the European growth area and there are expectations of greater institutional convergence with Europe, accompanied by an increased level of financial aid and technical co-operation. As a result of these conclusions, the study recommends greater regional integration at the institutional level in order to decrease the risk premium still further and thus increase the flows of DFI. Institutional adjustment and political credibility are therefore at the heart of the investment issue which, in any case, lies at the heart of every argument for the success of FTZs within the CSEM region.

Financial Co-operation and Political Conditionality

A novel kind of dual conditionality seems to have become the new key variable in the field of financial co-operation:

- Economic conditionality relates to the degree of implementation of structural reform measures to which CSEM governments have committed themselves. In future, those who fail to use their budget allocations under the MEDA programme by the end of the fiscal year may lose the balance to another partner whose economic performance, in terms of its commitment to the Process, is deemed more satisfactory.

14

- Outright political conditionality, which is now allied to economic conditionality, is essentially a new factor in Euro-Mediterranean relations. It relates to human rights and entails the possible suspension of financial aid following a qualified majority decision by the European Union, should human rights violations be revealed.

The problem here, however, is to determine how much deterrence political conditionality can actually generate and to establish to what extent it would provide an effective incentive for CSEM states to commit themselves to political reforms on human rights, fundamental freedoms, the rule-of-law and political pluralism. The extent to which this type of conditionality might buttress the actions of the various actors of civil society, who themselves are striving to establish the rule-of-law and democracy,[2] must also be considered.

Free Trade Adjustment and Politcal-institutional Convergence

The Euro-Mediterranean FTZ proposals, as laid down in the Barcelona Declaration, imply that the participating countries accept the basic principles of a market economy. This means that partners agree to abide by the same rules of trade as apply to all economic actors, institutions and agents. While the rules of free trade can, to a degree, be adapted to allow for to cultural diversity, they also imply a minimum degree of convergence at the level of institutions, in order to guarantee equal treatment for all. Thus, free trade adjustment (FTA) for the CSEM states may, as a precondition, involve the adoption of a minimum level of internal institutional transformation. Moreover, the Barcelona Declaration refers explicitly to institutional adjustment as necessary in order to promote free trade effectively. Free trade rules, in turn, imply political institutional structures which ensure the implementation and the respect of the rules themselves – independent judicial systems and the rule-of-law, political pluralism, financial and political transparency, as well as governmental accountability as the administrator of public property and the legal accountability of its institutions.

Institutional adjustment and minimal political and institutional convergence appear to be an explicit requirement under the terms of the economic basket of the Partnership, given its focus on the creation of FTZs. It is not clear whether the adjustment process undertaken by the CSEM states is expected to occur 'naturally' – as an unavoidable consequence of the very constraints imposed by free trade – whether it will be an objective consequence of the very existence of the FTZ, or whether it will be the product of specific and committed institutional reforms initiated by the CSEM governments themselves. This ambiguity, however, leads to several questions:

- To what extent can political dialogue allow a degree of political and institutional convergence between the partners and what would be the role of the various actors in civil society in this dialogue?

- Is it not political dialogue on human rights, together with the rule-of-law, democracy and pluralism, at the heart of the institutional mechanisms by which FTZs are implemented and therefore at the centre of institutional adjustment to free trade?

- Furthermore, can this political and institutional convergence adapt to cultural difference and to differences between the various political systems in the region? Is the search for minimal convergence likely to require that the existing politico-institutional systems of the CSEM be gradually recast in order to make them fit a European model which is now regarded as universal? How much importance should be granted to the universal dimension of such a paradigm and how much to specific local conditions? And what protective mechanisms exist to avoid loss of identity and cultural referents, which, if absent, would lead to the revival of profoundly destabilising and retrogressive reactions in the consequent search for identity?

These questions must be addressed within the political basket of the Barcelona Process and will involve actors from civil society as well. It is worth noting, however, that – contrary to the provisions of the Barcelona Declaration – a communication from the European Parliament and the Commission[3] states clearly that the FTZ is open to any country in the region which accepts the basic principles of market economy and political pluralism. The document highlights the links between the political dimension in terms of stability and security and the economic and social dimensions in terms of development and free trade, for the object is, according to the Barcelona Declaration, to, '... establish an area of stability and security by creating the necessary conditions for sustainable and rapid economic and social development. The most appropriate means of achieving this is to create a Euro-Mediterranean area characterised by free trade.'

In essence, this proposition entails the establishment of stability, peace and security in exchange for free trade accompanied by an improved financial aid package. The FTZ is regarded as a prerequisite to the realization of the objectives of the Barcelona Process and the appropriate instrument for the promotion of an area of shared prosperity, one of the cornerstones in the creation of an area of peace, stability and security. The resulting political equation behind the Process is, in other words: no peace, stability or security without shared prosperity brought about by free trade. Similarly and conversely, of course, no shared prosperity is possible without peace, stability and security in the Euro-Mediterranean region.

The reference, here, to the linked nature of market economies and political pluralism is quite explicit, as is the similar linkage between politico-institutional reform and economic reform. In the Barcelona Declaration, the formal reference to linkage is blurred and implicit in nhature, nor is it unambiguous and, for this reason, political dialogue will be required to remove such ambiguity. None the less, the political implications of the FTA concept are undeniable and political dialogue must take place if there is to be progress towards the required convergence at the political-institutional level.

Social Costs of FTZ Adjustment

The political implications of the FTZ concept are not the only ones that must be considered if the true consequences of the economic basket of the Barcelona Process are to be properly understood. There are social costs as well.

Economic Consequences and Social Impacts

Since the mid-1980s, most Mediterranean countries have adopted programmes of liberalization and adjustment in order to establish market mechanisms and free external trade, and to encourage private initiative and stimulate privatization. Thus, their progressive integration into the global economy is seen as irreversible. From this perspective, the option of a FTZ with the EU can be seen as a better way of putting down roots in the global economy and is in the nature of structural adjustment, mainly aimed at inducing a substantial effect of growth transfer as well as greater economic efficiency.

However, the establishment of a FTZ with the EU would significantly deregulate existing liberalisation policy mechanisms initiated by the authorities. Indeed, although for most CSEM states the choice of opening to the global economy is strategically irreversible, it is, none the less, endowed with some degree of realism in terms of its implementation. This has to be compatible with the means that can be mobilized to achieve the objective and, above all, implementation must take account of the fragility that characterizes these emerging economies. The FTZ alternative significantly speeds up liberalization, and act as a process initiated without properly identifying or mobilizing means to reduce costs and bring about conditions of success.

The FTZ, in effect, constitutes the trade basket of the Euro-Mediterranean Partnership agreement negotiated between the EU on the one hand, and each of the Mediterranean countries on the other. It has at least four specific characteristics: it is a FTZ between one country on the one hand and a group of countries on the other; between economies with unequal levels of development; between economies with unequal levels of integration; and between economies with unequal levels of mutual protection. These characteristics mean that the FTZ does not fit into the classic pattern of FTZ creation in which two or more countries with comparable levels of development and protection agree on the modalities of trade barrier removal. The implementation of the FTZ in the Barcelona context is therefore characterized by an obvious asymmetry. While the EU is already open to Mediterranean products (except for agricultural and some textile products), the CSEM states are faced with the unilateral dismantling of their protection mechanisms against imports from the EU. Thus, in view of its uniqueness and asymmetry, the implementation of the FTZ – which will be of unequal and uncertain impact on different CSEM states - must be qualified and the results of its impact assessment should be interpreted cautiously.

The analysis of social impact is closely linked with the economic effects of the FTZ, which are particularly evident in the domains of economic activity and public finance. These impacts generate, as responses, challenges the outcome of which will significantly condition the actual evolution and prospects of the FTZ in terms of economic and social development. Because of this factor, any analysis of the process must be speculative rather than prescriptive. However, it should none the less identify the major difficulties and constraints imposed by social parameters which are overwhelmed by economic and financial imperatives.

The creation of the FTZ between the CSEM and the EU requires the unilateral removal of trade barriers directed against European products without reciprocal action by the EU since nearly all manufactured goods from CSEM states already have free access to the European market. The only likely prospect for and increase in exports to the EU is in the realm of agricultural products, once the obstacles to trade have been eliminated. However, the fact that agricultural goods are currently excluded from the FTZ – discussions about their inclusion only began at the start of the year 2000 – nullifies this obvious advantage. Furthermore, the positive commercial effects expected from the creation of the FTZ, as far as manufactured goods are concerned, can only be indirect. For any country in this kind of partnership with the EU, such effects should come from the increased competitiveness associated with the fall in the price of goods imported from the EU and from the adjustments, for the sake of better productivity, generated by the removal of trade barriers.

The assessment of quantitative effects associated with the creation of a FTZ cannot be dissociated from the macro-economic policies which accompany the elimination of customs barriers. There are significant variations between the impacts depending on the hypothesis used to justify the FTZ concept. The hypothesis requiring official implementation of recessive supporting macro-economic measures – reductions in public spending or currency exchange rate adjustment – suggests that the overall effects on economic activity will be weak. They are likely to lead to general economic stagnation accompanied by differentiated sectoral growth, thus demonstrating the need for industrial restructuring and for labour relocation into more competitive sectors, with a overall increase in unemployment. Alternatively, the adoption of active macro-economic supporting measures designed to control the potential adverse effects of the FTZ might, for example, compensate for the loss of fiscal earnings due to the removal of trade barriers by a rise in indirect taxation or lead to positive adjustments to growth through a substantial increase in foreign investment. In this case, it should be noted that:

- Increasing indirect taxation whilst compensating for falls in customs revenues will generate side-effects which might severely affect economic growth. These could include price increases leading to a fall in investment and domestic demand as well as job losses, particularly for industries supplying the local market. Economic recession will cause a drop in fiscal revenues, as a result of the reduction in the tax base, even if there have been increases in tax rates, and thus increase unemployment. At the same time, such a recession would stimulate structures and mechanisms for spontaneous redeployment of labour by redirecting significant elements of the sector-based labour force.

- However, such macro-economic consequences could be reversed if adjustment was carried out with the help of capital inflows in the context of existing budgetary and monetary policies. Results obtained from the study of the impacts of the FTZ on the Tunisian economy[4] show accelerated growth, in response to substantial additional investment absorptive capacity in some sectors, together with falls in the rate of unemployment and growth in fiscal revenues.

The Social Impact of the FTA

The impact of a FTZ on economic activity and employment is, therefore, highly variable and depends on the capacity of the partner country to attract and mobilize a substantial flow of direct foreign investment. The effectiveness of this, in turn, will depend on the absorptive capacity of its industrial structure in handling significant variations in investment flows. The main challenge is to achieve economic flexibility in the transitional phase of trade liberalisation while preserving macro-economic equilibrium. During

FIGURE 1
DIFFICULTIES OF CONVERGENCE TO FREE TRADE

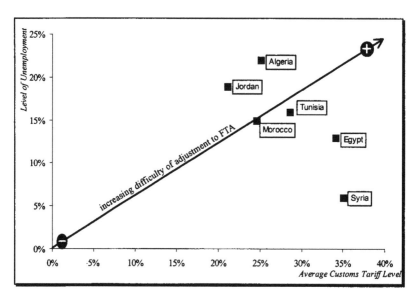

Source: Statistics: IMF & World Bank (1993–95)

this transitional phase, no country in a FTZ partnership with the EU can afford merely slow or moderate growth. The effort needed to succeed is made all the greater because its initial situation is characterised by wide-ranging protection mechanisms and a high rate of unemployment. The following graph, which plots average rates of customs tariffs (the protection indicator) horizontally and the rate of unemployment (the social indicator) vertically, illustrates the difficulties attached to the removal of protection barriers which has led to a loss of activities and jobs in six CSEM countries.

In the case of Tunisia, the portion of industrial production (approximately 10 per cent of GDP) threatened by the removal of tariffs on to imports from the EU has been estimated at 60 per cent of the total. Half of this output represents activities which are genuinely competitive in nature, whilst the remainder are protected and offer no real comparative advantage. This protection, following the establishment of a FTZ with the EU, can no longer be sustained and output can only be sustained if 30 per cent of national industrial activity is transferred into the competitive sector. This, in turn, will require that one third of the industrial sector will have to be abandoned, whilst another third will have to be redeployed into the third of the sector which is genuinely competitive in nature. This challenge will require a profound

20

change in the nature of the Tunisian economy and poses two important questions: to what extent is this formidable redeployment of productive resources possible for a competitive re-conversion of the Tunisian economy to take place? To what extent will the 'competitive third' remain competitive? In evaluating the answers to such questions, it should be borne in mind that they will will not take into account the additional stimulating effects of accompanying reform measures which will be implemented during the twelve-year transitional period provided for in the introduction of the FTZ.

For the CSEM states, the social impact of trade barrier removal is considerable. Over one quarter of the labour force currently employed in industrial activities which are increasingly unviable will have to be transferred to more competitive and profitable activities. Even if training programmes made it possible to achieve this tremendous movement of labour, the problems associated with the creation of competitive activities would still pose a problem. Currently, the main source of competitive activity for manufacturing industry in the CSEM region is the textile and clothing sector. In fact, competitiveness in this sector is really only sustained by preferential agreements with Europe. The sector will, therefore, have to undergo profound change if it is to survive, not just the establishment of the FTZ, but also the dismantling of the multi-fibre agreements which currently give it its competitive edge.

The social impact of the FTZ on the countries of the southern Mediterranean also has consequences for public finance, since customs revenues constitute an important budget resource for them. 'Budget vulnerability' to free trade and the difficulty for public finances to comply with the condition imposed by the FTZ because of the implied loss of revenues are reflected in the importance of customs revenues for fiscal balance and for public finance. The following graph illustrates the sensitivity of public finance to free trade for seven CSEM countries:

Countries such as Tunisia and Morocco, whose budgetary situation is difficult, with budget deficits often above to 4 per cent of GDP and a large portion of revenues depending on income and import taxes, have to make particularly intense efforts to reallocate budgetary resources to internal activities. This can only be done if two conditions are fulfilled; firstly thorough fiscal reform is essential and, secondly activities likely to generate fiscal revenues must be developed. Yet these requirements are not easily reconcilable with profound industrial change and labour redeployment that must involve, *inter alia*, the provision of tax incentives.

For most CSEM states, the loss of tax revenue implicit in the establishment of a FTZ with the EU, represents between 10 and 20 per cent of tax revenues. This presents government with a dilemma for it will be tempted to adopt a spontaneous policy of demand control which would result

FIGURE 2
BUDGETARY VULNERABILITY TO FREE TRADE (1995)

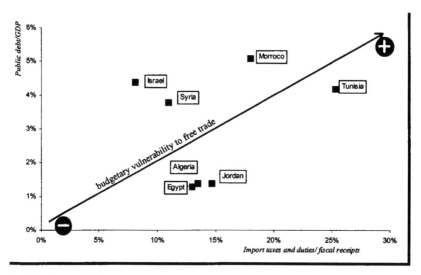

Statistical source: IMF.

in one of two outcomes: either government spending will be reduced or direct
and indirect taxation will be increased. In the first case, the fall in customs
revenues generated by the FTZ must translate into a considerable reduction of
public expenditure. Yet, since government spending is a prerequisite for the
creation of new productive resources, a policy of public expenditure cutbacks
is both incompatible with the principle of encouraging investment and
inappropriate in a context of industrial redeployment induced by the removal
of trade barriers which will necessitate more sustained budgetary support.
Thus, reaction to such a fall in tax revenue involving public expenditure
reduction would only lead to general recession. From a dynamic perspective,
such a recession would generate less fiscal revenue and therefore further
aggravate the consequences of this negative type of budget management.

In the second case, where the fall in tax revenues stimulates a search for
other compensatory tax resources through increasing indirect taxes, the
consequences would be similar, although the means would be different.
Indeed, increases in indirect taxation lead to demand control and thus to
restrictions on investment, production and employment. Even if the FTZ had
no effect over activity in a context of demand control – an unrealistic
hypothesis – the fiscal loss compensation induced by the removal of tariff
barriers will require raising rates to a level incompatible with political and
economic realities. In short, regardless of the impact of trade barrier removal

on public expenditure, there is a considerable risk that government expenditure on welfare will fall. In Tunisia, in the past, measures have been taken to minimise such consequences. The implementation of a structural adjustment programme at the end of the 1980s – which could have produced similar fiscal consequences – had no social cost because of the government's policy of social sector protection. This, however, led to a 14 per cent rise in public social expenditure in real terms, from 47.5 per cent of budget expenditure in 1987 to 52.5 per cent in 1993.[5] The establishment of the FTZ will, therefore, offer a new challenge in the domain of fiscal adjustment and social sector protection.

Emigration and Debt

In essence, this issue will involve furthering active co-operation in promoting human resources in the Euro-Mediterranean region. International migration is today, particularly in the Euro-Mediterranean context, an undeniable and fundamental fact of society, both in the country of origin and in the host country. Indeed, the migrant's virtual break from his or her country of origin is compounded by the difficulties or impossibility of integration in the new host country. The migration issue, therefore, is at the heart of the imposed interdependence across the Mediterranean, which has been difficult for partners in the North and South to accept, even though they are 'condemned' by history and geography into being strategic neighbours and having to cooperate in their efforts achieve development. This raises some important questions:

- how can the static or short term vision narrowly focused on migration as a security issue be avoided?

- how can a holistic vision of social integration across the Mediterranean be developed as a crucial dimension of cooperative relations between the Barcelona partners?

- why should the migration issue be the main bone of contention in such interdependent relations?

- could the issue of international migration be considered in the long term, as a historical and shared responsibility for the Barcelona partners which is also one of Europe's instruments for the promotion of human resources in countries of origin. Would it become the key to sustainable and shared development in political solidarity across the Mediterranean and thus a guarantee of stability and security for all?

- what would be the predictable effects of the FTZ on migration flows?

Migratory Pressure, the FTZ and Economic Convergence

Simulation models suggest that it will be difficult to guarantee a significant reduction in migration flows as a result of the establishment of the FTZ. The theoretical proposal that free trade, accompanied by substantial financial assistance, is an alternative to emigration can only be seriously considered to be an adjustment mechanism in the long term.[6] The underlying hypothesis here, which is often implicit, is that free trade (accompanied by significant foreign capital inflow) will contribute to the reduction of the income gap between Europe and the CSEM region and thus should reduce migration flows significantly. It is therefore a legitimate question to ask to what extent the economic partnership exemplified by the FTZ, together with economic and financial co-operation would stimulate economic convergence, in terms of a reduction of the lag in development in the South which would therefore deter further emigration? The gamble of economic partnership in seeking to build an area of shared prosperity is ultimately at the heart of the problem of economic convergence in the long term.

The Euro-Mediterranean issue initiated by the EU can be summed up in the following diagram:-

Disparities		**Migration pressure**		**PROBLEMS**
		$\triangledown$		
Poverty	➡	Side effects:	➡	Instability
		Criminality		Insecurity
Unemployment		Drugs		Tensions
		Extremism		
Dialogue		**Growth and convergence**		**GUARANTEES**
Partnership	➡	$\triangledown$	➡	Stability
		Reduction of migratory		Security
Co-operation		pressure		Peace

This issue was not a predominant concern during the integration of such countries as Greece, Spain and Portugal into the EU. Data on these countries show a significant, if gradual, tendency towards economic convergence. Indeed, an examination of the evolution of the GNP per capita (at purchasing power parity 'PPP' and with an index where 100 corresponds to the weighted average in EU countries) shows that for Portugal, the index rose from 26.3 before joining the EU (average for 1980–84) to 36.4 in the early 1990s (average for 1990–93). Spain experienced the same convergence (the indices for the same period are respectively 49.8 and 60.6). In the case of Greece, convergence was only observed from the beginning of the 1990s. The following table and figures illustrates the observed trends (detailed data can be found in the annex):

FIGURE 3
EVOLUTION OF PPP GNP PER CAPITA (BASE 100 = EU AVERAGE)

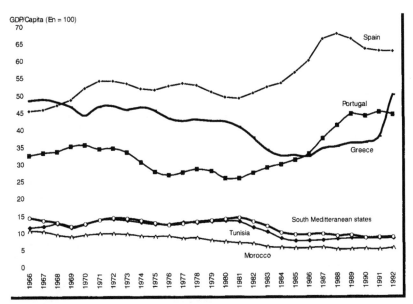

In the CSEM region this convergent tendency was observed between 1975 and 1985, probably as a result of the co-operation agreements signed in the mid-1970s. However, there was a clear divergence after 1986, although it seems to have been stabilised over the last few years. The CSEM GNP per capita index fell from 20 in 1985 to 15 in 1993 as an average for the CSEM region as a whole as individual states registered varying degrees of deterioration which reflected the income gaps between the two sides of the Mediterranean.

The case of Portugal provides a good illustration of this process. Since its integration within the EU, its gradual economic convergence has been accompanied by considerable inflows of foreign capital. DFI rose from $157 million to $1,300 million and there was a fourfold increase in net global flows, from $1,074 million in 1980 to $4,431 million in 1993. The data for the CSEM states shows that, in terms of net global flows or in terms of DFI, the results are alarming (except for Turkey). There has, in effect, been capital drain and the stagnation or reduction of DFI flows. The following table illustrates the comparison between the net flow of DFI towards three EU countries (Spain, Portugal and Greece) and those attracted by the CSEM region during the period from 1970–93. The evolution of net global transfers towards the CSEM region(for the six countries for which data are available) between 1980 and 1993 is illustrated in the following table:

FIGURE 4
EVOLUTION OF NET DFI FLOWS (in million US$)

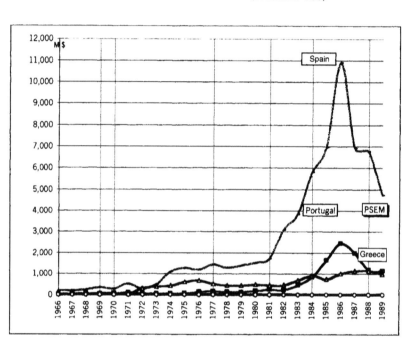

In 1993, global net transfers for the six countries under study represented less than one third of those of Portugal ($4.4 billion). Is the Euro-Mediterranean Partnership going to change this situation? Will the achievement of economic convergence run the risk of provoking a veritable meltdown amongst European partners as far as external capital flows, especially in DFI, are concerned? There is no way of knowing what the future will hold in this respect.

Debt or Debt Swaps – Human Resource Promotion

The data provided in the annex show that, apart from efforts to improve debt service terms, several CSEM states experience negative net transfers which affect their ability to attract the resources necessary to stimulate investment and job creation so as to reduce unemployment and minimise potential emigration. The following table illustrates the deterioration of the debt situation in five countries in the South Mediterranean region.

EVOLUTION OF FOREIGN DEBT

(Weighted average rates)

	1970–79	1980–89	1990–94
Tunisia			
Debt ratio	40%	59%	60%
Debt service ratio	14%	25%	24%
Mauritania			
Debt ratio	92%	193%	209%
Debt service ratio	26%	23%	26%
Morocco			
Debt ratio	40%	98%	80%
Debt service ratio	23%	45%	36%
Algeria			
Debt ratio	47%	40%	58%
Debt service ratio	20%	48%	71%
Egypt			
Debt ratio	66%	114%	88%
Debt service ratio	20%	31%	23%

The result is that CSEM states face and increasingly severe dual reality reflecting:

- Constraints in:
  - education-training-employment provision
  - debt servicing

- and consequences in:
  - unemployment (leading to potential emigration)
  - negative net transfers

The constraints are clearly inter-linked and, in the long-term can only be effectively managed through partnership arrangements across the

Mediterranean in which debtor and creditor cooperate. This will require that the following two objectives are achieved within the framework of such a partnership over the long-term:

- A rapid termination of net outward financial transfers from CSEM states and a significant reallocation of capital flows towards development based on human resources promotion.

- Partial or total debt cancellation or debt rescheduling over a thirty year period, which is the probable length of time before the reduction in demographic growth rates currently occurring manifests itself in the productive sectors of the economies in most CSEM states, so that there will be a real downturn in the level of additional employment demand. This will mean that debt service obligations could be reduced to a level compatible with a productive investment growth rate which, in turn, would satisfy employment demand and lead to a gradual reduction in absolute levels of unemployment.

In fact, both propositions would require agreement on the recycling of a substantial portion of the debt with the express purpose of promoting human resource development, in other words, the substitution of human resources promotion for debt. The necessary negotiations would deal with a dual concern. First, it would facilitate economic recovery in debt-ridden countries which are also experiencing net outward financial transfers, despite the counter-measures that may have been adopted. Second, it would give human resource development a prominent role in the new partnership, thus contributing to a reduction of the social cost of free trade and, in consequence, reducing the propensity for emigration from the South. Under current conditions, any consideration of the pattern of evolution of CSEM state social sector expenditure will demonstrate that there is, al best, stagnation and, in some cases, regression in real terms as a result of increasingly heavy debt servicing obligations. The available data (see annex) shows that, in three of the southern Mediterranean countries (Morocco, Tunisia and Egypt), per capita public expenditure on education, which in the 1970s was equivalent to almost twice the amount per capita spent on servicing, fell to only 60 per cent during the first half of the 1990s. Figure 5 illustrates this pattern.

External debt recycling in the CSEM region could be used to contribute towards the creation of a Euro-Mediterranean fund for the promotion of human resources where management principles and mechanisms should involve actors within civil society and should be negotiated between the partners on both sides of the Mediterranean. The objective of such a fund would be to contribute to:

FIGURE 5
PUBLIC EXPENDITURE FOR EDUCATION AND DEBT SERVICING

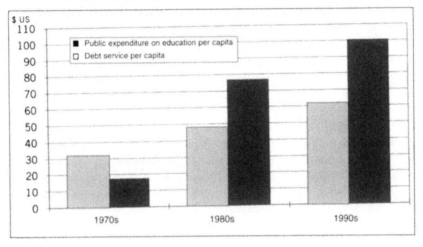

- the creation of productive employment opportunities, particularly in regions subject to strong migration pressures;

- the support of family planning policies;

- competitive economic restructuring in the CSEM region, since professional training must play a predominant role in transformation and reallocation of factors of production, particularly the industrial labour force.[7]

Professional training should be designed within the overall framework of labour qualification and mobility, since it concerns the whole of southern Mediterranean labour-force, whether in countries-of-origin or in host-countries. Thus, controlled and organized migration into European countries would allow for proper immigrant training programmes designed to facilitate eventual repatriation and the creation of micro-enterprises networks in countries-of-origin based on appropriate technology and commercial knowledge transfer. It would also provide trained managers for enterprises seeking to relocate into the CSEM region. Economic *rapprochement* across the Mediterranean, however, can only be completely successful if factors of production such as capital *and* labour are allowed to move freely within the Mediterranean region. Of course, this is not currently possible because of anxieties inside Europe over the social and political implications. As a result, during the transitional phase of the creation of a Euro-Mediterranean economic arena, a dynamic vision of the emigration issue, as suggested here,

29

would encourage a renewal of migration flows (which Europe will increasingly need as its own population ages). This could be organized so as to provide improved efficiency of control and training, in order to contribute to competitive economic re-conversion in the countries of the southern Mediterranean, while maintaining migration within the limits compatible with the EU's economic and social imperatives. In this respect, it would be interesting to examine closely the German experiment of the early 1970s, which offered vocational training to Portuguese workers residing in Germany.[8]

Finally, quite apart from considerations of immediate interest or ideological preconception, perhaps international migration should be viewed as a vector of social change and cultural interdependence. After all, the integration of migrant communities in host-countries is introducing profound social modification which raises questions about the fundamental values of European society, such as secularism, citizenship, and identity. It is stimulating a search for new patterns of social cohesion through the enlargement of the ethnic and cultural bases inside Europe itself. Immigration may thus may be contributing to the birth of a new European sense of citizenship, despite the immediate problems it may face. At the same time, the migrant experience of European cultural and political values may also act as a catalyst for the transition towards democracy in their countries-of-origin.

A Tentative Conclusion

For most CSEM states, integration into the Euro-Mediterranean arena will be costly, difficult and hazardous. Yet it will also provide a genuine opportunity for economic modernisation and restructuring which will better equip them to face the challenges of globalisation. Adjustment to such new situations also implies a substantial investment in human resources, infrastructure, the organization of production and institutions. The financial resources needed for these changes will exceed the capacities of the states involved and European participation is therefore essential. Such participation could occur in two ways:

- on a passive, short-term basis via compensation for the reduction of customs revenues as a result of the FTZ policy; or

- on an active, long-term basis via the financing of measures to improve national competitiveness, so that DFI, particularly from Europe, will be encouraged.

Another important facet of European support for CSEM economic restructuring would be the easing of trade constraints on agricultural produce and the food industry Since the FTZs introduced through the Barcelona

Process are restricted to industrial free trade, agricultural products are excluded. Their access to EU markets is still heavily constrained by quotas, customs tariffs, export schedules, target prices and quality standards, even though negotiations on liberalizing such restrictions began at the start of the year 2000. The social impact of these restrictions are crucial for they exclude the poorest social groups in the CSEM region who will not benefit from the FTZ as a result.

Conceptually, the Euro-Mediterranean Partnership project stems from a liberal vision. Yet, liberalism cannot be partial and discriminatory, for it will then contribute to regional destabilization instead of promoting a dynamic of progress. The Euro-Mediterranean Partnership project is also based on principles of co-operation and partnership, so that a permanent concern for equity must govern relations among partners, rather than considerations of balance of power. The construction of the Euro-Mediterranean region fits within a pattern of historic evolution. It is not merely an option but reflects that irreversible and inevitable evolution of regional economies as a result of liberalization which provides the only opportunity for creating regional stability, prosperity, and durable economic development. During its construction, a period of transition is necessary and inevitable and temporary negative outcomes may be difficult to avoid, even if they can be predicted in spheres such as industrial activity, public finance, employment, wages and revenues. The partners to the project must seek to mitigate such outcomes, they must try to shorten the transitional period, thus minimizing economic and social costs and optimizing the advent of genuine regional prosperity.

NOTES

1. D. Cogneau and J. Christophe, *Intégration régionale, investissements directs et migrations dans l'espace euro-méditerranéen: Enseignements d'un modèle d'équilibre général calculable*, Athens, 31 Oct. – 1 Nov. 1996.
2. 'Is this not a double-edged sword?', asks Fathia Talahite rightly, 'since by linking human rights to aid there is a real danger that the significance of this struggle may be corrupted and subjected to economic and financial pressures. Does the institution of a currency in a mechanism which, through aid, enables the EU to exert unilateral control over recipient countries, not run the risk of perpetuating relations of dependence, perverting the profound significance of human rights and delaying the day when this problem will be effectively acted upon by the societies concerned', *Maghreb-Machrek*, No.153, July–Sept. 1995.
3. Communication from the European Parliament and Council Commission: *Renforcement de la consolidation politique méditerranéenne de l'UE, établissement d'un partenariat euro-méditerranéen*, Brussels, 19 Oct. 1994.
4. See G. Kebabdjian, A. Mahjoub, H. Zaafrane et al., *Etude prospective de l'impact sur l'économie tunisienne de la mise en place d'une zone de libre-échange avec l'Union européenne*, COMETE, CEPEX, Nov. 1994.
5. See World Bank, *République Tunisienne, Allégement de la pauvreté: Bâtir sur les acquis pour préparer l'avenir*, April 1996.
6. 'The temporal horizon of the simulation models relied upon here does not allow for a full

understanding of the effects of free trade. This limitation is all the more worrying when one considers that potential migrants' anticipations of increased income and of job prospects in their country of origin constitute a critical factor in their decision to emigrate', G. Tapinos, 'La libéralisation des échanges et ses effets sur l'économie, l'emploi et les migrations dans le bassin méditerranéen', OECD, Athens, 31 Oct. – 1 Nov. 1996.

7. Two propositions made during the Barcelona Euro-Mediterranean forum of should be considered in this context: first, the creation of a Euro-Mediterranean in-service training institute; second, the establishment of an economic observatory for new communication technologies to be applied to education, professional training and scientific research in the Euro-Mediterranean.

8. See Luis Alberto Garcia Ferrero Morales: 'La création d'emplois au Maghreb dans la perspective d'un partenariat euro-maghrébin'. Second meeting of economic and social representatives from the countries of the Arab Maghreb Union and the European Community, Tunis, 8–10 Sept. 1993.

3

Foreign Investment and the Rule of Law

GEORGE JOFFÉ

En matière de régime des investissements étrangers, la plupart des PTM (pays tiers méditerranéens) ont adopté, depuis la fin des années 80, des codes d'investissements simplifiés offrant d'importants avantages fiscaux. Ces codes sont la plupart du temps reliés aux programmes de privatization. Mais la conversion radicale à l'accueil des investissements étrangers succède à plusieurs décennies de méfiance ... et les avantages maintenant proposés sont comparables à ceux de nombreux pays en développement. Il n'y a pas sur ce terrain d'avantage particulier.[1]

This statement, from a respected French commentator on the Mediterranean and on economic affairs, accurately sums up the current attitude towards the legal status of investment in the South Mediterranean region. However, the problems facing the private investor are far more complicated than he indicates. It is usually assumed that direct private foreign investment and portfolio equity investment, both of which fall under the rubric of 'foreign investment',[2] respond simply to the financial climate that exists in receiving countries. In fact, the situation that persuades an investor to invest is far more complex and the weighting given to different investment destinations and to different factors affecting investment varies from situation to situation. One highly important consideration is the legal status of institutions and of the political and economic environment in the investment destination under consideration. In this respect, the Middle East and North Africa has a series of acute problems to address if foreign investment is to reach the proportions sought within the Barcelona context. As mentioned above, two of the most important considerations relate to investor distrust and comparative advantage. Despite new and simplified investment codes designed to encourage the foreign investment decades of foreign distrust over political interference in the economic process and ideologies of state supervision have still to be effectively countered. In addition, these new investment codes have usually been produced to encourage the privatization of state assets but will do little to encourage investment outside this arena because the region as a whole lacks comparative advantage for the foreign investor, when compared with Latin America, South Asia or South East Asia.

The role of comparative advantage is, of course, important; China, for example, which has little formal guarantee of security of investment yet, none the less offers such financial comparative advantage that foreign investors are willing to accept a far higher level of risk than might otherwise be the case, as the massive inflows of direct foreign investment in recent years demonstrates. However, the ability of a host government to create a climate of investor confidence can, on occasion, be equally as important as the consequences of the October 1994 Mexico crash demonstrated. Mexico's rapid recovery was not only due to the safety-belt provided by the United States but was also a function of the speed with which the Mexican government responded, in creating an appropriate financial and economic environment to reassure investors and in providing appropriate legal infrastructures. The reverse can be equally true, as the crisis of confidence in the wake of the moral hazard manifested in the Asian financial collapse in 1997 demonstrated. On occasion, this can work in a regional context: the initiation of the Middle East peace process in 1993 caused a rush of foreign investment into Israel – as had occurred after the 1967 victory as well, albeit for different reasons – as investors assumed that Israel itself would become the gateway into a revived Middle East economic environment. Similarly, the difficulties encountered in pushing the process forward in 1995–96 resulted in a sudden dive in investment inflows there. Trust or, rather, confidence is, in short, probably the most important consideration as far as the Middle East and North Africa region is concerned, particularly if it wishes to significantly reverse its poor record in persuading foreign investors to accept the implicit risk of investment there. In part of course, this depends on the type of investment involved.

British Petroleum has not been deterred from making a massive $3.5 billion investment in the Algerian gas industry, despite the civil conflict there. Such investments, however, do little to alter the fundamental economic balances of the region; they allow governments to become rent-seekers rather than to encourage them to engage in creating conditions for productive investment. The reality is that, for the non-oil investor, the region has been distinctly unattractive for many years, largely because security of investment was perceived to be low – either because of arbitrary state action, particularly in nationalizing foreign assets, or because of difficulties of repatriation of profits and the constant threat of 'indigenization'.[3]

Regional governments – except Israel and, perhaps, Turkey, where appropriate conditions for foreign investors obtain – need to devote far more attention to creating investor confidence in terms other than the simple commercial environment. Investment codes, in short, are very important and a necessary but not sufficient condition to persuade the private investor to take risk. There is a crucial need to establish the independence of legal systems from government interference and the transparency and accountability of commercial administrations. Of course, it may be argued that this is an inevitable concomitant of economic liberalization and restructuring and of the development of international 'openness', to use the World Bank's term. This is not, however, self-evidently the case. Chile, after 1973, and Singapore suggest that other means also exist to create the climate of stability sought by the foreign investor. It therefore follows that, unless they wish to attempt the authoritarian approaches used there – which, in any case, have been responsible for significant economic and political inefficiencies in the past in terms of rent-seeking and political instability – governments in the Middle East and North Africa must actively promote steps to create political transparency, accountability and legitimacy for the very process of government itself, as much as they must ensure the independence of legal systems to which they themselves will also be accountable. In short, the political transformations required in the Middle East and North African region are as important as the specific economic measures now being undertaken by the majority, if not all of the countries concerned.

The Investor's Objectives

It is commonly thought that the primary consideration in potential investors' minds is simply the rate-of-return on investment to be expected from a particular investment destination. This is, of course, a consequence of investment opportunity itself – whether in the indigenous market or as an export generator – and of the economic environment of the country in which the investment is to be located. The latter consideration involves such factors as labour costs, input costs and availability, transport costs and the political climate for investment. The political climate is construed usually as issues such as the ability to repatriate profits and potential tax holidays, as well as other financial inducements to investors. There should, in short, be sufficient 'comparative advantage' making the investment attractive in financial terms.

There are, however, other acute considerations that affect investor decisions in choosing a destination for investment and determining the type and size of the investment to be made,[4] particularly if 'comparative advantage' is not the decisive consideration, as is the case in the Middle East and North Africa. One such consideration, for example – as suggested above – is that the rate-of-return, however high or low it may be in comparison with investments elsewhere, should be stable and predictable. This is particularly important in investments where the real benefit to the investor occurs only

35

FOREIGN INVESTMENT: DEVELOPING COUNTRIES BY REGION
($ BILLION)

	FDI	1993 (%)	PEI	(%)	1994 FDI	(%)
East Asia/Pacific	37.9	55.6	18.1	38.3	43.0	53.7
Latin America/Caribbean	15.7	23.0	25.1	53.1	20.8	26.0
Europe/Central Asia	**12.0	18.2	1.3	2.8	8.4	10.5
Sub-Saharan Africa	1.8	2.6	0.4	0.8	3.0	3.8
Middle East/North Africa	3.8	5.6	*0.4	0.8	3.7	4.6
South Asia	0.8	1.2	2.0	4.2	1.2	1.5
Total	**68.2**		**47.3**		**80.1**	

Source: COMET, 43 (May 1995); 21
   IBRD, Financial flows and the developing countries, August 1996;
   Table A11
Note: *World Bank projection
   **Includes Eastern Europe ($4.1 billion)

after the initial investment has been recovered, so that subsequent cash-flow streams are essentially profit. Major investments in hydrocarbons and other mining activities are a very good example of this. It should be borne in mind that high rates-of-return are often illusory, as – over time – returns tend to drift back to a basic norm related to government discount rates, according to the capital assets pricing model.

Outside the question of mining operations, decisions about investment in non-rent-related operations or in equity also often depend on considerations of long-term stability, since the real benefit to the investor will also be delayed until the initial investment is repaid. Immediate returns, therefore, are not necessarily the major consideration in making investment decisions. However, if long-term stability is a major concern, this also raises questions about both the legal status of foreign investment in a host country and about the political stability of the regime controlling it. Associated with these concerns are considerations of nationalization and compensation, as well as of the actual status of the rule of law. Indeed, the status of the legal system is a vital consideration, particularly its independence from government, as well as it ability to modify and moderate government action. In some respects, this consideration subsumes all others related to the political environment in which an investment is to be made for it will ultimately determine what that environment will be. In other words, political conditions in the Middle East and North Africa region are acutely important to the foreign investor today – outside, perhaps, the question of oil-related investment – and those conditions, in turn, are determined by the legal environment in which governments there operate, particularly the independence of the judiciary.

The Legal Status of Investment

If such independence is ensured, then one important aspect of this issue is the nature of the legal terms offered to foreign investors and guaranteed by the legal system.

Investment Codes

Until the 1980s, investment codes in developing countries, particularly in the Middle East and North Africa, were often seen to be restrictive and genuine liberalization of foreign investment codes only began towards the end of the decade.[5] Although there have been dramatic changes since then, the codes are often still seen by potential investors as restricted – Algeria's anxiety of economic sovereignty over the gas and oil sector is one good example. This is, of course, changing as the principles of modern economic liberalization are increasingly accepted by the governments concerned, but the South Mediterranean region continues to be one of the poorest in terms of foreign investment worldwide.

The actual levels of foreign investment inflows by country make clear the difficulties they face. Indeed, apart from Israel, Turkey, Morocco and Tunisia, foreign investment has been declining in the region – the Saudi figures are an aberration caused by the war against Iraq. Even in these three countries, the total amount of investment has been only around half of what had been anticipated or required despite modifications of law and regulation to encourage foreign investors. The picture when net foreign investment is considered is equally as depressing. The Middle East and North African region is grouped alongside South Asia and Africa in terms of its access to foreign investment world wide and, in many cases, early success in attracting foreign investment at the start of the decade has now begun to tail off. Furthermore, foreign investment is still predominantly in the form of direct investment and the very recent pick-up in portfolio equity investment in Egypt, Morocco and Tunisia reflects the one-time attraction of privatization programmes, rather than an ongoing commitment to economic arenas in which flexibility of investment offers its own rewards.

In fact, in a sample of 20 countries drawn from the Mediterranean, Latin America, the Far East and the three newest Mediterranean European Union members (Spain, Portugal and Greece), together with Eastern Europe and the former Soviet Union, the six major South Mediterranean states (Turkey, Israel, Egypt, Tunisia, Algeria and Morocco) only received seven per cent of accumulated direct private foreign investment receipts between 1971 and 1992. In comparison, 39 per cent went to South East Asia, 25 per cent to Latin America and seven per cent to the newest European Union members. Even worse, whereas the South Mediterranean states had received 11 per cent of

FOREIGN DIRECT INVESTMENT INFLOWS
($ MILLION)

	1989	1990	1991	1992	1993	1994
Algeria	12	6	10	12	15	18
Bahrain	181	–4	–7	–9		
Egypt	1250	734	253	459	493	530
Iran	–19	–362	23	–170	–50	–10
Iraq	3		–3			
Israel	125	101	351	539	555	406
Jordan	–1	38	–12	41	–34	–10
Lebanon	2	6	2	4	6	7
Libya	1225	159	24			
Kuwait	4	–1				
Mauritania	4		2	5	1	2
Morocco	167	165	320	424	522	550
Oman	112	144	149	87	99	130
Qatar	–1	16	43			
Saudi Arabia	–20	572	659	1873	–79	
Sudan	4			0	0	
Syria	74	71	62	67	70	72
Tunisia	79	75	150	379	239	275
Turkey	663	684	810	844	636	850
UAE	39	–116	–69			
Yemen	5			0		

Source: *Comet*, 41 (July 1994): 11.
IBRD, *World Development Report 1994*: 204–5
IBRD, *World Data 1995*, CD-ROM

these investment flows in the 1970s, between 1990 and 1992, they only received 4.1 per cent – much of which was, in any case directed towards the hydrocarbon sector. Migrant labour transfers during the same period were five times greater than direct private foreign investment, at $125 billion, compared with $24 billion – a pattern which was completely reversed in the case of South East Asia.[6]

In fact, it is difficult to see what these countries can do in addition to the measures they have already taken to persuade foreign investors to take up the opportunities they offer, unless they can create political and cultural conditions which encourage foreign investors far more quickly than they appear to be doing at present. The region is, in short, in crisis despite the valiant efforts made – in some cases for more than a decade – to achieve economic reform and restructuring which will promote economic development. Indeed, without adequate investment, it is most unlikely that these states can resolve their internal social problems, let alone begin to match the patterns of development experienced by the countries of the developed world or of the rapidly developing world of the Far East. Unless far more foreign investment – or official development aid, presumably from the

NET FOREIGN AND PORTFOLIO EQUITY INVESTMENT
($BILLION)

| | **FDI** | | | | **PEI** | | | |
	1991	**1992**	**1993**	**1994**	**1991**	**1992**	**1993**	**1994**
Algeria	−38.7	3	−2	0	0	0	0	1
Bahrain	−6.9	−8.5			−34.6			
Egypt	140.5	358.7	453.0	500.0				
Iran								
Iraq								
Israel*	−73.0	−112.1	−373.6	−420.5	548.4	−740.1	1750.3	2378.4
Jordan	26.0	45.0	20.0	25.0				
Kuwait*	−186.4	−1210.7	−848.1	−1074.5	−601.5	272.8	162.3	
Lebanon			902.0	1198.0				
Libya								
Mauritania	2.3	7.5	16.1	2.8				
Morocco	319.9	423.6	492.5	660.0	0	0	29.9	
Oman	149.0	87.4	98.8					
Qatar								
Saudi Arabia	160.2	−79.3	−79.3		−470.0	−3645.7	−8448.1	
Sudan								
Syria								
Tunisia	140.5	364.1	238.1	187.8	20.5	46.4	17.9	14.8
Turkey	783.0	779.0	622.0	559.0	623.0	2411.0	3917.0	
UAE								
Yemen	583.0	719.0	903.0	17.0				

Source: IBRD, *World Bank World Data 1995*, CD-ROM

Note: Negative, net direct foreign investment is due to outward investment:
Israel – (1991) $423.5mn, (1992) $650.7mn, (1993) $928.5 mn, (1994) $826.2mn;
Kuwait – (1991) $186.4mn, (1992) $1210.7mn, (1993) $848.4mn, (1994) $1074. 5mn.

THE ROLE OF DIRECT FOREIGN INVESTMENT 1986–91
FDI/GDCF– %

Middle East

Egypt	7.80
Oman	6.90
Tunisia	3.50
Morocco	2.60
Jordan	1.70
Yemen	0.90
Sudan	0.10
Algeria	0.05

Others – Europe

Belgium	16.00
United Kingdom	14.40
Netherlands	12.30

Others – Far East

Singapore	29.40
Hong Kong	12.10

Source: *Comet*, 41 (July 1994): 12.

Notes: FDI – Foreign direct investment
GDCF – Gross domestic capital formation

European Union[7] – is made available, genuine economic development seems unlikely to occur in any sense that will guarantee generalized economic growth in the countries concerned. Under present plans, the danger is that the alternative will be that enclave economies will be created in South Mediterranean states, designed to serve the European market and that the national economies will merely become states of the European Union without experiencing genuine economic development and the prosperity which should accompany it.

Yet, if the terms offered for foreign private investment have improved so significantly over the past decade and investment still does not come except to the oil and gas sectors in the amounts anticipated, then the reason must lie in other factors than the direct legal status conferred on foreign investment. Some of these problems are general to the whole phenomenon of foreign investment; other arise specifically from the conditions which exist in the Middle East and North Africa. As will be discussed below, the roots of these problems and difficulties reside largely in social and political issues, rather than in the directly economic sphere a consideration which underlines the urgent need for political and social reform throughout the region. At the same time, regional stability plays its part and outside actors, such as the European Union, need to pay far greater attention to participating actively in the resolution of regional problems, such as the continuing tensions between Israel and the Arab world, particularly with respect to the Palestinian issue, or the worsening crisis in Algeria.

The General Problems

One major concern arises for the status of foreign property rights. This is the question of providing legal guarantees of ownership to foreign nationals investing in a particular country. Since the original owner is, by definition, non-resident, he has little recourse except to withdraw future investment, if his investment is appropriated by legal or illegal means. It is an age-old problem that exists largely because few generalized instruments exist in international law to maintain such property rights and international law, itself is virtually without sanction against states and legal entities within them, except by agreement of the state concerned. Furthermore:

> ... foreign property rights grew out of reciprocal interests, but...they were one-sidedly extended to the developing countries. The capital exporters laid down the 'rules of the game'; the capital importers sought to undermine them. At first, the latter sought to establish the right not to be subject to military intervention at the time of investment disputes. Subsequently, they struggled for the right to nationalize foreign-

controlled, for whatever gains. By diplomatic co-operation developing countries gradually undercut the traditional property rights.[8]

Interestingly enough, one of the major efforts made by Western states since 1990 has been to enshrine foreign property rights in the legislation of both developing countries (including countries in the former centrally planned economies group) and to do the same in international fora. At present, a major row is developing between developing countries and the developed world over the latter's proposal to include a foreign investment code in the legislation of the World Trade Organisation – the Multilateral Investment Agreement that has been temporarily shelved as a result of French objections. This would allow for open access, whatever national legislation might dictate. It is being strongly resisted by developing countries, including Egypt. However, the countries concerned also need to recognize that their own legal systems are defective as far as the foreign investor is concerned, because their deficiencies increase the political risk of investment – despite recent initiatives to accept international procedures over litigation and dispute resolution.[9] This has a particular relevance to the issue of intellectual property rights, an area to which relatively little attention has been paid by South Mediterranean governments. Perhaps most immediate in this respect, however, is the continuing danger of state expropriation of private foreign assets, given the role of hydrocarbon investment in the region. Despite current assumptions that the era of nationalization has disappeared, the very nature of mining operations means that it is bound to re-emerge in the future and attention should be paid to this particular problem now, if the tensions and crises of the 1970s oil shocks are to be avoided next time round.

The Obsolescing Bargain

This problem gives rise to another, more specific issue: the 'sanctity of contract'. Foreign investors are anxious to be certain that a contract once entered into, will not be subject to change under pressure from domestic legislation. The classic dilemma in this respect is also best illustrated in the oil and gas sector which is subject, as are other mining operations, to the 'obsolescing bargain'. This provides for the fact that, when such an operation is planned, the risk of failure is clearly high for there is considerable uncertainty of profitable discoveries. Contract terms clearly have to reflect the high level of risk involved that the investment be unprofitable to both sides. However, once discovery has been made and exploitation has started, the risk element in the investment will have dropped significantly and the terms of the original contract seem increasingly unfair to the host country which sees the proportion of rent it receives as being unreasonably low in consequence.

Such contracts are notoriously subject to unilateral demands by host countries for change, demands which are often backed by the weight of domestic law and thus cannot be resisted. Although foreign investors attempt to allow for this by the inclusion of so-called 'stabilization clauses', the fact is that these can hardly ever be sustained against determined attack by the host country. This in-built lack of stability in the sanctity of contract is, of course a powerful dis-incentive to investment and its logical conclusion is nationalization. This, in turn, generates another problem for the foreign investor; namely, the mode of compensation he is to receive for his nationalized asset. International law demands that compensation should be 'fair and just'.

The problem is that there is no agreement on what these terms mean. The United States, supported by most developed states, has insisted that this term should be interpreted to mean the full value of the asset, as determined by discounted-cash-flow principles – as if the asset in question were to be valued for the purpose of private purchase. Developing countries have argued that net book value or some variant thereof is a fairer alternative. International tribunals have yet to establish what the standard of compensation should be.[10] The same problem, of course, exists in an attenuated form with non-oil properties, where it is known as 'the changing balance-of-power problem'. Furthermore, although nationalization as a technique in the hands of developing countries has declined significantly in recent years, there is every reason to suppose that, in a few years time, the problem will arise once again as developing countries perceive themselves to be unfairly disadvantaged by modern international investment codes, whether or not they are members of the World Trade Organization.

The Political Dimension

These problems are all rendered more acute by political considerations. One typical problem is that of sovereign immunity; namely when foreign entities are protected by their own governments so that a host state has to deal with another state in any dispute with an investor. This used to be a serious problem in the past and has slackened in recent years, largely because of customary international law. Nevertheless, treaty obligations can create such a situation in specific cases and with specific countries. The reverse of this problem is that of sanctions which renders foreign investors leery of what might otherwise be major investment opportunities which meet all other investment criteria.

The classical example of this type of problem is provided by the Helms-Burton and D' Amato-Kennedy legislation – better known as the Cuba Sanctions Act and the Iran–Libya Sanctions Act (ILSA) – in the United States which seeks to enshrine the principle of legal extra-territoriality for American federal law. The other typical example is the role of the United Nations or individual states in imposing sanctions on states such as Libya, Iran or Iraq. It should not be forgotten, for example, that a major investor in Egypt is Libya – which suggests that Egypt itself might fall under the constraints of American extra-territorial legislation or, until they were removed from Libya, United Nations sanctions, with all that that might imply for foreign private investors there. In effect, sanctions are considered by investors to be an unreasonable interference in legitimate economic activity but they are forced to comply because of the potential penalties under domestic legislation in the states applying sanctions.

Even United Nations sanctions operate under a similar legal regime. Investors face another problem, however these circumstances. This is that the host country for the investment may also levy penalties if the investor observes home country or third country legislation. Such penalties can involve financial loss, retention of profits or nationalization. Thus, investors tend to make careful evaluations of political risk in this case external political risk – as part of the basic investment decision. Often such calculations are absorbed into the proposed discount rate used to calculate expected returns and the financial value of the asset and this, in turn, can lead to problems over the 'obsolescing bargain'.

External political risk, however, is only one part of the political evaluation process. Two other aspects are of considerable interest to the investor and make their way into the discount rate. The first of these relates to the simple – and non-legal – question of political stability, clearly important in terms of the likely longevity of the investment. It does not follow, incidentally, that political instability disqualifies a particular country from receiving foreign investment, as is shown in the case of oil and gas investments in contemporary Algeria. It does, however, raise issues of legal continuity of sanctity of contract, hence the interest that potential investors take in consulting both governments and their oppositions! The most important aspect of political risk, however, is the actual status of a domestic legal code within the structure of a particular political regime. Ideally, governmental behaviour should be subject to the rule-of-law. In practice, however, this is often not the case, whatever governments may pretend. As a result, investors recognize that the process of investment becomes subject to the vagaries of governmental or individual whim. The most obvious example of this is the question of corruption, a widespread problem in the Middle Eastern and North African region.

Associated with this issue are the companion issues of corruption, smuggling, drugs and crime. They can all affect the status and effectiveness of domestic legislation and may even have more direct effects on investment. Governments, of course, try to respond, to the extent that they are able, given their own subjugation to the same problems. Sometimes, this can produce acute tensions within government, as some analysts allege occurred in 1971 in Morocco and as is said to have occurred in Tunisia in 1995 and, most particularly, in Algeria. Sometimes, it can result in campaigns designed to correct the original problem which incidentally also severely affect the investment climate. Something of the sort appears to have happened in connection with the Moroccan anti-drugs and anti-smuggling campaign in 1996. This may also turn out to be the case with the 1997 Moroccan anti-corruption campaign, simply because of the uncertainty it may introduce into the political process.

Law and Governance

One of the consequences of the Euro-Mediterranean Partnership initiative will eventually be to increase the significance of agreed standards of what the British government has called 'good governance'. By this term is meant the institution of governmental systems that are subject to the rule-of-law and do not engage in repression as a means of retaining power, being instead responsive and accountable to public pressure and to agreed norms of government. This will inevitably improve investor confidence as the level of transparency they require, both in commercial and political terms, will follow on from the creation of legal and judicial regimes which genuinely independent of the state and governmental structures. In this context, therefore, the political and security basket of the Barcelona Process had an immediate and important relevance to improving investor confidence and thus rendering the system introduced by the economic basket more viable.

Indeed, this issue highlights a profound difference between Europe and the United States over the ways in which political and economic transparency and accountability can be achieved. Europe generally argues that political initiatives are necessary to achieve this; government itself must be made accountable and, in a word, more democratic. This then leads to objective legal process and transparency which creates the conditions for sustained private investment. The American and – to some extent – British view is different. Here it is argued, along the lines of the 'economic theory of politics',[11] that the transparency imposed by the commercial world leads inexorably towards political transparency and accountability. Thus, through economic liberalization and the creation of appropriate legal structures to encourage this process, political liberalization will eventually be forced on reluctant governments – as occurred, for example in Chile.

In the South Mediterranean region, in reality, a combination of both processes is likely to force democratic change. The Barcelona Process, with its emphasis on eventual political change, largely because of regional security concerns if such change is not accomplished, is certainly one source of pressure, although its effectiveness will depend on the extent to which the European Union is willing to make it a priority within the Euro-Mediterranean Partnership initiative. At the same time, the economic changes being forced on South Mediterranean states as part of the transition process involved in the creation of the bilateral industrial free trade areas, will create their own imperative for legal change. One good example is the changes now required in customs tariff regimes and in domestic fiscal systems. The phased reductions in tariff barriers, which is an integral part of the free trade area process, will force governments to look for new sources of revenue, given the current importance in state finances played by tariffs. This will be buttressed by the introduction of Value Added Tax, as the main means of indirect taxation in most of the South Mediterranean countries as a result of World Bank pressure. This, in turn, will undoubtedly intensify social unrest in many states because VAT is a far more universal tax than most systems currently in place – and this, in turn, will force governments to become more responsive to public opinion unless they wish to face increasing political instability and consequent declines in foreign investor confidence.

Of course, this in part depends on the type of investment being made. It is notable, for example, that major investments in hydrocarbon assets seem to escape most of these political requirements entirely. It is as if either international oil companies do not bother over political risk, being uncertainty of economic return from investment, or consider that political risk is minimized by the fact that any government in whose territory they work will depend on access to oil rent to ensure its own survival. This certainly seems to be the case in Algeria currently, for example, where the British company BP has been prepared to risk a massive investment of $3.5 billion in political circumstances which are highly unpredictable. International oil companies are, in short, far more concerned about the misuse of the 'obsolescing bargain' and the threat of eventual nationalization than they are over issues of legal and political transparency and accountability.

For non-oil investors, however, this is not the case. They rely heavily on guaranteed political stability and legal transparency to ensure the predictability of the security of their anticipated return on investment. In their calculations of political risk, therefore, effective and independent legal structures are of crucial importance. They must also consider the ways in which other aspects of the Barcelona process are likely to affect investment. There is certain to be growing pressure for greater observance of human rights standards in the countries of the Southern Mediterranean, both from domestic and foreign sources, as the process of government accountability develops.

This is also likely to be partnered by growing domestic concerns over environmental and ecological issues – as was seen in the early 1990s, when a

Canadian company proposed waste dumping in the Western Sahara, only to see its contractual arrangements revoked by the Moroccan government. Similarly, consumer concerns over issues of labour abuse, which will be partnered by pressure from labour organizations in Europe because of the economic as well as the human rights implications, are bound to lead to increasingly complex patterns of legal controls over the freedoms of foreign investors, as will World Trade Organisation vigilance over the potential for economic dumping in European markets – although the comparative labour cost advantages of North African and Middle Eastern producers is likely to decline as development proceeds. None the less, the advent of government transparency and accountability will – certainly if it is accompanied by genuine economic development – result in a more complex legal framework for foreign investors, both guaranteeing their interests and circumscribing their freedoms of action – just as is the case in Europe!

Conclusion and Recommendations

The problems facing investment host countries as far as the legal status of investment is concerned fall into two groups. The first is one connected with the status of investment under international law and in the context of the 'obsolescing bargain'. This, in theory, could be dealt with through an international investment code operated by the World Trade Organisation and designed with the concerns of the developing world in mind. However, given the legal recognition of the sovereign immunity of states, difficulties reflecting differing perceptions of the inherent values of contracts will continue and the danger of nationalization will remain.

The second reflects the international political processes of host countries and the role played by domestic legal systems, particularly their independent status from government or regime. Unless such independence exists and is perceived to exist by potential investors, private investment will be discouraged. The process of investment thus links in to the problem of 'good governance' and thus forms an integral part of the Euro-Mediterranean partnership project. It remains to be seen to what extent both North and South Mediterranean partner-states are prepared to recognize the core role of the independent legal process, both in terms of political and economic development, and to what extent either side is prepared to confront the issue.

Of course, none of these developments will occur simply by themselves. To a large extent, the Euro-Mediterranean Partnership initiative should attempt to expand the role of its political and security basket to encourage the development of independent legal systems and transparency in the legal process. In part this will follow on from the process of democratization. However, there will also be a need to ensure that national legislation meets accepted international commercial legal standards. Care should also be taken to try to foster appropriate legislation to ensure that foreign investors cannot exploit labour, social and environmental legislation to their advantage. Above all, South Mediterranean governments should be encouraged to accept the crucial importance of effective and independent legal systems, untainted by official interference. Such changes require active European Union involvement and aid. It is unlikely that the MEDA programme, which forms part of the Euro-Mediterranean Partnership initiative will be able to provide such aid and consideration should be given to providing special funds – similar to the British government's 'know-how' fund for Eastern Europe.

There are also specific measures that could be considered by the European Union as part of its follow-up process to the Barcelona Conference in 1995. They relate to issues raised above:

(1) South Mediterranean governments should be encouraged to improve the status of foreign property rights in their countries by both improving legal protection provisions and arbitration procedures. These should be brought into line with European standards.

(2) Attention should be given to developing common standards and modes of compensation across the Mediterranean, both in the case of dispute and in the case of nationalization of foreign assets. Although this problem may appear to be remote at present, the very nature of the obsolescing bargain will force it to the forefront of the political and diplomatic stage by the early decades of the next century.

(3) European governments need to reconsider their views on the future role of economic sanctions in international relations, because of the adverse effects such regimes have on investor confidence – not just for the countries concerned, but for the region overall. This really forms part of the problem of political conditionality which still needs to be addressed within the context of the Barcelona Process.

(4) It is becoming increasingly clear that there is a close link between economic improvement and political change, particularly as far as attracting foreign investment is concerned. Thus the European Union should give greater prominence to encouraging increased 'good governance' as well as political transparency and accountability, as part of progress on the economic basket of the Barcelona Process.

(5) At the same time, the changes in tax structures required by the free trade area proposals will cause shortfalls in government revenues at a time

when adjustment will demand greater government expenditure on economic restructuring. The European Union should direct additional resources at easing this transition because of the adverse social consequences if this is not done, particularly in respect of restructuring fiscal systems and tax collection mechanisms.

(6) Environmental and ecological issues should be addressed by persuading South Mediterranean states to adhere to international conventions, particularly the convention on climate change, and to incorporate 'best practice' style legislation on environmental protection into their national legislations, so that common standards apply across the Mediterranean region.

(7) Similar 'best practice' style legislation should also be encouraged in terms of labour legislation and trade union legislation, even if this might imply a reduction in apparent comparative advantage, as this will tend to stabilize the political and social situation and will thus work to the benefit of the foreign investor in the medium to long term.

(8) In return for such adjustments, some of which will further erode the comparative advantage of the South Mediterranean region to foreign investors, the European Union should undertake to enforce appropriate legislation on a global basis through the World Trade Organisation.

(9) Foreign investors should also be encouraged by the provision of investment insurance systems, similar to those already provided by the World Bank, for investors in the South Mediterranean region. These should be in addition to insurance schemes already provided at a national level in Europe.

(10) In view of the increasing integration of North Africa into the European gas grid distribution system (via the TransMed and Trans-Maghreb pipeline systems), attention should be given to similar integration of electricity supply systems. This would provide an opportunity to stimulate investment into solar energy production in North Africa and the Middle East for electricity export to Europe.

Behind these considerations, there lie a set of essentially self-evident principles designed to ensure that foreign investors encounter stable and reproducible environments for investment, typified by the concept of the rule-of-law. Judicial systems must be independent of government in every meaningful way and government itself must be subordinate to established legal codes. This, in turn, implies that government must be committed to the principles of 'good governance' as generally understood to combine political participation and accountability to ensure social justice. More specifically, legal systems relating to commercial and financial activity must be transparent, simple and enforcible to be credible – the example of Egypt with its 65,000 laws, often in contradiction with each other is a case in point. Above all, the legal codes and system must be equitable, particularly in providing equal treatment to nationals and foreigners alike, whilst being reproducible, in that they are not subject to change at government whim but only by due process. The creation of a legal environment of this kind will do much to ensure that foreign investors see the Middle East and North African regions as viable investment destinations in future and it is that that should become one of the major objectives of the Barcelona Process.

NOTES

1. J. Ould Aoudia (1996), «'Les enjeux économiques de la nouvelle politique méditerranéenne de l'Europe', *Monde Arabe: Maghreb-Mashreq*, 153, July–Sept. 1996, p.33.
2. G. Bannock, R.E. Baxter and K. Rees (1978), *The Penguin Dictionary of Economics*, Harmondsworth: Penguin, p.189
3. The process whereby foreign investors are required to either take an indegenous partner, who is often the majority shareholder in a joint venture and thus can threaten the security of an investment, or are required to integrate local staff regardless of their levels of competence, as part of a process of assumed 'technology transfer'.
4. See, for example, J.S. Lizondo (1991), 'Foreign Direct Investment', in IMF, *Determinants and Systemic Consequences of International Capital Flows*, Occasional Paper 77, March 1991, pp.68–77.
5. E.G.H. Joffé (1992), 'Foreign Investment and Economic Liberalisation', *JIME Review*, 17 (Summer 1992), pp.24–5.
6. Aoudia, op. cit., pp.30–31.
7. European Union Official Development Assistance ran at four per cent of total aid for the South Mediterranean states between 1990 and 1993, rising to 29 per cent once bilateral official aid from European states was included. The Maghrib received the equivalent of $29 per head, whilst Israel, Egypt and Jordan received $90 per capita. However, in the Mashriq, Europe's role was even more restricted than in the Maghrib, providing only three per cent of multilateral aid from the European Union itself and 19 per cent, once bilateral official assistance was included. (See Aoudia, op. cit., pp.34–5.)
8. T. Andersson (1991), *Multinational Investment in Developing Countries: A Study of Taxation and Nationalization*, London and New York: Routledge, pp.11–12.
9. Aoudia, op. cit., p.33
10. For a detailed discussion of this issue with respect to oil and gas properties, see E. Penrose G. Joffé and P. Stevens (1992), 'Nationalisation of Foreign-Owned Property for a Public Purpose: An Economic Perspective on Appropriate Compensation', *The Modern Law Review* 55/3 (May 1992).
11. See, for example, A.O. Hirschman (1981), *Essays in Trespassing: Economics to Politics and Beyond*, Cambridge and London: Cambridge University Press and A. Foxley, M.S. McPherson and G. O'Donnell (1986), *Development, Democracy and the Art of Trespassing: Essays in Honor of Albert O.Hirschman*, Notre Dame, IN: University of Notre Dame Press.

The Political Process

4

Political Transition in the Middle East

MAY CHARTOUNI-DUBARRY

Following the ideological failure of communism and the concomitant rise of Islamism, the debate on civil society and the prospects for democracy in the Middle East and in the Maghreb has re-emerged in the West, as well as in the Arab world. The issue of democracy and its corollary, civil society, are omnipresent today in Arab political vocabulary and discourse, for they have replaced the mobilising slogans of the 1950s and 1960s concerned with socialism, pan-Arabism and national liberation. A plethora of studies on these issues has appeared in academic circles, both domestic and international, and the approaches they adopt vary widely. Some see civil society as the engine of political transition, others feel this role is played by the process of erosion of the authoritarian state in the Arab world, yet others consider the Islamist variable both as indicator and determinant of socio-political forces operating in the region. Although the question common to all these studies invariably revolves around the so-called 'Arab exception' to the world-wide wave of democratization of the 1980s, the academic responses designed to explain this democratic deficit vary considerably.

Since the practical objectives of the studies presented here excludes a strictly academic approach, the analysis adopted here is resolutely policy-oriented. The object is not to create paradigms by defining the necessary ingredients for democracy in the Middle East. Rather, it is to identify key elements among the most pertinent questions linked to the issue of political transition in the Middle East, in order to define and analyse the mechanisms of what will necessarily be a long process with uncertain outcomes and whose nature and intensity can vary from country to country. In other words, although an identical system of analysis has been used to examine countries as different as Lebanon, Jordan, Egypt, Syria or the Palestinian Entity, the method used must remain as empirical as possible. It must integrate the multiplicity of political situations and patterns of evolutions as well as their increasingly significant differences.

It goes without saying that the area under scrutiny in this study, although limited to the Middle Eastern states involved in the Barcelona Process, is neither a closed area nor a monolithic bloc. The division of the overall analysis of political transition in the South Mediterranean into two parts, one dealing with the Maghreb and the other with the Mashreq, has no scientific significance. Indeed, in order to be coherent and as exhaustive as possible, the analysis must in essence draw on comparative and conceptual elements in each case study.

The task is difficult, for the issue of analytical subjectivity constitutes a fundamental obstacle. Democracy, with its strong normative and ideological content, confronts North–South perceptions and revives a gamut of deeply embedded prejudices and assumptions. As with everything that relates to political-cultural representations on either side of the Mediterranean, it is an area in which the trans-Mediterranean dialogue is particularly delicate and where mutual resentment and criticism perpetuate cultural blockages and negative perceptions, which are detrimental to political dialogue. The second difficulty has to do with epistemology and relates to the very definition of the term democracy, which has a self-evident significance on the northern bank of the Mediterranean, is more problematic in meaning once transposed into Arab-Islamic lands. In more concrete terms, one must ask whether democratic developments in a given Arab state should be measured against the Western model of liberal and representative democracy, as well as the historical context in which it emerged. Such a static approach would only lead to yet another negative and pessimistic view of the prospects for democracy in the region. Only a dynamic and integrated approach, focused on the process of political change *per se* rather than its presumed outcome, can lead to constructive dialogue. As a result, this contribution first seeks to examine the complexity of the debate among intellectuals and social scientists on the subject of democracy in the Arab world. It then seeks to determine the real content and the consequences of the current wave of liberalization there, before focusing on its major implications for the Euro-Mediterranean dialogue.

The Persistence of Authoritarianism in the Arab World

Political upheaval in Eastern Europe has legitimized, at least domestically, the debate on the prospects for democracy in the Middle East, although it is not directly responsible for initiating it. This interest is linked to internal factors and is a consequence of the failure of Nasserist socialist models which have dominated the political scene over the last 30 to 40 years. The 1980s dealt a serious blow to the very logic of authoritarianism with the appearance of two new factors: the end of the rentier economy in its purest form and the rise of the largest-ever contemporary popular protest movement, usually referred to by the shorthand term of 'Islamism'. The erosion of the state and its legitimacy is central to the socio-political evolution of the states in the region.

Few studies are now devoted to the examination of authoritarianism *per se* in the Arab world.[1] A fashionable topic in the 1960s and until the early 1970s, it lost its appeal mainly because of the stabilization of authoritarian regimes so that they became a 'natural' component of the regional political scene. The attention of researchers – and politicians – is now focused on whatever signs of weakness – or 'liberalization' – might emanate from regimes in difficulties and apparently on the verge of collapse, or about to be forced into political liberalization as their only means of survival. While for some the erosion of these regimes should necessarily lead (by virtue of an historical determinism) to a linear and universal transition to democracy, others consider the political itinerary of these societies as 'culturally genetic' and would therefore argue they are organically resistant to democracy.

This study supports neither theory. It does not take for granted the evolutionist presupposition according to which Arab societies are 'naturally' moving towards the same democratic outcome which is now presented as the common destiny of humanity. The relativization of the democratic paradigm as universal or the rejection of the uniqueness of the Arab world – and of the Middle East in this case – is not to denigrate the virtues of democracy nor is it a denial of the existence of regional specificities which could explain the persistence of authoritarianism. But authoritarianism is neither a matter of chance nor the result of some implacable fate and less still the product of Arab-Islamic culture, as some Orientalists – be they specialists of Islam, anthropologists or sociologists – still persist in believing.[2] It is due to the convergence and complex interaction – which vary country-by-country – of a number of historical, economic and socio-political factors linked to the evolution of the state, its institutions and its relation to civil society.

The Culturalist Approach

One of the most widely held ideas, both within Western public opinion – for whom it appears to be 'common sense' – and the intelligentsia which tries to rationalize this belief, is that of the so-called intrinsic incompatibility between Islam on the one hand and modernity, progress and democracy on the other. This approach which tries to explain the nature of a system or political regime through cultural parameters continues to be dominant in Western analysis. The theory that all Arab-Islamic societies are naturally or culturally[3] incompatible with democracy has pervaded Orientalist literature for decades.[4] According to it, authoritarianism has its origins within Islam itself, which is *din wa dawla*, religion and state – according to the cliché which still sustains this kind of studies. It states that the intrinsic specificity of this religion alone explains democratic lacunae in the Arab-Muslim world. The argument usually includes factors such as the non-separation of church and state, the absence of key-concepts in Islamic tradition such as that of citizenship, individualism and popular sovereignty, the confusion of the public and the private, or the weakness of civil society.

This theory does not belong exclusively to the Western vision. Some Arab intellectuals also maintain that authoritarianism has its roots in the patriarchal tradition of power, which is strongly anchored in Arab-Islamic civilization. Some underline the tradition of reverence and the need for submission, which characterize the ruler–ruled relationship, attitudes which can rapidly lead to fear and terror.[5] Others have underlined the weight of inherited authoritarianism on a political culture subjected to an undiluted patrimonial state system for centuries.[6] Some even wonder whether there actually exists a need or a demand for democracy within Arab societies.[7]

It must be noted that this culturalist explanation has its counterpart south of the Mediterranean where it has popular appeal. Cultural 'authenticity' is often held as a sacrosanct dogma and legitimizes the rejection of imported political models such as representative democracy, denounced as the ultimate assault of Western cultural imperialism. Thus, this essentialist logic is at the heart of the Islamist discourse, which extols the specificity of Arab-Islamic civilization, without, as we will see later, rejecting the values inherent to political pluralism for it seeks to re-appropriate them instead.

The Army and Rent – Ingredients of the Authoritarian State

The alliance of rent and repression has ensured that authoritarian regimes should flourish. With the help of the economic rents – whether from oil, financial (transfers of migrant labour, transit rights for the Suez canal), or geo-strategic sources (US aid to Egypt, aid from the oil-rich Gulf states to the confrontation states) – these regimes were able to invest into expensive military programmes while still providing for their populations and remaining unaccountable to them. This is why the petrol era induced the state into political irresponsibility and the society into a form of anomy towards political life. While oil revenues endowed the state with considerable financial resources, they also enabled it to monopolize the arena of symbolic production and to proceed with its strategy of the 'de-politicization' of society. Indeed, oil revenues kept alive the leaders' promises of rapid development while at the same time they neutralized the demand for political participation.[8] The oil economy has, according to some authors, rendered the correlation between the level of taxation and that of representation (the 'no representation without taxation' paradigm) inoperative.[9]

The role of the army – as both an instrument of security and a vehicle for the populist ideology of liberation and national integration – is equally crucial in the understanding of the legitimization mechanisms of authoritarianism. The myth of the army was strongly influenced by the development and modernization ideologies of the 1950s and 1960s, which endowed the modern state with unlimited capabilities to achieve economic and social progress.[10] The 1967 defeat, compounded by the military's inability to fulfil social promises, contributed significantly to the army's loss of its sacrosanct status and to the erosion of the 'Arab Socialist' model.[11] But this loss of legitimacy was not accompanied by in-depth demilitarization of the regimes through a reduction in troops or real depoliticization, despite a move towards greater military professionalization.[12] Nor did it moderate the existing regimes' rhetoric as they continued to justify their refusal to engage in political reforms with the same dominant national defence and security imperatives. These issues seem to have retained their full mobilising potential with Arab populations. In other words, the erosion of the legitimacy of authoritarian regimes, notably because of their inability to achieve the 'sacred' objectives they set themselves, was not accompanied by a loss of legitimacy of the objectives themselves.[13] This explains why Islamists have been able to successfully adopt them as their own.

The collapse of the alliance between military force and revenue, therefore, contributed to the reinforcement of legitimizing mechanisms which allowed Arab states to justify their authoritarian rule. This, however, does not mean that these regimes are irremediably condemned. On the contrary, they are showing remarkable longevity, which could be partly attributed to their institutionalization of repression. Indeed, repression has given political violence its own momentum, whether such violence is systematic or sporadic.[14] But these regimes are now looking for new sources of legitimization, demonstrated by the growing significance of religion in official ideology and discourse, as well as the state's determination to establish total control of religious matters, thus confronting its main Islamist political rivals.

The Controversy Over Civil Society: Strong State Against Weak Society?

The external and superimposed position of the state in relation to society and the 'integration' of the former into the latter are the most common explanations for the absence or weakness of civil society in the region and therefore, of the persistence of authoritarianism. The military and bureaucratic outgrowths of the state apparatus as well as the absolute monopoly over the political and institutional apparatus have guaranteed total control of an Arab society which is often described as fragmented, de-structured and lacking integration and political 'culture'. The expression 'Arab masses', widely used by the Western media during the Gulf War, is significant in this respect. The Arab intelligentsia also contributed to the debate on the interaction between the state and society with the idea of the 'imported' Arab state whose 'cannibalistic' nature (for it devours social resources) hinders the development of civil society.[15]

The concept of civil society, which is always linked with democracy, is now highly valued by academics and social scientists. This interest, however, has not fostered a better understanding of the concept itself. Nor has it ended the debate between those who reject the very use of this term in relation to the Arab world and those who see in the creation of charitable, human rights and professional associations as well as various pressure groups, the emergence or re-emergence of the nuclei of civil society in the region.[16] Others have underlined the difference in Arabic between *al-mujtama' al ahli* (civil society) and *al mujtama' al madani* (civic society). This distinction seeks to demonstrate that, whereas civic society refers to 'modern values' such as secularism and citizenship, civil society considers society as a whole, integrating its surviving traditional or pre-state structures, whether confessional, tribal or regional (*'assabiyya* or 'esprit de corps').[17]

The debate on civil society, therefore, raises the much thornier issue of whether or not to recognize the social and cultural pluralism which underlies Middle Eastern societies and which has been systematically denied and stifled by regimes in the name of modernity, with the exception of Lebanon and, to a lesser extent, Yemen. Admittedly, the lack of national cohesion and profound social segmentation which characterize many countries in the region have often been considered as factors in the emergence of 'strong' states. The use and institutionalization of repression are then perceived as the natural and sometimes legitimate response from countries engaged in state- and nation-building.

The issues at stake as Arab societies become autonomous from the state also raise the question of the role of the middle classes or the new bourgeoisie in the transition to democracy. The economic explanation, which establishes a direct link between economic liberalism and the degree of democratization, was very fashionable when development theories dominated sociology. It has now lost ground and does not seem applicable to the Middle East where the state bourgeoisie as well as the private sector bourgeoisie are currently too dependent on the state – when they have not actually sworn complete allegiance to it (since they share its interests and have the same sense of identity) – to attempt political emancipation and act as a catalyst of civil society and become democracy's 'natural ally'.[18] The drawing in of both the over-mighty public sector and the nascent private sector as clients of the state, has, according to some, contributed to blurring the dividing line between public and private and thus prevented the emergence of an external political arena independent from the state and able to contain its power.[19]

The Internal–External Interaction

An internal–external interaction between state and region and within the state itself takes place on two levels One is strategic in nature, whereas the other is 'civilizational'; both play a part in explaining the nature of Arab regimes. This explanation, however, must be used with care because it has also been exploited by established regimes. The causality is not to be found in official discourse, which regularly denounces foreign conspiracies, but at the level of collective perceptions and local political culture. Arab societies remain, as a whole, fundamentally suspicious of and even hostile to any form of Western intervention, especially when it occurs in the name of international law or the right of intervention. The second Gulf War as well as the subsequent international embargo and attempted tutelage over Iraq have reinforced this suspicion. The West is accused of seeking new ways to impose its hegemony while hiding behind the pretext of democratic principles and their universality. Thus, the weak support for democracy in the Arab world could be explained partly by the fact that the democratic model is too closely associated with the West to find a more enthusiastic echo in the Arab world.[20]

The strategic impact of the external variable – regional and international – on domestic equilibrium is crucial in the Mashreq. This may be what constitutes the essential specificity of the Mashreq, or at least, what distinguishes it from the Maghreb, which is also subject to important external constraints, albeit of a different nature and intensity. It is due to regional factors (the Israeli–Arab conflict, oil, over-armament, border disputes, water, for example), which have provoked a level of intervention rarely seen in the rest of the world. The region's potential for conflict does not aid the creation of an environment favourable to political liberalization. Instead, it has exacerbated the sense of insecurity and vulnerability felt by regimes there, by encouraging them to protect themselves against the threat of domestic subversion.[21] This is illustrated by the correlation between the persistence and aggravation of regional sources of tension and the strengthening of authoritarian regimes. However, the reversibility of this causality relationship (in other words, reductions in external tensions would lead necessarily to liberalization and internal political stability) cannot be taken for granted.

Case Studies: Comparative Experiences of Liberalizations

The complexity of the multi-faceted debate over the persistence of authoritarianism and, above all, over its complexity and powerful emotional and polemic content, argues for caution in interpreting the short and medium term significance of the minor waves of political liberalization, for, since the mid-1980s, these initiatives have hardly affected the exclusive political monopoly of the state. However, two consequences have emerged. The first relates to the present crisis of the Arab state. Although it does not imply a qualitative transformation of the fundamentally authoritarian nature of the regime, it does, however, question the durability of present political structures.[22] The second is that formal democratization, initiated and orchestrated entirely from the top in most cases, resembles a power strategy rather than a response to a truly popular demand for democracy. Furthermore, the experience of political pluralism (*al-ta'adudiyya* in the official Arabic rhetoric) is limited to passive representation and participation. Legal opposition parties – when they exist – are co-opted by the regime and obey the rules of a game it has devised. In such circumstances no peaceful and institutional alternative to the present regimes, brought about by free elections, can be seriously contemplated.

This is the general trend in the Arab world where elections, despite being commonplace, appear to be attempts to preserve existing political systems rather than to liberalize them. A close examination of the five case studies selected here reveals, however, contrasting realities and suggests a more qualified and multiple approach to such experiments in democratization. Indeed, they vary with each country in relation to the interaction of the variables mentioned earlier: the nature of the regime, the role of the military, the strength of civil society, the level of national cohesion and the weight of external constraints. If the interaction between these variables determines the causes and nature of these processes of pluralization, its evolution and outcome depend largely on the importance accorded to the Islamists and their integration, exclusion or co-optation by existing regimes. Aware of their new vulnerability, these states seem less willing to embark on genuine political reform since they are now confronted with a powerful political protest movement which, despite a lack of enthusiasm for and ambivalence towards democracy, remains the only alternative to secular Nasserist or left-wing opposition parties, which, in any case, have been severely weakened by years of repression.

A Variable Geometry of Democracy

Each state in this study – except for Syria – has experienced some level of pluralism or democratization. In 1989, Jordan followed Egypt by launching its own limited and controlled programme of political pluralism; the end of the war in Lebanon enabled the country to return to its traditional consensual democracy; and the Palestinian entity held its first 'free' elections on 20 January 1996. It is possible to measure the degree of democratization in these states by means of quantifiable criteria such as elections, public and political freedoms, the importance of association networks and the independence of trade unions. A comparative approach was therefore chosen because it facilitates the identification of common dynamics and the appraisal of the diversity of situations.

Despite differences in their degrees of liberalization, Egypt, Jordan, the Palestinian Authority, Lebanon and Syria share, among other things, their weak commitment to democratic principles, philosophy and ethics. Indeed, although Western democracy is characterized by a number of practices that constitute the foundation of a political system, it is also a system of values and norms. This is something that these states lack. Another common characteristic that they share is the 'red line' that under no circumstances must be transgressed and that forbids criticism of the ruler.[23] This limits the extent to which democratic practices may take place, in so far as the opposition, even though it may tolerated or even legal, must still swear unconditional allegiance to the head of state.

- Both the Palestinian and Lebanese cases present some similarities which set them apart from the models of liberalization that dominate the rest of the Arab world today – the absence of a territorially sovereign state on the one hand, and the blatant weakness of the state structure on the other; a relatively strong civil society due in part to the vitality and autonomy of Lebanese community structures and to the historical national mobilization of the Palestinian community; and the particularly significant impact of external constraints on the mechanisms of democracy in practice. In both cases it is obvious that democratization was not imposed from the top and drip-fed by an omnipotent state. In Lebanon, for example, it was not imposed out of choice or democratic conviction, but out of necessity to meet specific considerations linked to the religious configuration of Lebanese society and the need to guarantee inter-communal coexistence. Democratization also met the practical requirements which accompanied the emergence of the territorial Palestinian entity and the imperative need to give it constitutional substance to consolidate the legitimacy of the Palestinian Authority, established in Palestine in the summer of 1994, in disjointed areas between Gaza and Jericho.

- *Palestine:* The main question regarding the case of Palestine is to what extent the Oslo Agreement, the establishment of the Palestinian Authority and the 20 January 1996 elections – which have provided it with a president and a cabinet – have stimulated a true process of democratization. The simultaneous existence of three equally precarious processes – state and nation building, application of the Oslo Accords and democratic transition – is so intricately interwoven that it would be hazardous to rely on the example of Palestine to support the theory that there is a mechanical relationship of cause and effect between the advent of peace and the establishment of democracy in the region. Quite apart from the spasmodic nature and underlying regressive nature of the Oslo

Process, the pattern of democratization in Palestine, a phenomenon which was unknown in any institutionalized form before, is in many ways reminiscent of the political practice and culture which dominates the region in which national interest and the interest of the ruling elite eventually become fused. Yasser Arafat's lapses into authoritarian practices have already been documented.[24] Excessive budgetary commitment to the establishment of a security apparatus, the frequent use of emergency laws to arrest and imprison peace process opponents as well as the rapid expansion of the bureaucracy through co-optation conforms to the models of such omnipotent and centralized states as Iraq, Syria, Egypt and Algeria.[25]

- *Lebanon*: After receiving much praise from its many supporters as the only real Arab democracy, consociational Lebanese democracy, which was founded on a balance-of-power among the various communities in the country, became, with the outbreak of the civil war in 1975, the perfect 'anti-model'. Lebanon's descent into chaos partly legitimized, or at least restored, the credibility of military authoritarianism and reinstated it as the only political system capable of dealing with the region's profoundly segmented societies and as the only guarantee of internal political stability.[26] However, once the war ended, the Lebanese system showed a surprising ability to survive. Since then, the Lebanese model has been rehabilitated because it validates, to a certain extent, the theory – increasingly relied upon in academic circles – that pre-electoral national pacts can be instrumental in the democratic transition of Arab states. The Lebanese system, however, is far from being a panacea and it is flawed both in theory and practice. Indeed, Lebanese democracy was never an end in itself. It is today, as in the past, the only peaceful means of resolving conflicts between the many communities that form both the basic political unit and the true source of legitimacy in Lebanon. The way in which Lebanese communities operate internally – each one a law unto itself – remains strongly marked by political feudalism and untouched by democratic traditions. In practice, several distortions of the 1989 Taif constitutional reforms[27] emerged to corrupt the democratic process. Thus, the concern for representation was taken so far as to immobilize the political process, which is now rocked by power struggles within the triumvirate formed by the president of the republic (Maronite), the prime minister (Sunni) and the speaker of parliament (Shi'i). These conflicts are usually only resolved by Syrian intervention.

- The cases of Egypt and Jordan constitute more classical examples of liberalization. Measures leading to political liberalization (multi-party elections, legalization of opposition parties, greater public liberties, freedom of association) have accompanied the process of economic liberalization in both countries. *Infitah* (opening-up) in both countries was the consequence of the failure of centrally-controlled economic growth and the resulting economic quagmire. In the face of sporadic but violent urban rioting, democratization seemed to provide a safety valve, an instrument of legitimization and domestic stability, as well as a means of broadening the regimes' support-bases by co-opting larger sections of civil society to share the responsibility for crisis management and the unpopular austerity measures dictated by the IMF and the World Bank. The main reason behind Egypt's and Jordan's decision to organize multi-party elections – from the mid-1970s and, more decisively, after 1984 in Egypt and in 1989 in Jordan – stemmed from their respective needs to resolve serious social crises.

- *Egypt*: The Egyptian state was, in effect, a pioneer of this mode of 'authoritarian liberalization'. Defined and controlled by a regime eager to defuse and channel popular discontent since President Sadat's rise to power, the aim of this liberalization process was to strengthen both its domestic and international legitimacy. The case of Egypt is therefore the best illustration of the contradictions, hedging and precariousness inherent in 'authoritarian liberalization'. Neither the periodical nature of elections, the existence of over ten legally recognized political parties[28] and of an opposition press, the relative autonomy of the judiciary,[29] nor the vitality of the associational network have affected the hegemonic position of the ruling party, the National Democratic Party (NPD), altered the bureaucratic and military structure of power, or even tempered the inordinate power of the head of state who has not yet lifted the state of emergency imposed in 1967. This failure is compounded by the low level of electoral participation – a symptom of disaffection, if not cynicism, towards politics on the part of most Egyptians[30] – and the powerful appeal of the Islamist opposition. The leadership's inability to include the legally recognized wing of the *Ikhwan al-Muslimin* within the formal political process since the beginning of the 1990s clearly shows that cosmetic Egyptian democratization has led to a political impasse.

- *Jordan*: The Jordanian experience of democratization is characterized – apart from the issue of the integration of Islamists, which will be examined later – by the fact that it was imposed through the interaction between internal and external constraints. Indeed, the beginning of the democratization process in 1989 responded to the urgent need to face the joint threat posed by the Palestinian uprising (the *intifada*) and the

Jordanian option (the creation of a Palestinian state in Jordan) – preferred by Israel – to national cohesion and even the viability of the Jordanian entity. The abandonment of claims to the West Bank intensified socio-economic tensions and alerted the leadership to the need to strengthen the state from within, through a better integration of the Palestinian community within Jordan and by giving the Islamist movement a legal status. The need to pacify the domestic front grew more vital as the external threat intensified. Thus, in an attempt to control the domestic economic and social crisis, linked to the regional situation, King Hussein authorized the November 1989 elections which were among the most open in the Arab world at the time. The position of Jordan – a long-time Western ally – during the Gulf War revealed how viable and genuine the democratization option had become, since the state conceded to the pro-Iraq sentiments of the public at large. However, the terms of the peace treaty with Israel soon upset the national consensus on foreign policy and this explains, to a certain extent, why the king then adopted a tougher approach, implementing his own decisions in foreign policy matters regardless of public opinion. This provides further evidence of the existence of 'red lines' limiting the democratization process in Middle Eastern states and puts the significance of liberalization in Jordan into perspective. Despite the abolition of emergency laws, the creation of a national charter and the organization of the 1993 elections, Jordan is still a long way from genuine constitutional monarchy.

• *Syria*: Syria stands apart from other Arab states in so far as its two phases of *infitah* (economic liberalization) and the development of a private sector did not lead to significant political liberalization.[31] Together with Iraq, Syria continues to epitomize authoritarianism in the Arab world. The Syrian state has invaded society and the associational networks inherent in civil society are almost non-existent. There are no political parties nor a free press, trade unions are incorporated within the state's single political party and the president holds absolute powers. The function of the *Majlis al-Sha'ab* remains purely consultative and is limited to non-political issues. According to President Asad, Syria has developed its own form of democracy and will not import a foreign model.

Islamism in Political Transition

Although Islamism is fully acknowledged as the main political and ideological force in the Arab world today, its significance and, above all, its place in the democratization process are perceived differently. It is seen intermittently either as a regression in the process of political transition or, on the contrary, as the most visible sign of the emergence of civil society and of the articulation in religious terms (the most familiar, popular and legitimate language) of a form of political mobilization. Does the rise of Islamism reflect a return to a sense of identity enshrined in a mythical past as a reaction to the deterioration in socio-economic conditions, or is it the only real political alternative to regimes that have lost their legitimacy? Is it simply a manifestation of the multifarious crisis that is affecting Arab countries, or could it, at last, signal the emergence of civil society in a region which has always been dominated by strong states and weak societies? Should, therefore, the movement be politically channelled by integrating the Islamists into the legal political arena or should they be prevented, at all costs, from seizing a power they would be incapable of sharing? In other words, should these movements be treated as a threat to be eradicated, as the Egyptian (since 1992), Algerian and Syrian regimes have done or should they be considered as an integral part of the national political scene, as in the case of Morocco, Jordan, Lebanon and Yemen?[32]

The debate over integrating the Islamists into the liberalization process is far from over. It has, in fact, become more acute because of the dramatic situation in Algeria between 1992 and 1999. But the Algerian situation cannot be used as an example of the nature and evolution of the relations between the state and the Islamist movement in the rest of the Arab world. Indeed, the violent polarization of politics in Algeria appears to be the exception rather than the rule. The general trend – should there be one – within the Islamist movement is one of pragmatism revealing a clear intention to participate in the electoral process and therefore, to enter the sphere of legal political activity. The spread – and in certain cases, the fact that it has almost become a banality – of Islamist protest over the last few years has progressively underlined the complexity of a phenomenon which, far from being global or monolithic, varies considerably from country to country in its twofold relationship with civil society and the state. In other words, although the Islamist movement remains united on ideology (application of the *Shari'a* as a prerequisite for the establishment of an Islamic state with divine sovereignty), there are, however, diverse Islamist players who have had to adapt to their respective national constraints. Likewise, Arab states have formulated various strategies and responses to Islamist protest. The spectrum of these strategies spans from repression and exclusion (or eradiction) to co-optation and integration. The interaction between the state and the Islamist movement depends on a series of internal and external variables: the political nature and legitimacy of the regime, the level of social and national cohesion, the role of religion within power structures, the strength and depth of implantation of the Islamist movement and, of course, external constraints. All these factors are intertwined in such a way that each country's relationship with Islamism is affected differently: the experiences do not stem from the same causes and do not lead to the same results. This heterogeneity shows the obvious limitations of viewing political Islam as a security issue by considering the movement solely as a powerfully uniform and trans-national threat. This is, however, a view still favoured by some Western experts, echoing the repressive attitudes inherent in the rhetoric of the Algerian and Egyptian regimes, which revolves around the demonization of the Islamists who are portrayed as a handful of marginal terrorists in the pay of hostile foreign powers.

Yet, each of the five cases studied here illustrates a specific type of relationship between the state and the Islamist movements, in which, each case must be considered as atypical, even unique or, at least, exceptional in specific respects.

- *Lebanon*: The Lebanese case – the least known – is an example of the relatively easy integration of Islamists, whether Shi'i (*Hizbullah*) or Sunni (*al-Jamaa al-Islamiyya*), into the body politic. Active in parliament since 1992, the Islamists supported the inter-confessional system as reinstated after the Taif Agreement, although they had earlier fought against it during the 15-year war and had derived their legitimacy from this opposition. The external variable of Syrian hegemony over the power structure largely explains the Islamist strategic turnaround. But the reasons behind the success of this political reversal, although paradoxical, lie in the confessional nature of the Lebanese state. The participation of the Islamists in the political process did not emerge as a strategic and vertical decision made by the state. Instead, it was initiated by the popular base of society and regulated by competition within each community. The state, because of its function as a distributor, only controls the degree of representation to which such new political forces are entitled.[33]

- *Jordan*: Jordan offers another example of the successful integration of Islamists in the democratization process initiated by King Hussein in 1989. It is a model of peaceful electoral and institutional containment. Jordan is one of the few states which avoided violence in its management of the Islamist challenge. This is due to a series of factors related to the nature of the Jordanian Islamist movement and its privileged relationship with the Hashemite dynasty over the last forty years. Deeply rooted within Jordanian society, the Jordanian *Ikhwan al-Muslimin*[34] has enjoyed considerable freedom of action in the spheres of culture, education and public morality in exchange for the movement's loyalty to the monarchy. Its social activism has enabled it, as in Egypt, to develop a large parallel social services network, consistent with its peaceful and law-abiding strategy for a gradual Islamization of society. Until the movement's full integration into the democratization process, it did not regard politics as important. Its participation, however, in the 1989 general elections turned it into the main political force as well as the best structured parliamentary group and its members did not hesitate to make alliances with secular or opposition parties. Jordanian Islamists, like their Lebanese counterparts, cannot question the legitimacy of a system of which they are an integral part without running the risk of signing their own death warrants.

As the king's allies – and clients – they scrupulously respect the rules of the political game and the parameters of national dialogue as defined unilaterally by the leadership. Thus they have always refrained from commenting on or criticising the main orientations of the king's foreign policy. The peace treaty with Israel, however, is proving a serious strain on the strength of this alliance, which is one of the key ingredients of the kingdom's domestic stability. King Hussein did not hesitate to react to their untimely opposition to the normalization process with Israel in a speech far less indulgent towards them than had been the case in the past. Indeed, the movement's fall from royal grace resulted, above all, in the clear erosion of its position within the new parliamentary chamber, elected in 1993.

• *Egypt*: The Egyptian regime's change of strategy towards the Islamist movement in the 1990s reflects the ambiguity which has marked the process of democratization since its inception.[35] After spending the last two decades trying to divide the Islamist movement between its moderate law-abiding wing, represented by the *Ikhwan al-Muslimin* which enjoyed some degree of legitimate political integration, and its radical and violent wing, the Egyptian regime has returned, since the beginning of the 1990s, to Nasser's confrontational strategy towards the movement as a whole. The Algerian crisis and the wave of terrorist attacks which shook the country between 1992 and 1994 radically modified the regime's perception of the Islamist challenge. The earlier strategy of semi-integration of the law-abiding wing of the Islamist movement primarily consisted in using it as a counterweight to Nasserist and leftist forces. The Mubarak regime sought to maintain the balance between the secular and the Islamist opposition.

The main weakness of this strategy, originally initiated by Anwar Sadat and then continued by his successor, Husni Mubarak, is that both leaders rejected requests for legalization made by the *Ikhwan al-Muslimin* either for rehabilitation as an association[36] or for recognition as a political party. This semi-legal situation did not, however, prevent the movement's considerable expansion in the 1980s when it not only took over many governmental and non-governmental organizations[37] but also entered the political arena. Indeed, in 1984, the *Ikhwan al-Muslimin* managed to circumvent the law which forbade it from becoming a political party and entered parliament through its alliance with the Wafd. Then in 1987, the Islamic alliance which brought together the Liberal Party, the Labour Socialist Party and the *Ikhwan al-Muslimin*, enabled the latter to run in the elections.[38] But this infiltration of established political parties did not open the way to full integration in the multi-party system. Despite this, the legalist leadership of the movement has not departed from its traditional pragmatic stance, in spite of the serious dissentions and ruptures which have punctuated its history. Nonetheless, although it lacks its own dedicated press organ, the *Ikhwan al-Muslimin* is still able to express itself freely in various sectors of the media and thus acts as an opposition movement in complete legality and in accordance with Egyptian democratic rules.[39] The movement puts pressure on the regime for a gradual application of the *Shari'a*, a move supported by Article 2 of the Egyptian constitution which states that Islamic law constitutes the only source of legislation in the country. But moderation and compromise have been insufficient to bring it closer to a regime which regards it, above all, as a formidable opponent. It is true that its implantation in the social arena, providing for the poorest, satisfies – and therefore, underlines – a need inadequately addressed by the state. The *Ikhwan al-Muslimin* also has a strong following among the urban middle class which has traditionally constituted the support base of the regime. This staggering rise was probably one of the reasons for the leadership's sudden change of attitude towards the moderates of the *Ikhwan al-Muslimin* in the mid-1990s. Today, the leadership of the regime is convinced that, instead of contributing to the isolation of the extremists, moderate Islamists actually actively or implicitly support them. Thus, the moderates have become the main target of security activity and this is bound to have an impact on the liberalization process.

There is a great deal to learn from the way in which the Egyptian leadership has dealt with the Islamist movement. Its strategy, essentially an attempt to weaken and divide the Islamist movement, has, as yet, been unsuccessful both in its repression of the extremist wing (although the major Islamist group declared a unilateral truce in 1999) and its policy of containment of the moderates. In order to have some chance of success, this policy should have been extended to include the complete integration of the *Ikhwan al-Muslimin* into the legal political arena. The institutional-ization of the Islamist opposition could help clarify the blurred dividing line between moderates and extremists. Instead, the refusal to grant the *Ikhwan al-Muslimin* full legal status has enabled the movement to retain its reputation for morality and political credibility, untouched by the corruption which has invaded Egyptian politics.

- *Palestine*: The relations between the Palestinian Authority and the Islamist movement, embodied by *Hamas* and *Jihad*, are atypical and do not fit into the traditional leadership/opposition pattern present in most other Arab states. The main reason for this is the absence of sovereignty of the Palestinian Authority both internally and externally, making Israel a full partner in a three-way relationship. This triangular relationship cannot, however, conceal the fact that what is at stake in the competition between the two Palestinian players – secular and Islamist – remains the recognition of their historical legitimacy as the main resistance and national liberation movement.

- *Syria*: Syria counters the example of the Algerian experience in so far as the regime's strategy of exclusion and repression seems to have led to the effective eradication of the Islamist movement as an opposition force. Although the phenomenon of gradual Islamization did not spare Syria, it has remained the only country in the region which has not been affected by Islamist agitation. Since the decapitation of the powerful *Ikhwan al-Muslimin*, through the 1982 Hama massacre carried out by the Syrian army, the Asad regime has been able to eliminate the Islamist threat without opening the way to political liberalization. Apart from the use of terror, the regime, in its attempt to emasculate the Islamist opposition, resorted to the usual stratagems: stringent control of the official Sunni religious and institutional structures and the co-optation and clientalization of some sectors of the population, such as the commercial bourgeoisie. But the greatest originality and success of the Syrian strategy reside in the fact that President Asad, while intransigent towards the Syrian *Ikhwan al-Muslimin*, has established links with foreign groups or governments such as Iran, *Hamas* and *Hizbullah*. This has enabled him to maximize his regional influence, while at the same time keeping communication channels open with Syrian Islamists. Finally, there is an obvious link between the silencing of the Islamist opposition and the profound lethargy of Syrian politics.

The Impact of the Euro-Mediterranean Partnership on Middle East Democratic Transitions

The consensus on democracy and human rights reached by the 27 signatories to the Barcelona Declaration in their founding conference in 1995 has a strong symbolic value. Defining common political and cultural values gives moral content to the global framework of the Euro-Mediterranean Partnership. The fact that it may also be wishful thinking is irrelevant. Indeed, the same criticism would also apply to the structure designed by the Barcelona

Declaration, for its political and cultural agendas remain to be defined. Pragmatism must, therefore, prevail in the same way as it already does in the economic and financial spheres of the Process. Yet, to speak of pragmatism when dealing with values and principles such as the rule-of-law, democracy or human rights, which have become intangible and inviolable in international law, may seem contradictory. However, it seems that only political realism, devoid of any complacency, can enable this dialogue to acquire credibility and thus generate its own momentum. This is precisely where the potential link between Euro-Mediterranean Partnership and the political transition process lies: it makes more sense to rely on the long-term cumulative effect of one dynamic over another, rather than on some mechanical and improbable correlation. In more concrete terms, this implies a permanent monitoring of the Barcelona dialogue, given the fact that its bases and priorities have already been established. The purpose here, therefore, is to prepare the ground by identifying some of the priorities of the dialogue on democracy and human rights, while constantly endeavouring to identify the common stereotypes on the region.

Ambiguity, Unpredictability and Reversibility in Democratic Transition

The socio-political realities of the Arab world are much more complex and multifarious than any foreign observer would expect. National political itineraries and democratization experiences are increasingly distinct. Arab societies have become more complex over the last two decades and this *de facto* pluralization of societies underlines the erosion of the centralized authoritarian state. It also emphasizes the failure of the Arab state to suppress old and new *asab'iyat*, whose emergence it had encouraged through attempts at co-opting and clientalising social groups engendered by policies of economic liberalization. But the erosion and weakening of the state do not necessarily imply its destruction. The crisis of legitimacy experienced by Middle Eastern leaderships is unprecedented but civil society does not seem to be in a position to demand its own political forum and thus provide a counterweight to the state apparatus. There are, at present, no organized forces (whether among intellectuals, the private sector bourgeoisie or the middle classes) to sustain democracy and the probabilities of a popular uprising against existing regimes remain almost non-existent (urban uprisings have been, until now, easily contained). Since the people has not participated in the elaboration of the rules defining the democratic process, the state remains the only source of liberalization. The future of this process seems closely linked, for better or for worse, to the attitude of a state remarkably lacking in resources to achieve it. By and large, the transition to democracy in the Middle East does not seem to be considered as an end in itself but rather as a process which is bound to be very slow and whose outcome is uncertain and, above all, reversible. But, whatever shape it takes in the Middle East, democracy will not be achieved against the state but *with* it because the relationship between the state and society cannot be characterized as lacking positive, productive aspects. Likewise, it is unlikely to be achieved without the Islamists who have become the main political players.

The Democratic Pact

The idea of the democratic pact is not new. It was inspired by the contractual tradition initiated by Rousseau, Hobbes and Locke. But it has become more topical and valid because of the impasse in which Arab regimes now find themselves. It is based on a rational and instrumental approach to democracy which stems from necessity rather than choice and appears as the only means of guaranteeing civil peace between the *assab'iyat*, or rival groups.[40] This proposition seems very bold – even subversive according to some – in the face of the ambient conservative consensus on the specific conditions and mechamisms of the establishment of a democratic regime. Only Lebanon and, to a lesser extent, Jordan have experienced it; the Palestinian experience is still unfinished. Power-sharing between Middle Eastern states and their main Islamist political rivals through pre-electoral pacts is difficult to imagine. It would only occur if the regimes were forced into such situations by a combination of domestic and foreign pressures (failure of repression, civil conflict, survival imperative, pressure from the international community, regional or international foreign intervention, for example). Under these circumstances, a power-sharing agreement would provide a strategic means of conflict resolution – with international guarantees – rather than the starting point of a peaceful transition to democracy.

The Issues at Stake in Islamic Protest

The Islamist phenomenon can no longer be considered as a self-contained entity arisen from the 'depths of fundamentalism', a conclusion that should be emphasized to politicians, academics and experts on fundamentalism and terrorism. The Islamist movement's intimate involvement in socio-political dynamics and its presence in the history of each Middle Eastern state means that the phenomenon cannot be isolated from its context. As an opposition movement, it must be understood in the context of both its relationship with the regime in power and of its interaction with civil society. Misguided analyses and approaches to the problem are often linked to the confusion between intensely ideological Islamist discourse, centred on Islamic culture and tradition, and the actual political nature and objectives of the Islamist movement. We are simply witnessing a classic political struggle for the appropriation and control of state resources. Arab states themselves are forced to acknowledge, at least implicitly, the Islamists as their primary challenge, even when there is no bipolar confrontation, as in Algeria. The Islamists have become the main targets of co-optation strategies and of repression. The argument, put forward by some states, that the fundamentally totalitarian nature of these movements justifies their political exclusion is no longer convincing in the light of the liberalization carried out by these very states themselves with the sole purpose of re-establishing their own eroded authoritarian power. Moreover, experience has shown that Islamist integration into a suitably transparent and credible political arena has a moderating effect.

The Significance of the Cultural Argument

The side-effects of culturalism have been emphasized above, but is worth bearing in mind that culture has become a tool as easily manipulated by regimes as well as by their oppositions. In fact, this is the arena in which the confrontation between the regimes and the Islamists takes place. Yet the intense conversion of tradition into ideology can be explained by two factors: the de-politicization of the social body and the de-legitimization of politics monopolized by the leadership. Such exclusion from the political field leads the main actors to over-invest in the cultural and symbolic arenas, both strategically and rhetorically. Care must therefore be taken that the focus of the socio-political debate is not shifted towards exclusively cultural and identity issues.

The External Variable

Here too, it is important to dispute the received wisdom that an almost natural correlation exists between regional *detente* and democratization. The peace process, with all its fluctuations and difficulties, places regimes in an awkward position as far public opinion is concerned, for generally, it continues to be largely hostile to the normalization of relations with Israel. Democratization implies opening a forum for the expression of opposition to the peace process and to the predominant American role in the region, as well as to the strong dependency on American support this has caused for some states, such as Jordan and, above all, Egypt. For nearly half a century, the dominance of the conflict with Israel has justified and legitimized all sorts of abuse by political leaderships in the Middle East and thus allowed the regimes to move towards increased militarization in accordance with their concept of the security state. In short, these regimes built their *raison d'être* and their legitimacy on the principle of the paramount need to defend themselves against the existential threat posed to the Arab nation by Israel. The prospects for peace are now forcing them to redefine themselves and this is likely to reinforce their sense of internal vulnerability.

Indeed, the main fragility of these regimes resides precisely in the inadequacy of their internal and external sources of legitimacy. This explains the reserve, even the extreme caution, of some states towards the peace process, as illustrated by Syria. The question is not to what extent American policies encourage democracy in the Arab world, since they have shown their preference, on more than one occasion, for the authoritarian but stable and predictable state over chaotic and unmanageable democracy. Furthermore, it would be a mistake to endow the US with the capacity to impact significantly on the domestic political situations of states in the region. The real question regarding the impact of the external variable on democratization lies elsewhere. It concerns the intensity of interaction between the internal sources of tension and external challenges. It also lies in the ability of regimes to regulate democratization by a gradual introduction of basic political and institutional reforms. In fact, Islamist protest – and this is what gives it strength – is situated precisely at the junction between internal tensions and external constraints.

NOTES

1. Note, however the article by Jill Crystal, 'Authoritarianism and Its Adversaries in the Arab World', *World Politics*, 46, Jan. 1994, pp.262–89.
2. Among these well-known Orientalists, one finds Bernard Lewis, *Islam and the West*, New York: Harper Torchbooks, 1964; Samuel Huntington, *The Third Wave: Democratization in the Late Twentieth Century*, Norman, OK and London: University of Oklahoma Press; and Elie Kedourie, *Democracy and Arab Political Culture*, Washington, DC: Washington Institute for Near East Policy, 1992.
3. Generally presented as antagonistic, the notions of nature and culture are in this context almost synonymous, in so far as culture is understood as something intangible and immutable on which history has no effect.
4. The best analysis of Orientalism is still Edward W. Said's, *Orientalism: Western Conceptions of the Orient*, London: Penguin Books, 1977, 1995. For a sharper view, see Yahya Sadowski, 'The New Orientalism and the Democracy Debate', *Middle East Report*, July–Aug. 1993, in which the author dismantles, with considerable irony, the intellectual opportunism of Orientalists who have managed to adapt their essentialism to the evolution of sociology. When the consensus among social scientists linked the rise of democracy and development to the active participation of cohesive and specific social groups, Orientalists insisted on the absence of such groups in Islamic societies. Now that some thinkers have developed the opposite theory, that is to say that development occurs in passive and quietist societies, a new generation of Orientalists portrays Muslim societies as governed by anarchical and powerful solidarities.
5. Hisham Sharabi, *Neo-Patriarchy: A Theory of Distorted Change in the Arab World*, Oxford and New York: Oxford University Press, 1988. Saad Eddine Ibrahim (ed.), *Al-Mujtama' al madani wal tahawul al dimuqrati fil watan al arabi*, Cairo: Markaz ibn Khaldun, 1993.
6. Abdallah Laraoui, *Islam et modernité*, Paris: La découverte, 1987.
7. Labib al-Tahir, '*Hal al-dimuqratiyya matlab ijtimai'?*' (Is Democracy a Social Request?), in Said al-Alawi, *Al-mujtama' al-madani fil-watan al-'arabi* ... (Civil Society and Its Role in the Fulfilment of the Arab Nation), Beirut: Centre d'Etudes pour l'Unité Arabe, 1992.
8. The most extreme example of the obsession of authoritarian regimes with ensuring the highest possible living standards for its people is that of Ba'thist Iraq which, according to Samir al-Khalil himself – the author of *The Republic of Fear: The Politics of Modern Iraq*,

Berkeley, CA: University of California Press, 1989 – has achieved real progress in national wealth redistribution.

9. Giacomo Luciani in 'Economic Foundations of Democracy and Authoritarianism in Comparative Perspective', *Arab Quarterly*, 10/4 1988: Huntington, op. cit., uses the same argument in order to illustrate his theory of Arab-Islamic 'exceptionalism': oil revenues accrue to the state, they therefore increase the power of state bureaucracy and, because they reduce or eliminate the need for taxation, they also reduce the need for the government to solicit the acquiescence of its subjects to taxation. The lower the level of taxation, the less reason for the public to demand representation. 'No taxation without representation' was a political demand; 'no representation without taxation' is a political reality.

10. Migdal Joel, *Strong Societies and Weak States: State–Society Relations and States Capabilities in the Third World*, Princeton, NJ: Princeton Universtiy Press, 1988.

11. Ghassan Salamé, 'Sur la causalité d'un manque: Pourquoi le monde Arabe n'est-il donc pas démocratique?' *Revue Française de Science Politique*, 41/3 (June), pp.307–41. The author explains the legitimization mechanisms of military authoritarianism by the adoption of a model composed of neo-patrimonialism, Stalinist decisional centralism and military authoritarianism.

12. See Elizabeth Picard, 'The Arab Military in Politics: From Revolutionary Plot to Authoritarian State', in Adeed Dawisha and William Zartman (eds.), *Beyond Coercion: The Durability of the Arab State*, London: Croom Helm, 1988.

13. John Waterbury underlines this point, which he places among the 'unique' factors preventing democratic transition in the Middle East. John Waterbury, 'Une démocratie sans démocrates? Le potentiel de libéralisme politique au Moyen-Orient', in Ghassan Salamé, *Démocratie sans démocrates. Politiques d'ouverture dans le monde arabe et islamique* (Political Liberalisation in the Arab and Islamic World), Paris: Fayard, 1994.

14. Crystal, op. cit.

15. Muhammad Abid al-Jabiri, 'Ishkaliyyat al-dimuqratiyya wal-mujtama' al-madani fil-watan al-'arabi', *al Mustaqbal al-'arabi*, No.155, Jan. 1993, Abdallah Laraoui, op. cit.

16. Gudrun Krämer, 'Liberalization and Democracy in the Arab World', *Middle East Report*, 187, Jan.–Feb. 1992. For a rehabilitation of the role of civil society in the Middle East, see Richard Augustus Norton (ed.), *Civil Society in the Middle East*, Leiden: E.J. Brill, 1995.

17. Nazih Ayubih, *Overstating the Arab State, Politics and Society in the Middle East*, London: IB Tauris, 1995. According to the author, civic society creates the best political and institutional borders for civil society: Civic society 'is the realm of public debate and conscious collective action or, in a word, of citizenship ... The civic realm is that part of the public space that is not colonised by state bureaucracy and the system of public administration' (p.440).

18. This democratic half-heartedness – or political ambivalence – was well described by Alan Richards and John Waterbury, in *A Political Economy of the Middle East*, Boulder, CO: Westview Press, 1990.

19. Michel Camau, *Changements politiques au Maghreb*, Paris: Editions du CNRS, 1991.

20. This is the theory defended by Ghassan Salamé who insists on the ambiguity and the powerful emotional content which characterize the relations between Europe and the Arab-Islamic world and which, according to him, constitute a serious obstacle to the propagation and implantation of the democratic model in the region. Ghassan Salamé, 'Où sont les démocrates?', in Salamé, *Démocraties sans démocrates*, op. cit.

21. Bassma Kodmani-Darwish and May Chartouni-Dubarry (eds.), *Perceptions de sécurité et stratégies nationales au Moyen-Orient* (Perceptions of Security and National Strategies in the Middle East), Paris: Masson, 1994.

22. Dawisha and Zartman (eds.), *Beyond Coercion*, op. cit.; Ghassan Salamé, *The Foundations of the Arab State*, London: Croom Helm, 1988. See also Michael C. Hudson, *Arab Politics: The Search for Legitimacy*, New Haven, CT: Yale University, 1977 and Roger Owen, *State, Power and Politics in the Making of the Modern Middle East*, London: Routledge, 1995.

23. Krämer, op. cit. It must be said, with regard to Lebanon, that although the president – who holds executive power in accordance with the Taif Agreement – and his policies are criticized by the parliamentary opposition, Syria, as personified by its president, is regularly and unanimously praised by Lebanese deputies. This goes beyond strategic constraints and the transformation of Lebanon into a satellite state by Syria, for it denotes a lack of democratic culture and tradition among Lebanese politicians.

24. Ahmad S. Khalidi, 'The Palestinians' First Excursion into Democracy', *Journal of Palestine Studies*, No.4, Summer 1996, pp.20–28.

25. See Bassma Kodmani-Darwish, 'L'espace national à construire', in *La Diaspora palestinienne* (Chapter 9), Paris: PUF, 1997; On the relations with the Islamist opposition, see by the same author, 'Palestine: des rapports pouvoir-opposition ou un parternariat?' , in Bassma Kodmani-Darwish and May Chartouni-Dubarry, *Les états arabes face à la contestation islamiste* (The Arab States Faced with Islamist Protest), Travaux et Recherches de l'IFRI, Paris: Colin, 1997.

26. The fact that the present Algerian regime uses the same argument in order to rally domestic and international support by brandishing the threat of chaos is significant.

27. The October 1989 Taif national *entente* pact reinstated the confessional system but transferred what had been Maronite prerogatives to the Sunni and Shi'ite communities.

28. It must be noted that the law on political parties is very selective and restrictive regarding both the creation and the organization of parties which can only be legally recognized by a tribunal composed of five magistrates from the state council and five other personalities. Moreover, they are not allowed to hold public meetings and their internal mode of operation is undemocratic. By and large, their programmes remain vague, they are dominated by the personalities of their leaders and their recruiting abilities are very restricted.

29. Egypt is one of the most advanced Arab countries in this respect, as is illustrated by the increasing role of magistrates in politics and in particular with regard to the constitutionality of laws.

30. Iman Farag, 'La politique à l'égyptienne: lecture des élections législatives', *Monde Arabe: Maghreb-Machrek*, 135, July–Sept. 1991. Out of 45 per cent of registered voters, less than 40 per cent, on average, participate effectively in the elections.

31. See Volker Perthes, 'Le secteur privé, la libéralisation économique et les perspectives de démocratisation: le cas de la Syrie et certains autres pays arabes', in Salamé, *Démocratie sans démocrates*, op. cit., pp.335–71.

32. There is, on this subject, a large number of works of unequal quality. Among the reference works are: Sami Zubaida, *The People and the State*, London: IB Tauris, 1993; Abdel Salam Sid Ahmed and Anoushiravan Ehteshami (eds.), *Islamic Fundamentalism*, Boulder, CO: Westview Press, 1996; François Burgat, *L'islamisme en face*, Paris: La Découverte, 1996; Dale F. Eickelman and James Piscatori, *Muslim Politics*, Princeton, NJ: Princetion University Press, 1996; Laura Guazzone (ed.), *The Islamist Dilemma: The Political Role of Islamist Movements in the Contemporary Arab World*, Reading: Ithaca Press, 1996.

33. May Chartouni-Dubarry, 'Pluralisme communautaire dans la République libanaise de Taëf', in Kodmani-Darwish and Chartouni-Dubarry (eds.), *Les Etats arabes face à la contestation islamiste* (Arab States and Islamist Protest), op. cit.

34. The *Ikhwan al-Muslimin* was officially recognized in January 1945. It is now predominant in the majority of student groups, professional organizations and trade unions and controls a number of Islamic schools (madrasa al-Aqsa).

35. The Egyptian Islamist movement is the oldest, the most important and the most heterogenous in the Middle East. See May Chartouni-Dubarry, 'Egypte: une stabilité ébranlée?', *Ramsès 1995*, IFRI, Dunod.

36. Founded in 1928 by Hassan al-Banna, it was dissolved in 1954 by Nasser.

37. Twenty-seven per cent of Egyptian associations have some religious reference. See Sarah ben Nefissa-Paris, 'Le mouvement associatif égyten et l'islam', *Monde Arabe: Maghreb-Machrek*, 135, Jan.–March 1992, pp.19–36.

38. The alliance with the Wafd enabled them to win 15 per cent of the seats in 1984 and the Islamic Alliance gave them 18 per cent in 1987.
39. Among the intellectuals who express themselves mostly through the press are Tariq al-Bishri (an old Marxist, now close to the *Ikhwan al-Muslimin*) and Fahmi Howeidi. These authors, who denounce the use of violence, are favourable to the integration of Islamists within an authentically democratic regime, that is to say one that is intrinsically Islamic and based on the *Shari'a* alone.
40. This is the theory central to the work edited by Salamé, *Démocracies sans démocrates*, op. cit., in which the author evokes 'the possiblity of a democratic political organization, even without enthusiastic advocates to defend it, even without previous normativist ideologization of its values' (p.8).

5

Democratization in the Mashreq:
The Role of External Factors

MUSTAFA HAMARNEH

Political democracy evolved along with the unique historic phenomenon of capitalism, which first occurred in Western Europe. This phenomenon is referred to in the social sciences as the process of modernization. Although initially industrialization and capitalism, not unlike other political forces, were brutally painful to certain social strata, modernization ultimately represented a fundamental break with tradition and involved a significant improvement in the quality of life of the citizens of Western societies. Thus it is valid to conclude that the expansion of the critical space[1] between society and the state, involving participatory government, accountability, tolerance, civility – essential ingredients for the development of democratic rule – were, to a large extent, by-products of capitalist development in the West.

Today the Arab Mashreq, like the rest of the south, is affected by the global wave of political liberalization. This brief essay aims at explicating the dialectical tensions and interplay between internal dynamics and external variables. One of the arguments advanced is that no clear understanding may be achieved without examining the role of capitalist distortion and the colonial legacy, though internal dynamics need to be taken into account. This essay will further analyse the debate between those scholars who advance explanations based on external or internal reasoning and proffer a synthesis between the two differing schools. The goal is to provide an overall view of the process of political liberalization and the main reasons inhibiting this process.

Capitalist penetration , in the rest of the world, so far, however, has not led to the reproduction of this unique historic process of modernity, though some scholars believe that a new wave – the Third Wave – is sweeping some parts of the developing world.[2] The development of events and conditions outside Western Europe took a different course. The majority of the states that today comprise what is called the periphery, or the Third World, were formed with the help of a powerful outside factor, namely the expansion of Europe. The exigencies of the Eurocentric European model introduced a form of capitalism into these areas where direct contact took place. The result was a distorted form of capitalism, and the early assumption that development of political democracy would be a by-product of penetration did not materialize, as proved to be the case in, for example, Korea, Singapore and Latin America.

Since the Second World War, two main methodological currents have been employed to understand problems related to socio-political development in the Third World. The first current, in an attempt at explaining the effects of the process of development in these societies, reduces the debate to internal variables. Therefore, the focus is on values and attitudes of the peoples and how these became factors inhibiting the modernization of these societies. The second current takes the opposite view in that it deals with the problems facing these societies in their attempt at modernization as external to society, which is located within an international context.

Since the collapse of the Soviet Union and the subsequent changes that have taken place in Eastern Europe, a universal interest in democracy and civil society ensued. In the specific case of Arab and Muslim societies, that debate has been divided along the same line as the developmental debate. Hence it was logical that the first current produced the theory of the Arab and Muslim 'exception'. The 'absence' of democracy, as was said to have been the case with earlier attempts at exploring the 'backwardness' of these societies, was the result of internal cultural factors.[3] The externalist approach in analysing the problems of backwardness treated these societies (the Third World societies) as part of a larger international structure where external factors have had a negative impact on its socio-economic development.

Although there is extensive literature on. the impact of the external factor on. the social and economic structure, little has been. written on the effect this interaction has had on the political development in the societies themselves. The process of economic distortion in these societies has had an impact on the process of political development as well.

Unlike the West, the historic process of development in most of the rest of the world inhibited the development of fully-fledged social classes, and social structures remained weak but complex. Social life in the periphery is more dependent upon non-class social alignments (race, religion, age, ethnicity) than it is in the Western world. Thus a similar process of distortion as occurred in. the economic sphere has taken place in the political sphere.

Like the Third World itself, the Arab Mashreq is not monolithic. Political openness in the Third World, whether it took place as a result of domestic factors, outside pressure or a combination of both, produced forms of government that varied from 'full' authoritarian regimes to 'benevolent totalitarianism' and consociational democracy. In the specific case of the Arab Mashreq, the First World War – an important external factor – was a major watershed. The Ottoman *wilayat* of Syria was divided by the colonial powers of Britain and France, and subsequently several entities emerged: Lebanon, Syria and Jordan along with what today constitutes Israel and the Palestinian territories.

As a result of this break-up, parts of the hinterland and the *badia* were isolated from major Arab cities and towns. Furthermore, the different, often competing, colonial interests, operating within the context of the new boundaries that were created as a result, gave rise to different system of government and different economic structures. The largely decentralized and fractional system of government in Lebanon differed fundamentally from the strong and centralized system of government in Jordan. In Syria, the failure of colonial rule, which was never able to root itself deeply in Syrian society, paved the way for the development of the autocratic Syrian state. In Palestine, the British objective of setting up a Jewish entity had a devastating impact on Palestinian society which was eventually uprooted and scattered over the region and the wider world.

In the post-independence era, the external factor – referred to here as the network of political, economic and social relations between the North and the South – had, in the context of the cold war, a negative impact on the development of modern systems of governance, and the process of the evolution of civil society in general. The external powers during this period were more interested in 'stability' rather than in promoting economic development and democratization.[4] Furthermore, the Arab–Israeli conflict and the war for Palestine provided the regimes with a powerful mobilization agenda that led either to a single-party political structure or to equally autocratic systems; the critical space between state and society was often considerably reduced.

The Transition

The widely accepted notion that the process of political liberalization in the Arab countries began with the Gulf War needs to be reassessed critically. There is no evidence to support this claim, at least in relation to the Arab Mashreq. The limited economic liberalization in Syria has not been matched by political liberalization, it is true, and the Syrian state has so far successfully resisted outside pressure. However, in Jordan, political liberalization started before the Second Gulf War, and although the process gained momentum during the war, it was for different reasons than those usually advanced.

In both Lebanon and Palestine, the complexities of their domestic scenes and the network of external factors linked to them requires a different periodization in order to understand the dynamism of both societies. Palestinian society on the West Bank and Gaza has experienced an *intifada* and the thrust of its mobilizational effort was directed towards protecting and liberating itself from Israel occupation. Legislative elections were only possible as a result of a process of negotiations between Israel and the Palestine Liberation Organization (PLO), which took place under American tutelage. In Lebanon the dynamism that ended the civil war and the reintroduction of participatory government were rooted more in Syrian–Lebanese relations and their interaction with regional factors than with the Gulf War.

Among the Arab Mashreq countries, the Jordanian experiment in political liberalization and its process of transition since 1989 offers the analyst a valuable case study. The country is relatively stable. Both the state and society are going through a profound process of social change with far-reaching consequences, not only for its own population but also for neighbouring countries. It is the only state that so far has had two consecutive elections in the last eight years – the third was held at the end of the twentieth century – that were generally characterized as fair and free, and in which political Islam was the dominant political force in the first election in 1989 and a major factor in the elections of 1993.

Jordan is also implementing an economic restructuring programme involving severe austerity measures. In addition, the country, as a result of the economic restructuring, has witnessed an increase in the number of its non-governmental organizations (NGOs). Furthermore, Jordan signed a peace treaty with Israel in 1994, thus formally ending the state of belligerency with the Jewish state. The collective impact of these major factors has been felt by all strata of Jordanian society and is changing gradually the relationship between state and society. The Jordanian case serves as a critical example to shed light on the process of political liberalization in the Arab arena. Although this short essay will focus mainly on Jordan, it will refer to and use insights from other case studies in the Arab Mashreq to complement the analysis.

Civil Society

As mentioned above, for a proper understanding the process of liberalization, it is essential to analyse the relationship between external factors and domestic dynamism. The pressure to politically liberalize is the result of two factors: (1) the end of the cold war and the subsequent global wave for liberalization; and (2) the failure of statist policies as

TABLE 1
POPULAR ORGANISATIONS AND PROFESSIONAL
ASSOCIATIONS IN SYRIA

No.	Name of Organisation
1	General Federation of Workers' Syndicates
2	General Federation of Fanners
3	Federation of the Revolution's Youth
4	National Federation of Syria's Students
5	Teachers Syndicate
6	General Women's Federation
8	Al-Baath Youth Organisation
9	General Sports Federation
10	Federation of Arab Writers
11	Housing Co-operative Federation
12	Syndicate of Engineers
13	Syndicate d Physicians
14	Syndicate of Agricultural Engineers
15	Syndicate of Dentist
16	Syndicate of Pharmacists
17	Syndicate of Lawyers
18	Union of Journalists
19	Fine Arts Syndicate
20	Syndicate of Artists

Source: Arab Baath Socialist Party, *Al-Harakah al-Tashihíyah al-Majidah* (Gloríous Corrective Movement), Damascus, National Headquarters Printing Press, 1995, pp.183–364.

applied in some countries, such as Syria and Jordan, despite their different ideological leanings. Syria's and Jordan's economic failure and their inability to continue to provide goods and services without any consideration as to their real cost has brought both countries under unprecedented pressure to liberalize their economies more than at any other time in their history. However, in Syria 'authoritarian rule appears remarkably durable in-spite of increasing socio-economic modernization'[5] (see Table 1).

While the Syrian state today is not a military dictatorship, the military and security apparatus exercise considerable influence. By 1990 there were 35 members of the armed forces to every 1000 citizens.[6] The roots of this development can be traced to the nationalist crisis of the 1950s, on both the political and economic levels, and to the Arab–Israeli conflict. The overwhelming desire to reverse the situation in Palestine, reunite the homeland and defeat Western interests in the region, provided the argument for establishing a strong central government capable of mobilizing resources for economic development and liberation legitimacy. And in this process, the critical space between society and state was reduced to a minimum.

This statist thrust gained momentum after the coup of 1966, and the Baath regime succeeded in controlling organizations such as the unions and professional associations. In the rural areas, the state was successful in mobilizing the peasantry who were alienated under the colonial administration and the nationalist government of the post-world war eras. The leadership of those associations were militants of the ruling party – and, therefore, 'partners' in government. They had access to power and at the same time executed the policies of the regime. Thus the associations and unions were not 'voluntary associations' of citizens promoting their interests, but frameworks for mobilization that were used by the regime as a means of implementing the power of the state.[7]

Yet legislative elections have taken place and the Syrian press and television often report on select parliamentary activities. In reality, however, everybody is aware that not only the executive power but also the legislative power lies in the hands of the president. Political parties in Syria are either 'junior partners' with no independent popular base or, as in the case of Islamists, banned, (see Table 2). The ability of the Syrian regime to mobilize in Syria is so great that during the Gulf War, this Arab nationalist regime, which fought with Allied troops led by the United States in an anti-Arab nationalist cause, was able to neutralize all domestic opposition. The only opposition force that exists today in Syria is provided by the Islamists, although a series of violent confrontations with the state has rendered them ineffective.

TABLE 2
POLITICAL PARTIES IN THE RULING COALITION IN SYRIA
(NATIONAL PROGRESSIVE FRONT)

No.	Name of Political Organizalion
1	Arab Socialist Baalh Party
2	Arab Socialist Union Party
3	Syrian Communist Party*
4	Syrian Communist Party (Yousef Faisal)
5	Socialist Unionists Party
6	Arab Socialist Movement
7	Unionist Socialist Democratic Party

*Khalid Bakdash died on 25 July 1995 and was succeeded as party leader by his wife.

Source: Arab Baath Socialist Party, *Al-Harakah al-Tashjhiyah al-Majidah* (Glorious Corrective
Móvement), Damascus: National Headquarters Printing Press: 1995, pp.128–44.

In neighbouring Jordan, however, events took a different direction. Historically, except for brief moments, the professional associations for most of their history had had an antagonistic relationship with the state. Unlike the situation in Syria, most leaders of these associations were also leaders of the opposition. With political parties banned and underground for the entire period between 1957 and 1967 and again between 1970 and 1989, the professional associations became arenas of competition for the political forces in the country and forums of expressions for anti-state politics. Thus the critical space between state and society in Jordan remained relatively wider than was the case in Syria, enabling 'political life' to exist within society. This difference sheds considerable light on the different political systems in the two neighbouring states of Syria and Jordan.

Furthermore, despite the presence of a relatively strong public sector, the Jordanian state was more permissive in introducing decentralizing technologies. Telexes, photocopying machines and later facsimile machines, in addition to their economic utility, facilitated the dissemination of political statements and other political literature by the underground organizations. 'Punishment' for political 'crimes' was never as severe as in Syria and other neighbouring countries. The Jordanian state before 1989 may best be described as benign authoritarianism, not as totalitarian. It is here that most of the explanation as to why the process of political liberalization took place in Jordan and not in other neighbouring Arab countries lies.

Thus, it is safe to assume that 'reform depend[ed] as much on the will of the citizens as on the willingness of the government'.[8] As a result of the crisis and riots of 1989, 659 candidates presented themselves for the 80 seats in parliament in the 1989 elections, and in 1993 the number of candidates was 537. Both the 1989 and the 1993 campaigns were boisterous, whilst the number of political slogans was overwhelming and severely critical of the performance of past governments, offering instead promises to put an end to all corruption and make government accountable.

Thus the new parliamentary deputies had a strong mandate. Elections were free and fair, and, coupled with the representation of all political forces in the country (except for the Tahrir party) they gave parliament, as an institution, credibility. Following the elections of 1989, martial law was abolished, while a new party law and a press and publications law were enacted by parliament. The nascent democracy also passed its first test: the Gulf War. Professional associations, university students, voluntary neighbourhood initiatives and political party activists were mobilized against the Allied Forces in support of Iraq. It appeared then that the entire political atmosphere in the country was changing and the critical space was expanding. Political party material was available without restriction, and freedom to express opinions and to assemble were now guaranteed by law. But the liberalization process then began to slow down and today, eight years later, there is clearly a regression.

In Lebanon and in the Palestinian territories elections have also been held and, to some degree, democratically elected legislative bodies have been put in place. It appears, however, that today the situation in all these entities has stagnated. In Jordan the stagnation is the result of the fact that civil society institutions, despite the wide coverage their activists and statements receive in the printed press, are limited in their ability to mobilize both their memberships and citizens in general. Thus these institutions have not been able to reverse regressive tendencies or influence the course of social change in a meaningful way. The opposition forces, led by Islamists, have, in their campaigns, been successful at dispensing promises and criticizing unpopular policies. They have not, however, been able to provide alternative programmes in response to the ones implemented by successive governments since 1989. A major exception to this is the small business community. For the first time in the history of Jordan, industrialists and leading merchants have been voicing their opinions in an open and systematic way concerning not only issues related to economic policy such as the debate on the introduction of a sales tax but also concerning foreign policy. The chambers of industry and commerce in Amman opposed very strongly the shift in policy towards Iraq. They called for a policy of co-operation with Iraq, for their interests clearly lay in maintaining very strong and friendly relations with Iraq.

The first powerful signal from above that the process of liberalization would be a long one came in June of 1993 when, by royal decree, King Hussein introduced an amendment to the election law that effectively reduced the number of Islamic deputies in the 1993 parliament. It also prevented other opposition figures from being re-elected. This move was highly unpopular and was totally rejected by the majority of the political elite in the country.[9] Four years of political activity to reform the law by the opposition have, however, been fruitless. The second blow came on the eve of the signing of the peace treaty between Jordan and Israel. The Jordanian state in its effort to secure the ratification of the treaty by the Jordanian parliament, resorted to 'pre-democratic' means of mobilization and control. Opposition views were banned from the only (state owned) television and radio station. Demonstrations and public assembly were, for the most part, either banned or strongly discouraged.

These measures were even extended to the mosques, where collective prayers in open public spaces were banned. On the day of ratification, a police cordon was installed in the areas around Parliament, which had the effect of intimidating MP's and prevented immediate contact between those who gathered outside Parliament to protest the treaty and the legislators. Furthermore, the government moved to curb and manage the process of political liberalization by amending the press and publications law. The objective was not to restrict the political party press but rather the established daily newspapers and the weekly newspapers that have flourished and increased in numbers. The first attempt to introduce changes in the press and publications law under the government of Sharif Zeid ben Shaker during the second half of 1995 was postponed. However, in May 1997, and while Parliament was in recess, a temporary law signed by the king was issued. The amendments included articles which would have restricted the freedom of the press. The response was immediate; in protest, the entire board, except for the president, of the Jordan Press Association resigned, and in a further escalation of protest over the law, the council of the Federation of Professional Associations in the country threatened to resign. They gave the government six days to rescind the amendments. This measure, however, was criticized by an important segment of public opinion so that the threatened resignations were withdrawn. The leadership, nevertheless, opted for resignation rather than use other legal measures to pressure the government.[10]

These reactions provide additional evidence that the institutions of civil society in Jordan, despite their role in the country's political and social life, were incapable of mobilizing popular support to counter the government's attempt at controlling and managing the process of political liberalization. The key question is, therefore, why have modern political frameworks of mobilization and participation not developed? Jordan's contemporary history is full of mass demonstrations and association efforts in support of Arab causes. Public opinion in the country was the single most imported factor in preventing the country from joining the Baghdad Pact in the 1950s. The organized 'street' stood very firmly alongside President Nasser in his struggles, from the nationalization of the Suez Canal Company and the war with Israel, Britain and France, to its support for the Algerian struggle for independence and all other Arab nationalist causes of the period, including the latest example; the Second Gulf War in which the 'street' was solidly on the side of Iraq.

The reason why the political domestic scene in Jordan was different in the 1950s and 1960s, can simply be explained by the existence of sweeping pan-Arab ideologies that found a receptive audience amongst Jordanians. This factor, which was also external in nature, played a critical role in 'convincing' the monarchy not to liberalize lest its political stability and survival be adversely affected. Furthermore, an analysis of the interaction of such external factors with the inner dynamism of the Jordanian political experiment is of use, not only for the detached analyst but also for pro-democracy activists. Political analysts, 'enlightened' tribal activists and commentators in general predicted that the elections of 1989, which began the process of liberalization, would be the last elections in which tribal affiliation would play a significant role in determining voting patterns. To the disappointment of these actors, the 1993 elections turned out to be more tribal and parochial than those held four years earlier.

The explanation for the tribalization of politics and the, re-emergence of pre-modem forms of mobilization is not wholly rooted in local conditions. It is maintained here that the complexity of the social structure, which is the result of the distorted process of development, is the single most important factor inhibiting the development of social classes. The process of political openness did not lead, as was expected, to the development of strong political parties neither old nor new. Instead, a new hybrid system of participatory frameworks developed (see Table 3).

In today's Jordan, one of the most important factors determining voting patterns is kinship.[11] However, as a result of the erosion of the power-base of established sheikhdoms which traditional provided popular leadership, the emergence of new challenges to this existing tribal leadership brought about an interesting development. In some localities in the north, where informal selection processes were unsuccessful in determining the tribal candidate, 'primaries' were conducted to determine who would represent the 'collectivity' in the parliamentary elections. In one case, tribal candidates paid fees and ballot boxes were distributed in the villages of the tribe. A tribal committee oversaw the entire process and declared, as a result of the primary,

TABLE 3
PROPORTIONAL DISTRIBUTION OF ACCORDING TO AFFILIATION

Political Party Affiliation at any time	Poll of 1997	Poll of 1996	Poll of 1995
Yes	1.0	1.3	2.2
No	97.8	98.1	97.5
Refused to Answer	1.0	0.6	0.4
Unknown	0.1	–	–
Total=100%	973	1200	2000

Source: Public Opinion Poll on Democracy in Jordan (1997), Centre for Strategic Studies, University of Jordan, May 1997.

who was to be the 'official' tribal candidate. Women were excluded from participating in this 'family' affair.[12]

The process of selecting the tribal candidates, however, was not always harmonious. In certain localities consensus was not possible, and several candidates presented themselves. A different method was employed in other parts of the country. In Karak, for example, tribal congresses were convened to 'elect' who would become 'their' candidate in the general elections. In fact, this process of regression and the continued ascendancy of 'collective' affiliation is not unique to Jordan. A similar process takes place in the Palestinian territory on a different level. In Lebanon it is doubtful that the Lebanese system ever separated itself from the collectivity. The Lebanese system is still very much entrenched in the sectarian-tribal and communal social structure. Similarly, observers have noted a deterioration and regression in political practice in the Palestinian territories.[13] In Syria it remains to be seen what course political parties will take if a process of political liberalization takes place there. Thus one needs to examine carefully the relevance of formal institutions imported from the West, such as political parties, as frameworks for participation in the context of societies analysed here.

The expansion of the critical space between society and the state, participatory government, accountability, tolerance, civility – all essential ingredients for the development of democratic rule – cannot develop without a strong civil society. For a strong civil society to develop an adequate framework for mobilization and participation must also develop. This also questions the role of members-of-parliament who collectively assume legislative power but who do not represent the objective interests of the people who elected them. Furthermore, it is necessary to discuss the issue of 'accepted' political values. In the West, a new system of values accompanied the process of capitalist evolution and this was to become the foundation of morality in society there. Most of these values cannot be transplanted into other regions of the world as they stand, although this should not be construed as an argument to support values and practices that promote oppression and strengthen authoritarianism in the name of authenticity.

In the Palestinian territories the same process of regression is taking place. The professional associations, trade unions, student unions, and women's organizations originally flourished inside and outside Palestine as a result of strong PLO involvement.[14] These were not voluntary associations designed simply to promote and protect membership interests, but their establishment was a strong statement about political identity. In addition, the strong and organized PLO presence within these organizations gave them the characteristics of similar organizations in Syria and other one-party states. With the creation of the Palestinian National Authority, these associations became an arm of Yasir Arafat's system of rule. The widely-reported strike in 1997 by teachers on the West Bank was a case in point. Eleven thousand teachers went on strike demanding higher wages, whilst their 'union' was opposed to their action![15]

The Islamists

The size of the Islamist victory in 1989 in Jordan surprised political observers, including the Royal Palace. The Muslim Brotherhood won 20 seats out of 22 candidates on the Muslim Brotherhood list, and the multi-voting system allowed them to capture 12 other seats for Islamists or candidates with Islamist leanings. Their support was also instrumental in electing several minority (Christian) candidates (see Table 4). The victory not only confirmed what the Muslim Brotherhood had been claiming about the size of its popular support, but now gave it legitimacy as a leading factor in political life and allowed it to attempt to fulfil its Islamist agenda through legislation.

The phenomenon of Islamists contesting elections in Jordan and joining the cabinet was described initially as the 'politics of inclusion'. The relationship between the Jordanian state and the Islamists was at the time unique amongst the states of the Middle East and Islamist tactics in Jordan were based on 'reforming' the system from within. While in Syria, for example, the relationship is one of violent confrontation, in Jordan the Islamists represented a major political player in their ability of being able to oppose or support the government as well. In Syria, however, the Islamists

TABLE 4
ELEVENTH HOUSE OF DEPUTIES (1989)

Islamist	Conservative and Centre	Nationalist and Leftist
32 seats (20 Muslim Brotherhood) (12 independent Islamists)	33 seats	15 seats

Source: Hussein Abu Rumman, 'First Reading in Jordan's 1989 Parliamentary Elections', in *New Jordan Magazine*, No.15–16, 1990, pp.25–42.

reject the vary nature and existence of the Bathi'st regime, using extralegal means to contest the legitimacy of the Syrian government. This distinction sheds light on the issue of 'legitimacy' which confronts the two political systems in Syria and Jordan. On the whole, the Jordanian government is seen to be legitimate, while the opposite is true in the case of Syria.

Behind the apparent similarities between the Brotherhood movements in Syria, Jordan and Palestine lie important differences, particularly between the Syrian Brotherhood and its Jordanian counterpart. The most important difference arises from the type of relationship each movement has with the state. In Syria, the movement opposed the 'socialist' policy of the Arab nationalists whether under the local Baath or the Nasserite model. The confrontation between the Brotherhood and Arab nationalism, which began in Egypt in the 1940s and 1950s, later spread to the rest of the Arab World, including Syria. During this early period in the confrontation, the Jordanian state provided the movement with a safe haven in the country and the Brotherhood was, as a result, a powerful domestic ally of the Hashemites.

While members of the Muslim Brotherhood were being purged and jailed in Syria, in Jordan they fought alongside the monarchy in all its battles against the forces of Arab nationalism, Palestinian nationalism and communism. Thus they had no history of opposition to the regime in Jordan, and the policy of inclusion in Jordan did not in fact start until 1989 because it was simply unnecessary. Members of the Brotherhood held leading positions in the Jordanian bureaucracy before the process of liberalization began. The situation was very different in Palestine, where the Brotherhood split and its activist wing, Hamas, has had a relationship with the Palestinian National Authority which was not harmonious and which, furthermore was further complicated by an external factor – Israel. Israel, in any case, is not interested in promoting democratization in the Palestinian territories but rather in promoting 'stability' to protect its interests and it was for this reason that it tolerated the original activities of the Brotherhood and even the Hamas split, as it saw it as a way of weakening the PLO.[16]

Yet despite the close relationship between the Hashemites and the Muslim Brotherhood, the regime has, in more recent times, followed a policy of being opposed to what it regards as major political organizations. In 1993, by Royal decree, the election law in Jordan was changed in order to reduce the ability of the Brotherhood to mobilize as effectively as it had done in 1989. The consequence was that this move reduced the number of seats the organization and its allies gained in the 1993 elections (see Table 5). Under the old system, the number of seats allocated varied from one district to the other. In some districts the number allocated was nine while in others, it was five or even three. Voters could vote for any number of candidates. The new system allowed voters to cast ballots for only one candidate. The result was that Islamist representation inside Parliament was now reduced to a level similar to the movement's degree of support in the country as a whole. The new election law also reduced the chances of victory for independent candidates who did not have a wide tribal base of support. Although the change was implemented according to the Jordanian constitution, it was undemocratic in its intentions and its consequences.

None the less, the overall consequence has been that the policy of inclusion in Jordan has, so far, been successful. The move by the king to change the election law put the Islamists on the defensive and, unlike the 1989 Parliament, in its 1993 successor, the Islamist agenda was almost absent. In 1989, the Brotherhood members-of-parliament and their allies – Islamists and others – had pushed for legislation to ban the manufacture and sale of alcohol in the country. They had also demanded the segregation of the sexes in schools beyond the fourth grade and had also pushed for strict legislation to restrict interaction of the sexes in public places, on the premise that such rules were consistent with Sharia law, which, they claimed, also required segregation at recreational facilities.[17]

TABLE 5
TWELFTH HOUSE OF DEPUTIES (1993)

Islamist	Conservative and Centre	Nationalist and Leftist
22 seats (16 Muslim Brotherhood)	47 seats	11 seats

Source: Taleb Award *et al.*, 'Jordan's 1993 Elections: Analytical Numerical Study', 2nd edition, *Civic Society and Political Life in Jordan* (Amman: New Jordan Studies Centre, Sept. 1994), pp.31–4.

The Role of External Factors

Since an historical analysis of the impact of external factors has been given here, starting with the beginning of the process of state formation in the Mashreq, the fragmentation of Syria by colonial powers has to be the point of departure for the discussion. The colonial intervention, and the subsequent process of development combined with the interaction between other regional conflicts, such as the Arab–Israeli conflict and international factors, such as the cold war, have had a decisive impact on the relationship between rulers and ruled in the Arab Mashreq. The evidence suggests that external factors, will continue to have the same impact as in the past.

Western powers, particularly the United States, are engaged in promoting their perceived national interests rather than in advancing democratization. A case in point is the American relationship with Jordan. Between 1989 and 1993, when Jordan was going through one of the most democratic phases in its history, it was also being punished by the United States because of its policy towards Iraq. Another aspect of this external factor is the effect of the economic restructuring programme on Jordan. The World Bank has called for an expanded role for NGOs in the country in the process of development something which will become inevitable as a result of the dismantling of the public sector. Yet this is a policy of doubtful utility to Jordan, for it is based on the unequal relations that exist between the North and the South. In reality, both economically and politically, the countries of the South should follow an independent route. However, this will not be permitted and hence the conditions that have been reproduced in the past will continue to exist and the process of socio-economic, and political distortion will accelerate.

Economic aid or any other kind of co-operation should be provided to address needs that are rooted in local conditions and are linked to a specific process of reform, in order to avoid the perpetuation of distortions that have been the result of other links established between North and South in the past. Of course, it is important in this context that the kind of economic aid characteristic of the era that followed the Second World War should be avoided for such aid was, for the most part, self-serving and designed to promote 'stability' rather than reform. It was a decisive factor in strengthening the coercive apparatus of the states to which it was supplied and had a negative impact on the process of the evolution of civil society in the South as a result. In fact, the most important aspect of foreign aid in the past was the way in which it helped the consolidation of the coercive powers of the rentier state over civil society. Rents, especially foreign aid, enabled Third World regimes to acquire and maintain a margin of autonomy in relation to society, so that the latter was weakened and marginalized in the process.[18]

Contemporary patterns of co-operation and aid in support of democratization could have a similar distorting impact if they do not take into account the specific historical pattern of state formation and its subsequent development in the South. Local academics, intellectual politicians and activists should therefore have a larger role in drawing plans for action and determining the methods to implement reform. Indeed, a condition for avoiding the reproduction of the modernization debate of the 1950s, 1960s and 1970s, and imposing it on the debate on the evolution of civil society in the South is that the first steps in such a debate should take place through a South–South dialogue. Independent actors in the South are better equipped to analyse the existing social, political and economic structures that exist there and to devise plans of action in order to expand the critical space between societies and the state in their own countries. As a first stage in what will prove to be a long process of cooperation, they also need to be exposed to experiences of others in the region. This will enable them to incorporate ideas suitable to their environment as a result of an expanding epistemological debate on issues related to participation, mobilization, accountability, and citizenship. This will ultimately yield better results by conditioning the collective efforts of these independent actors in reforming their societies. Yet it is also imperative that independent actors from the South become partners with their counterparts and agencies in the North in designing programmes and strategies for action to promote democratization in the South.

NOTES

1. What I mean by critical space is the extent and degree of autonomy that civil society tends to have *vis-à-vis* the state.
2. See Huntington, *The Third Wave: Democratisation in the Late Twentieth Century*, Norman, OK and London: University of Oklahoma Press, 1991.
3. For a good overview on this debate see: Kedourie, *Democracy and Arab Political Culture*, Washington, DC: Washington Institute for Near East Policy, 1992.
4. There is extensive literature on this issue, for a discussion on the specific case of an Arab country (Egypt) see: Moheb, *Civil Society and Democratisation in Egypt 1981–1994*, Dar al-Katub, Cairo, 1994.
5. Hinnebusch, State and Civil Society in Syria, *Middle East Journal*, 47/2, Spring M3, pp.243–4.
6. Perthes, 'State Building, National Security and War Preparation in Syria, or Si vis stabilitatem', para bellum, unpublished paper, p.3.
7. Hinnebush, op. cit. No.248–250.
8. Schwedler, *Toward Civil Society in the Middle East? A Primer*, Boulder, CO: Lynne Rienner, 1995.
9. For the details of the reaction to the move to change the election law §M the Statements of leading politicians in the local press.
10. *Al-Ra'i* (Arabic), daily, Amman, 19 May 1997, following intense debate the members of board of the Jordanian Press Association rescinded their resignations. However, Hussein Mjali, President of The Bar Association, resigned.
11. The Centre for Strategic Studies (CSS) bas been conducting polls on issues related to

democracy. This has been one of the major findings of the surveys conducted by the CSS on 'Democracy' from 1993 till 1997. The CSS has been conducting polls since 1993 on issues related to people's attitude towards civil institutions in general; political parties, voluntary associations, press, etc. Also measuring people's participation in primordial activities.

12. Interview with Professor Azzam himself a candidate in one of the premier in the fall of 1993.
13. See Lecture by Professor Jirbawi, Abdul Hameed Shoman Foundation, Amman, Jordan, 5 June 1997.
14. On the situation of the process of liberalization in the Palestinian territories see: Abu Amr, *Al-Mujtama' al-Madani wal-Tahawwul al-Dïmoqrati fi Filistïn*, Cairo: Ibn Khaldoun Centre for Development Studies, 1995, also on the debate over democratization. in Palestine see: Budeiri and others, *Al-Dimoqratiyah al-Filistïniyah: Awräq Naqdjyah, A Critical Perspective on Palestinian Democracy*, Muwatin: The Palestinian Institute for the Study of Democracy, April 1995.
15. Panorama, Palestinian Information Centre, Vol.6, year 1, 1997, p.29.
16. The two leading Islamist organizations in the Palestinian territories, Hamas and Jihad,officially boycotted the 1996 elections. However, six independent Islamist in the Palestinian legislative council see: Shikaki, *Al-Intikhäbät al-Filistïniyah al-Ülah: al-Bï'ah al-Siyäsiyah, al-Sulük al-Intikhäbi, wal-Natä'ej*, Nablus: Center for Palestine Research and Studies, 1997.
17. For an extensive analysis o(the debate over the Islamists' agenda in the 1989 parliament see minutes of the sessions, 19 Feb. 1992, 27 Jan. M3 and 10 March 1993.
18. For more detailed analysis of the Jordanian case see: Brand, *Jordan's International Relations: The Political Economy of Alliance Making*, New York: Columbia University Press, 1995.

REFERENCES

Abu Amr, Ziyad, *Al-Mujtama' al-Madani wal-Tahawwul al-Dimoqrati fi Filistïn*, Cairo: Ibn Khaldoun Center for Development Studies, 1995.

Al-Abdullat, Marwan, *Kharitat al-Ahzab Assiyasiyah fi al-Urdun*, Amman, 1992.

Al-Khatib, Ranad Ayyadh, *Attayyarat Assiyasiyah fi al-Urdun wa-Nass* Qanun al-Ahzab, Amman, 1992.

Al-Ma'aytah, Sameeh, *Al-Tajrubah Assiyasiyah lil-Harakah al-Islamiyah fi al-Urdun*, Dar al-Bashir, Amman, 1994.

Al-Sayyid, Mustapha K., 'A Civil Society in Egypt', *The Middle East Journal*, 47/2, Spring 1993, pp.228–42.

Al-Tohleh, Zaki, 'Mawagef al-Harakat Assiyasiyah al-Islamiyah fi al-Mujtama' al-Urduni min al-Dimoqratiyah' , Master's thesis, University of Jordan, Amman, 1996.

Bartlett, Robert V., 1990, 'Comprehensive Environmental Decision Making: Can It Work', in Norman Vig and Michael Kraft (eds.), *Environmental Policy in the 1990s: Toward a New Agenda*, Washington, DC: Congressional Quarterly Press, pp.235–54.

Bidas, Ashraf, 'Harakat al-Mujtama' al-Madani', *Majalat al-Mujtama' al-Madani*, Ibn Khaldoun Centre for Development Studies, No.62, 1997, pp.14–16.

Brand, Laurie A., 'The Quest for Civil Society in Jordan', unpublished paper.

Brynen, Rex *et al.*, *Political Liberalisation and Democratisation in the Arab World*, Boulder, CO: Lynne Rienner, 1995.

Centre for Strategic Studies, University of Jordan, *Public Opinion Poll on Democracy in Jordan*, Amman, 1993.

Centre for Strategic Studies, University of Jordan, *Public Opinion Poll on Democracy in Jordan*, Amman, 1995.

Centre for Strategic Studies, University of Jordan, *Public Opinion Poll on Democracy in Jordan*, Amman, 1996.

Centre for Strategic Studies, University of Jordan, *Public Opinion Poll on Democracy in Jordan*, Amman, 1997.

Chomsky, Noam, *Deterring Democracy*, New York: Hill & Wang, 1992.

Commonwealth of Australia, 1996, *Australia's Report for the United Nations Commission on Sustainable Development*, Canberra: DEST.

Dar al-Uroubah, *Lildirasat wal-Istisharat al-I'lamiyah*, Addalil Assiyasi al, Amman, 1994.

Department of th eEnvironment, Sport and Territories, 1998, *Reform of Commonwealth Environment Legislation: Consultation Paper*, Canberra: Department of the Environment.

Department of th eEnvironment, Sport and Territories, 1998a, *National Strategy for Ecologically Sustainable Development* (http://kaos.erin.gov.au/portfolio/esd/nsesd/nsesd.htm\).

Farhati, Omar, 'Ishkaliyat al-Dimoqratiyah fi al-Jaza'er', Masters thesis, University of Algeria, 1992.

Ghalyoun, Burhan, 'Bina' al-Mujtama' al-Madani al-'Arabi: Dawr al-' Awamel al-Dakhiliyah wal Kharijiyah', *Majalat al-Mustaqbal Al-' Arabi*, 4/158, 1992, pp.105–24.

Halpern, M., *The Politics of Social Change in the Middle East and the Arab World*, Princeton, 1962.

Hamarneh, Mustafa B., *Al-Mujtama' al-Madani wal Tahawwul al-Dimoqrati fi al-Watan al-Arabi: Halat al-Urdun*, Cairo: Ibn Khaldoun Centre for Development Studies, 1995.

Hanf Theodor and Bernard Sabella, *A Date with Democracy: Palestinians on Society and Politics – An Empirical Survey*, Arnold-Bergstraesser-Institut, Freiburg I. Br., 1996.

Harrison, Kathryn, 1996, *Passing the Buck: Federation and Canadian Environmental Policy*, Vancouver: UBC Press.

Hinnebusch, Raymond A., 'State and Civil Society in Syria', *Middle East Journal*, 47/2, Spring 1993.

Hourani, Hani *et al.*, *Al-Murshed ela al-Hizb Assiyasi*, Dar al-Sindibad, Amman, 1995.

Ibrahim, Sa'd Eddin *et al.*, *Mustaqbal al-Mujtama wal-Dawlah fi al Watan al-'Arabi*, Arab Thought Forum, Amman, 1988.

Ibrahim, Saad Eddin, 'Crises, Elites, and Democratisation in the Arab World', *Middle East Journal*, 47/2, Spring 1993, pp.292–305.

Ibrahim, Saad Eddin, *Al-Mujtama' al-Madani wal-Tahawwul al-Dimoqrati fi al-Watan al-'Arabi*, Cairo: Ibn Khaldoun Centre for Development Studies, 1992.

Imam, Abdul Fattah, 'Masirat al-Dimoqratiyah ... Ru'yah Falsafiyah', *'alam al-Fikr*, 2, Kuwait, 1993.

Kellow, Aynsley, 1996, 'Thinking Globally and Acting Federally: Intergovernmental Relations and Environmental Protection in Australia', in Kenneth M. Holland, F.L. Morton and Brian Galligan (eds.), *Federalism and the Environment: Environmental Policymaking in Ausxtralia, Canada, and the United States*, Westport, CT: Greenwood Press, pp.135–56.

Khleifat, Sahban, *Al-Dimoqratiyah fi al-Urdun Siyaqiha al-Dawli wa-Shurutiha al-Mawdu'iyah*, Dar Afaq, Amman, 1994.

Khouri, Tareq, *Mustaqbal al-Urdun: al-Dimoqratiyah, al-Hawiyah*, al-Tahidiyat Tahidiyat, Amman, 1990.

Muslih, Muhammad, 'Palestinian Civil Society', *Middle East Journal*, 47/2, Spring 1993, pp.258–74.

Norton, Agustus Richard, 'The Future of Civil Society in the Middle East' 1993, *Middle East Journal*, 47/2, Spring 1993, pp.205–16.

Norton, R., 'Introduction to a Social Issue on Civil Society in the Mddle East', *Middle East Journal*, Spring, 1993.

Orum, A.M., *Introduction to Political Sociology*, Englewood Cliffs, NJ, 1987.

Owen, Roger, *State, Power, and Politics in the Making of the Modem Middle East*, London: Routledge, 1992.

Perthes, Volker, 'State Building, National Security and Preparation in Syria', unpublished paper.

Perthes, Volker, *The Political Economy of Syria under Asad*, London: I.B. Tauris, 1995.

Piscatori, James, *Islamic Fundamentalism and the Gulf Crisis*, American Academy of Arts and Sciences, 1991.

RIVM, 1997, *Milieubalans 97. Het Nederlandse Milieu Verklaard*, Alphen aan den Rijn: Samsom/H.D. Tjeenk Wllink bv.

Sa'b, Hassan, *al-'Amaliyah al-Intikhabiyah wal-Dimoqratiyah fi Lubnan*, al-Mu'assasah al-Jami'eyah, Beirut, 1987.

94

Sawalha, Leah, *The Jordanian Women's Movement*, Jordanian Women Union, Amman, 1995.

Schwedler, Jillian (ed.), *Toward Civil Society in the Middle East*, Boulder, CO: Lynne Rienner Publishers, 1995.

Seminar on 'Political Pluralism', Ibrahim, Saad Eddin, Amman, 1989.

Seminar on 'The Civil Society in the Arab World and its role in achieving democracy, 20–23 January 1992', Arab Unity Research Centre, Beirut, 1992.

Seminar on 'Which Elections for More Democracy in Lebanon?', Beirut: Arab Unity Research Centre, 1992.

Shikaki, Khalil, *Al-Intikhabat al-Filistiniyah al-Ulah: al-Bi'ah Assiyasiyah, Assuluk al-Intikhabi, wal Nata'ej*, Nablus: Centre for Palestinian Research, 1997.

Skogstad, Grace, 1996, 'Intergovernmental Relations and the Politics of Environmental Protection in Canada', in Holland, Morton and Galligan [*1996: 103–34*].

Tetreault, Mary Ann, 'Civil Society in Kuwait: Protected Spaces and Women's Rights', *Middle East Journal*, 47/2, Spring 1993, pp.275–91.

Toner, Geln, 1996, 'Environment Canada's Continuing Roller Coaster Ride', in Gene Swimnmer (ed.), *How Ottawa Spends 1996–97. Life Under the Knife*, Ottawa: Carleton University Press, pp.99–132.

Wallace, David, 1995, *Environmental Policy and Industrial Innovation: Strategies in Europe, the USA and Japan*, London: Earthscan Publications.

Zaki, Moheb, *Civil Society and Democratisation in Egypt 1981–1994*, Cairo: Dar al-Kutub, 1994.

6

Political Reform and Social Change in the Maghreb

GEMA MARTIN-MUÑOZ

Not surprisingly, international and regional relations were profoundly affected by the end of the cold war in 1990 and the parallel end of the global balance of power which had persisted throughout the cold war era. The disappearance of global military threat and enhanced co-operation between states have also modified our concepts of security and have initiated new trends in international affairs, such as strengthened economic interdependence and more importantly, a redefinition of internal and regional stability through the restructuring of internal socio-political processes.

The revival of the Euro-Mediterranean dialogue, via the Barcelona Declaration, is a part of this new momentum that began to emerge long before but also developed throughout the 1980s. Unlike previous initiatives, in which co-operation between the European Union and the Mediterranean region was almost exclusively based upon economic relations, this new policy initiative emphasizes the link between political and economic liberalization. Thus, while the economic factor remains crucial within the policy, it is not pivotal to the Euro-Mediterranean Partnership as defined in the Barcelona Declaration, which describes a project based on a global vision that requires the redefinition of relations in the Mediterranean region.

Traditional interpretations of the economic problems and risks facing the Mediterranean region are generally accepted by specialists and by the international community as a whole. The traditional concept that economic take-off alone can provide a solution to both social and political problems has been one of the essential theoretical foundations of North–South relations. However, the Barcelona Declaration highlights the fact that political and social dialogue between Europe and the Southern Mediterranean is also the basis for consensus and the solution to imbalances between these two political entities. The reason for this is partly that, if liberal economic reforms are accompanied by a democratic deficit, their positive effects in terms of

96

political integration are minimized whilst the social costs of restructuring can have a destabilising effect. In other words, it is imperative for the state to convince people of its political credibility and institutional efficiency if they are to accept such costs.

Over the past 20 years, the populations of the Maghreb countries – Morocco, Algeria and Tunisia – have experienced considerable social upheaval although the situation of the political elites has remained unaffected. This discordance has gradually created a gap between the elites and society and, in view of the predominance of the young as a social group, this socio-political breakdown has largely taken the shape of a generation gap. The direction in which socio-political stability will evolve depends largely on the political and economic system in which this new generation develops. On the one hand, in closed political systems where the social integration of youth – through education, work and political participation – has been prevented, this group may become a significant destabilizing force. Islamist movements are more likely to develop in parallel with such a development, particularly in the form of mass protest movements whose identity is marked by nationalist, Third World and anti-Western outlooks. On the other hand, where an open and pluralist political framework exists, social mobility and the participation of new elites can be expected and the tensions generated by the generation gap and Islamism are therefore likely to be neutralized. Profound and irreversible political integration is a powerful factor in political stability.

The social debate in Maghrebi societies, in consequence, no longer focuses on the issue of modernization but is instead concerned with the introduction of moral content into the political and socio-economic order. This is mainly intended to counter the corruption and social marginalization engendered by the state, which has divided integrated and marginalized social groups from each other. Furthermore, political relations between the state and citizens must be revived and developed in a legitimate and sustainable framework, involving consensus and reliable institutional structures. Indeed, institutional reforms have been initiated in the Maghreb and have enabled populations there to vote on constitutional reforms leading to general elections in 1997 in Morocco and Algeria. In Tunisia, the president announced in December 1996 reforms to come into operation the following year. However, whether these developments mean that democracy is really taking hold in the region can only be ascertained by examining each country individually.

Virtues and Shortcomings of Consensus in Morocco

Since the constitutional revisions of 1992, Morocco has engaged in a reform process which culminated in King Hassan II's invitation to the opposition to form a government after the 1993 elections. In these elections, for the first time in over 30 years, the main two opposition parties, the *Union Socialiste des Forces Populaires* (Socialist Union of Popular Forces, USFP) and *Istiqlal*,[1] formed a front (*al-Kutla al-Dimuqratiyya* – Democratic Bloc) and their representatives won 91 of the 222 seats elected by universal suffrage. Two-thirds of the single-chamber parliamentary assembly was, at that time, elected directly and the remaining one third of the seats were filled by indirect election. After lengthy deliberations, however, the opposition turned down the king's invitation in early 1995 and refused to govern without a majority in parliament – especially since subsequent indirect elections had invalidated the result of direct elections and deprived *al-Kutla*[2] of its overall majority.

A period of political pessimism, lasting for a year-and-a-half, followed the breakdown in communications between the Royal leadership and the opposition. It was compounded by a loss of faith in the economic situation following a critical World Bank report in October 1995. This stated that, if Morocco 'failed to invest in human capital (which would imply a profound educational reform) and to correct the bureaucratic and legal archaisms of its excessively centralized administration, it would be unable to adapt to economic growth and this would increase social and economic inequalities'.[3]

Amid concerns about his health, the king himself became increasingly anxious to complete his political heritage for his successor. Indeed, Prince Sidi Muhammad (now king) entered political life in 1995 and has since been on official visits, participated in the negotiations with the Polisario Front and, up to his accession to the throne in July 1999, was involved in important aspects of relations with the socialist opposition. Even though his father made many changes, he did not complete his reform project. As a result, the new king, Muhammad VI, is still left with a major political issue to resolve – the Western Sahara conflict. A strong national consensus will be all the more important if the Western Sahara conflict is to be resolved. The situation there fluctuated between the 1996 collapse in dialogue between Morocco and the Polisario Front and the 1997 resumption of dialogue as a result of mediation by James Baker, the former American secretary-of-state under President Bush and now the United Nations secretary-general's special envoy over the issue. At the start of the new millennium, the conflict was still unresolved, however.

These events led the Moroccan elite to the conclusion that, given the profound changes affecting the country, it would have to redefine itself through institutional reform. Furthermore, national aspirations for economic development and closer relations with Europe could only be fulfilled if its economic and financial fabric were consolidated, integrated and rendered efficient in order to make the country's commercial sector competitive. On 20 August 1996, the Moroccan monarch announced in a speech to the nation the reforms proposed to achieve this; they were to start with a new amendment of the Constitution which would lead to general elections in May 1997. In practice, however, the reform programme slipped and elections only occurred at the end of that year.

On 13 September 1997, the reform of the Fundamental Law, which sought political reform by creating a bicameral parliamentary assembly and administrative decentralization through regionalization – was approved by referendum with a 99.5 percent vote in favour. The amended constitution benefited from two fundamental new factors: indirect suffrage in the legislative elections was eliminated and the proposed constitutional changes enjoyed the opposition's endorsement. Opposition parties urged their voters to support the new constitution, even though they had not participated in drawing it up. In proposing these constitutional changes, the regime acknowledged the structural crisis it had previously ignored and, in accepting them the opposition, characterized in the past by its constant rejection of decisions made by the state, accepted reform. The reluctance shown by trade unionists and younger members of the USFP (*Union Socialiste des Forces Populaires*) did not alter this situation despite the outright rejection of it by the radical OADP (*Organisation de l'Action Démocratique et Populaire*) leadership. Indeed, the OADP then split and the PSD (*Parti Social-Démocratique*) was created from its remnants.

Although Morocco's pluralist political system had been devised as a way of combating the groups that evolved from the National Movement[4] and despite the fact that the monolithic character of the royalist leadership always thwarted their development, nationalist parties were able to find a place within Moroccan society and to be legitimized by the opposition discourse which had sustained them for several decades. Thus, even though these parties played no role in political decision-making (except for the *Istiqlal* which participated in the government between 1961 and 1963 and again between 1977 and 1984), relations between the leadership and the opposition were never fully severed, as both sides were aware that they might need each other's support in the future in order to normalize political life. The new impulse given to political reform at the end of 1996 showed that the leadership needed to consolidate channels of mediation and to delegate part of its responsibilities. As for the opposition, its approval of proposals made by the regime was a measure of its need for a wider field of action if it were to reassert its position, particularly in view of its loss of support among the poorer segments of the young generations emerging into political activity.

The cautious optimism generated by these events, both in and outside the country, was less the result of their immediate consequences than of their symbolic value since, for the first time since the advent of Independence, it was possible to discern signs of a consensus between the opposition and the leadership. This was to end the *status quo* in Moroccan political life, which had caused the stagnation of meaningful activity within the party political framework and had been characterized by an irreconcilable duality between the parties descended from the nationalist movement and the *Makhzen.*[5] The opposition's request for direct universal suffrage was thus fulfilled, even though the originally unicameral Chamber of Representatives was now joined by a new second chamber. The new chamber, far from playing the secondary role of a senate, was designed to be a powerful institution able to present draft laws, set up inquiries on important matters and pass a vote of no-confidence on the government with a qualified majority of three quarters of its members. These prerogatives undermined those of the Chamber of Representatives, particularly when the fact that the new superior chamber was elected by indirect suffrage was taken into account. Some 60 per cent of its delegates were to be elected by the recently created Regional Assemblies and the remainder by trade and employers' unions, as had been the case with the indirect elections under the old unicameral system.

King Hassan, in a speech in August 1997, explained the purpose of the new powerful indirectly-elected Upper Chamber as follows:

> In order to make this Chamber more attractive to candidates, we have decided to make it different from chambers in other constitutions. In doing this, we shall demonstrate that Morocco is not satisfied with drawing inspiration from other existing entities, but that it will adapt other countries' models and ideas to its own realities. What are, then, the characteristics of the second Chamber? The first one is that its composition will be the result of a triple election: separate elections will be organized by local communities, wage-earners, and professional chambers. The representatives elected by these groups will elect regional representatives who will, in turn, choose the members of the second Chamber.

The aim of regionalization – not to be confused with regionalism, as the authorities stressed at the time – was to decentralize and reform Moroccan administration, whilst encouraging the creation of new regional elites at a time when the balance traditionally established by the *Makhzen* had become fragile because its ability to distribute power and patronage from the centre had decreased. For the Moroccan government, much of the 1980s were spent stabilising the public finances and, above all, in seeking a solution to the foreign debt problem. Structural adjustment – theoretically completed in 1992 – the withdrawal of the state from the economy and economic austerity fed the protest movement which culminated in the 1981 and 1984 riots and was compounded by the failed *coup d'état* by General Dlimi in January 1983. The 1990s began with a widespread strike, which led to violent repression in December 1990 and was enhanced by the tensions which preceded the Gulf

War. This situation was further compounded by the start of the civil war in neighbouring Algeria.

These events clearly showed up the fragility of leadership stability, in the face of a new generation largely made up of unemployed young people that now formed the most excluded and the largest social group in Moroccan society. Those under 30 years of age now form two-thirds of the population; they are the victims of a inefficient educational system and of a social framework unable to satisfy the expectations of social development that it had itself fostered – for instance, according to official figures, 33 per cent of graduates are unemployed.[6] This new potential for mass action and a marked resistance to party militancy led to widespread social change as well. Young people, together with Morocco's working class, have recently become noticeably more defiant towards politicians who were previously able to channel their claims and aspirations. Sociological research carried out during the 1993 elections showed that the population no longer identified with the political parties participating in the elections. Furthermore, the National Union of Students – traditionally controlled by the political left – had gradually been taken over by Islamist groups. The result was a profound gulf between the political parties and political groupings involving youth. The generation gap between these two political groups became clear during clashes between Islamists and members of the USFP at Rabat University in May 1996, when a series of demonstrations were organized outside the control of the student union which represented the majority of students. The lesson to Morocco's political leaders and the Royal palace was clear; they had to take a greater interest in youth for its grievances must be addressed and controlled.

This specific political situation was compounded both by international economic realities which require a complete overhaul of Morocco's human infrastructure, particularly education and the administration, and by the inevitable impact such reforms would have on the elite. There was also the question of the diplomatic choices made by Morocco – which were often criticized at home – but which have always endeared it to the West. Examples of such choices are the country's wholehearted adoption of the capitalist model and of economic liberalism – the leader of the USFP himself, following an ideological U-turn for the USFP is traditionally a socialist party, eventually declared his support for liberalism[7] – its moderate position on the Arab–Israeli conflict, its acceptance of structural adjustment programmes and its pro-Western attitude during the Gulf War. These positions earned Morocco financial rewards: between 1983 and 1992, its official foreign debt was rescheduled six times, its bank debt three times and it was granted credit facilities by the IMF and the World Bank.[8]

In addition to these factors, Morocco, in the mid-1990s was also counting on its future integration into Europe with which it has always sought a privileged relationship. This integration, which would extend beyond that developed in the framework of European Union–Maghreb relations, was to provide an institutional, political, economic and financial guarantee for the national reforms. Besides the bilateral agreements, which have existed since 1969, closer relations were also to be encouraged by the November 1995 free-trade agreement with the European Union, in the context of the Barcelona Process. The agreement was seen as the means by which Morocco would eliminate constraints on private sector competitiveness, reform an inefficient and ill-trained administration, remove the legal lacunae which hamper commerce and generate a stable economic policy, despite the sluggishness of structural reform. Thus, Moroccan entrepreneurs' suddenly became aware of the importance of the rule-of-law, which could end legal insecurity that has profoundly hindered national economic activity.

Such changes, however, will inevitably create new socio-political allegiances and alliances and economic openness also carried the risk of affecting relations with the national leadership as well as threatening prominent political players, given growing domestic unrest as economic change continued. It was, therefore, logical for the Moroccan leadership and the *Makhzen* to seek political and financial support from new players and institutions. This was the context in which the reform process in Morocco had to be understood. The then interior minister, Driss Basri, and the king's adviser, André Azoulay, prepared the way for reform by neutralising conflict both nationally and internationally and promoting the economic reform programme in political and business circles. The interior minister himself entered into a "gentleman's agreement", on behalf of the government, designed to improve the climate in the business world and with the union movements. Following a period of widespread social unrest which led to a general strike organized by the UGTM (*Union Générale des Travailleurs Marocains*) and the CDT (*Confedération Démocratique du Travail*) on 5 June 1996, a tripartite outline agreement was signed on 1 August 1996 between the government, the management and trade unions. This marked the beginning of a social dialogue which had a substantial psychological impact since, until then, labour and management had virtually never been seen together, let alone share the same objectives.[9] This agreement was a victory for trade unions because it was an acknowledgement on the part of both the employers' federation and the government, of the unions' social importance and thus provided them with improved legitimacy. As far as the government was concerned, the dialogue limited the impact of social issues on politics, particularly in view of the political reforms then being designed. The fact that Driss Basri was present at the CDT national congress in March 1997 – he was invited by the union's secretary general, Noubir al-Amaoui, imprisoned four years before for criticising Moroccan politicians – illustrated the political changes that had taken place in Morocco as well as underlining Driss Basri's aspiration to be the "catalyst of transition". Similarly, the role of the interior minister as the king's political right-hand was highlighted by the joint declaration signed on 28 February 1997 by Driss Basri on behalf of the government with the parties, which guaranteed fair elections.[10]

The Opposition Challenge

The bipolarity which, until recently, characterized Moroccan politics – the legal opposition movement, stemming from the old nationalist movement on the one hand and the Royal Palace on the other – disappeared when the opposition gradually ceased to monopolize channels of protest and popular frustration was increasingly expressed through the Islamist movement which became a real, if moderate, opposition to the regime. As in other Arab states, this has led to the Islamization of some opposition parties, a development which demonstrates that Islamism is present in Morocco at both a social and political level.

The *Istiqlal* party, for example, which, in religious terms, can be regarded as a traditionalist party has sought to appropriate the Islamist social base by reactivating its conservative Islamic discourse and by presenting itself as the upholder of Islamic values. However, it refused to make an alliance with *al-Tawhid wa'l-Tajdid* (Unity and Renovation), an Islamist group which was attempting to legalize itself with a view to entering the political arena.[11] The USFP and its trade union branch, the CDT, have accepted individual Islamists as members but the party has also suffered an internal power struggle between partisans and opponents of this new approach. Furthermore, the integration of *al-Tawhid wa'l-Tajdid*[12] into the *Mouvement Populaire Démocratique et Constitutionnel* (MPDC), a legal party led by the old nationalist leader Dr Khatib,[13] provoked a lively debate on the Moroccan political scene as well as a great deal of anxiety in neighbouring Maghrebi states.

Faced with a dual challenge – from the regime and from the new opposition – the traditional parties decided to form a coalition and, on 26 May 1996, they formed the 'Bloc Démocratique' (*al-Kutla*) in order to focus their activities.[14] There is no doubt that King Hassan approved of this development for he had frequently expressed his support for a bipolar party political system and the new *al-Kutla* coalition formed an ideal partner in such an arrangement with *al-Wifaq* (l'Entente), the grouping formed in 1993 by those parties which enjoyed tacit government patronage.[15] These two groupings, however, should not be seen as two poles, one progressive, the other conservative, an arrangement that would eventually ensure their identity and survival in the long-term. They are, in reality, simply the representatives of the regime on the one hand, and of the opposition on the other (the *Istiqlal*, in particular, cannot really be labelled a left-wing party) Thus, once political 'alternance' – the term is used in Morocco to describe the consecutive alternation as the party of government between two such political tendencies – is achieved, the two groupings would be expected to lose their original identity and even their political purpose.[16]

The local elections on 13 June 1997 confirmed this was the actual situation and that its implications were also understood by the electorate *Al-Kutla* was unable to participate as a single party because of grass-roots opposition in most constituencies where real political significance was attached to its individual party members, rather than to the coalition as a whole. As for the *Rassemblement National des Independents* (RNI), the major independent party outside the *Wifaq*, it seemed keen to become a middle-of-the-road party claiming to draw on social liberalism to define itself as 'a party open towards civil society which aims to unite all those who no longer identify with traditional left or right-wing parties'.[17]

Al-Kutla – without the OADP but with the PSD – accepted the political and constitutional reform proposals put forward in 1996, not only because it was the best offer that had been made by the regime, but also because its leadership realized that a degree of realism and pragmatism was needed in order to go beyond the dualism of government and permanent opposition which had previously characterized Morocco's political history. The proposals gave the opposition the opportunity to enter government and to avoid being constantly disadvantaged by its status as perpetual opponent. As it was constantly excluded from decision-making processes, it was consequently becoming increasingly isolated from its popular support base as well. It was for this reason that the three major opposition parties called for a vote in favour of the reform proposals in the 13 September 1996 constitutional reform referendum, despite the fact that they had not participated in drawing the proposals up. The USFP leadership also pointed out that the wider political context had played a more significant role in their decision than 'the analysis of the constitutional document, which was relegated to the background'.

There would have been disastrous consequences , had this process failed, which would have provoked internal conflict within the USFP[18] where support for reform was divided, much like the party itself. This is particularly true in view of the confirmed June 1997 local election results which showed that, even though *al-Kutla* had increased its percentage of the vote, this increase was by no means spectacular, particularly for the USFP where many young militants were perplexed because they had thought that the *al-Kutla* strategy was unlikely to be applied as it stood. In any case, as far as political forces in the local context were concerned, it was clear that no single political group had obtained a real majority (*Wifaq*: 30.26 per cent; *al-Kutla*: 31.71 per cent;

centre parties: 26.43 per cent; others: 11.6 per cent).[19] If the reforms were successful, there clearly would be, therefore, two major modifications to the political scene. Firstly, the traditional opposition parties would move into the political majority, whilst the Islamist movement would become the main opposition focus. Secondly, whilst Abdallilah Benkirane, the leader of *al-Tawhid wa'l-Tajdid*, would be integrated into this system, Abdessalam Yassin, the leader of *al-'Adl wa'l-Islah* (Justice et Charité), the original Islamist movement in Morocco which was far less willing to compound with Royal power would remain outside it. It was not a movement that could be ignored, as the February 1997 student demonstrations at Hassan II University in Casablanca and elsewhere in the country demonstrated. Although the demonstrations were partly caused by to the university system's own shortcomings, they also demonstrated the extent of the Islamist influence through *al-'Adl wa'l-Islah* inside the educational sector. Indeed, the demonstrations may even have been a show of force, designed to highlight the organization's existence and presence, in order to counter the fact that it had been excluded from the reform process. The challenge thereafter for the state would be to find ways in which it could gradually integrate this group into the legal political system.

The 1997 General Elections: Top-Down Political Change

The general elections which took place between November and December 1997 and which, in many respects were a mechanism to legitimize political reform and the change of government which had occurred a year earlier, did not deliver the triumph expected by the opposition. It was not possible, therefore, for the Royal Palace to base the political transformation it sought on the electoral process. Direct elections to the 325-member Chamber of Representatives took place on 14 November 1997, on the basis of a first-past-the-post system. No independent candidates were allowed to participate and the *Al-Kutla* parties, who had been unable to form common candidate lists, ran independently of each other. The USFP won the largest number of votes and seats (57 seats), followed by the leading member of the *Wifaq*, the UC (*Union Constitutionelle*; 50 seats) and the RNI (46 seats). *Istiqlal*'s results were disappointing (32 seats) and it lost 500,000 votes compared to its results in the 13 June 1997 local elections. This put the party in a difficult position at the special congress demanded by its younger militants immediately after its electoral disappointments, where the party leadership tried to check the pro-electoral boycott faction of the party. To everyone's surprise, the three main coalitions (*al-Kutla, al-Wifaq* and the Centre) more or less maintained their respective positions in terms of the votes they received, despite some adjustments within the blocs themselves. *Al-Kutla* and other left-wing parties won 116 seats (35.7per cent), while the centre, the right and the Islamists won 209 seats – two thirds of the assembly seats. The left-wing splinter groups also managed to obtain seats, with results that were either nearly as good (*Front des Forces Démocratiques* – FFD) or better (PSD) than those of their parent parties (the PRP – *Parti de Renouveau et du Progrès* – originally Morocco's communist party, and the OADP respectively)

TABLE 1
ELECTION STATISTICS

Constituencies	325
Participation percentage	58.3
Registered voters	12,790, 631
Votes cast	7,456,996
Invalid votes	1,085,366
Valid votes	6,371,630

The election, for the first time in Moroccan political history, of nine Islamist deputies was unprecedented and had they had one extra seat, they would have been able to constitute their own parliamentary group. In fact, the party claimed they should have had two more seats, those for Casablanca and Fez. Nevertheless, *al-Tawhid wa'l-Tajdid*, Abdelillah Benkirane's own party, obtained its main political objective for many years; a role on the legitimate political stage. The moderate Islamist movement only gained this recognition, however, through the alliance it was allowed to make with a legal party. The Royal Palace was thus able to avoid the question of legalization of the Islamists as a political force in their own right but, at the same time, to grant political participation to a new political elite, which has a significant support-base inside contemporary Moroccan society. This approach also allowed the Palace to isolate and divide Abdel Salam Yassin's *al-'Adl wa'l-Ihsah*, the other Islamist group increasingly eager for a role in political life, despite its leader's continuing opposition to the regime. In fact, *al-Tawhid wa'l-Tajdid* had linked to the *Mouvement Populaire Constitutionel Démocratique* (MPCD), which had been founded in 1967 by Abdelkrim Khatib, a participant in the nationalist struggle and a strong supporter of the monarchy who had also been known for many years for his activities in the Islamic world. These developments, however, did not mean that the Islamist issue had been solved for Morocco, even though the entry of a small number into parliament defused tensions. There remains the question of how to deal with the much larger movement that still remains outside the formal political process, despite its ability to mobilize the population.

The direct elections were followed, on 5 December 1997, by indirect elections to the upper house. The result of these elections diminished the impact of the direct elections, for the *Al-Kutla* bloc obtained only 44 seats (16 per cent of the seats available) and the balance went to the Centre (90 seats) and to government supporters. The RNI obtained the most votes with 16 per cent of the total (46 seats), followed by the MDS (*Mouvement Démocrate-Socialiste*), the UC, the *Istiqlal* and the PND. The USFP came in seventh place. Despite the disappointments, these elections constituted definite progress in terms of dialogue, as well as in the government's procedural transparency and neutrality because of the agreements made by the administration and the political parties before the elections. However, the practice of vote buying within the electoral constituencies had a significant impact on the results and deprived the opposition of many votes. There were other problems as well, not least the fact that participation in the elections continued to be poor – at 58 per cent of the electorate, five percentage points below the 1993 level. This relatively poor turnout underlined the lack of credibility of this particular form of political participation, for it has long had little meaning for the population-at-large. This problem, which is really one of legitimization opf the electoral process in the eyes of the electorate, was emphasized by the high percentage of invalid votes (14.5 per cent), particularly in towns and cities.

The fact cannot be ignored that the boundary definition of electoral constituencies carried out by the Mininstry of Interior made a major contribution to the outcome of the electoral process overall. Interestingly enough, the results obtained by the three main political blocs – al-Kutla, Wifaq and the Centre – which, in effect and somewhat artificially brought together most of the 17 political groups involved in the elections, were more or less the same. In the Chamber of Representatives, the USFP obtained the largest number of seats, whereas the largest number of seats in the upper chamber were obtained by the RNI with 90 seats – Wifaq won 76 seatsand al-Kutla only 44. The rightwing and centre parties, the latter dominated by the RNI, obtained together a majority in the bicameral parliament, with 88 deputies for the RNI, 78 for the UC, 73 for the USFP (plus 11 deputies from the CDT trade union which is allied to it), 67 for the MP, 65 for the MDS and 53 for the *Istiqlal* (plus three from its allied trade unions). This was not the result that the opposition had anticipated and it was overcome by disappointment and confusion. Its expectations of electoral victory and entry into government, thus fulfilling its acceptance of the principles of political *alternance* four years earlier, were dashed. Instead, it was the victim of electoral fraud, so it claimed, although it knew that the real measure of its failure was its loss of grass-roots support. As a result, the leader of the USFP, Abderrahman Yusufi, went into a symbolic self-imposed exile for two months.

TABLE 2
ANALYSIS OF THE INDIRECT ELECTIONS (5 December 1997)

	Local administration professional boards Seats	Workers representatives Seats	Total Seats	%
Results per bloc:				
al-Wifaq	76		76	28.1
al-Kutla	44		44	16.3
Centre	90		90	33.3
Other left-wing parties	16		16	5.9
Other independents	17		17	6.3
Results per main party:				
<u>*al-Kutla*</u>				
Istiqlal	21		21	7.8
USFP	16		16	5.9
PPS		7	7	2.6
OADP		–	–	–
<u>Other Left-wing parties</u>				
FFD	12		12	4.4
PSD		4	4	1.5
<u>Centre</u>				
RNI	42		42	15.6
MDS	33		33	12.2
MNP	15		15	5.5
<u>*al-Wifaq*</u>				
MP	27		27	10.0
UC	28		28	10.4
PND	21		21	7.8
<u>Other</u>				
Independents	–		–	–
PA	13		13	4.8
PDI	4		4	1.5
MPCD (Islamists)	–		–	–
<u>Trade Unions</u>				
CDT		11	11	4.1
UMT		8	8	2.9
UGTM		3	3	1.1
COM		1	1	0.4
USP		1	1	0.4
SND		1	1	0.4
UNTM		1	1	0.4
UDT		1	1	0.4
TOTAL	**243**	**27**	**270**	**100.0**

TABLE 3
CHAMBER OF REPRESENTATIVES: 1993 AND 1997

	Unicameral parliament 1993		Bicameral parliament 1997	
	%	*Seats*	*%*	*Seats*
Electoral Bloc				
al-Wifaq	39.1	129	30.8	100
al-Kutla	36.4	120	31.4	102
Left-wing parties	4.3	14	4.9	16
Centre	20.0	66	29.8	97
Other	4.5	15	3.1	10
Seats per party				
Istiqlal (*al-Kutla*)		52		32
USFP (*al-Kutla*)		56		57
PPS/PRP (*al-Kutla*)		10		9
FFD (close to *al-Kutla*)				9
OADP (*al-Kutla*)		2		4
PSD (close to the *al-Kutla*)				5
RNI (centre)		41		46
MDS (Centre)				32
MNP (Centre)		25		19
MP (*al-Wifaq*)		51		40
UC (*al-Wifaq*)		54		50
PND (*al-Wifaq*)		24		10
PA		2		2
PDI		9		1
MPCD (Islamists)				9
Total:		**330**		**325**

Note: The above table presents the seat distribution and percentages in relation to the directly elected chambers only, although it includes the indirectly elected members in 1993. In 1993, parliament was unicameral and contained 330 seats, 220 of which were elected directly and 110 indirectly.

The new enlarged bicameral parliament, with its 595 members – 45 per cent of whom were elected indirectly – clearly showed that the country's political make-up had hardly changed since 1993. The Centre and the Right still held the majority in both chambers and in the same proportions as in the previous parliament. The new parliament was even more fragmented than before with its 16 parties as well as eight groups of affiliated trade unions. Furthermore, the abstention rate and the high percentage of spoiled ballots, in both local and general elections, showed how disillusioned the population had become with such elections. These considerations had an immediate effect on the opposition as a whole, with criticism of the electoral process emerging as a result of disappointment and frustration. Some groups within the USFP (the youth organization and the trade union branch) and the *Istiqlal* wanted to denounce the elections as electoral fraud and boycott participation in the government – thus, incidentally, perpetuating their role as permanent opponents of the regime.

The period that followed the elections opened a phase of uncertainty for the opposition. It was faced with a difficult dilemma: should it resume its former attitude of rejection and non-collaboration or should it take up a difficult challenge with all the inevitable costs? Had it not accepted to play the electoral game, knowing that the rules had been set by the *Makhzen*? Could it afford not to seize the opportunity of helping political change in Morocco? Would it be able to accept the price of the kind of political change which is not based on electoral results? Could it afford to perpetuate a political crisis less than a year before the referendum on the Western Sahara was ostensibly due?

Throughout December and January, there were unusually tense discussions within *al-Kutla* parties. At first, internal debates gave rise to warnings of party splits. This gradually gave way to a more moderate discourse from party leaderships. In mid-December, following the intervention of personalities close to the palace, such as André Azoulay, and contacts with various social-democrat parties abroad, the leadership of the USFP announced it was ready to participate in the government. Other left-wing parties, except for the OADP, followed suit. Following a special congress held on 14 December 1997, the *Istiqlal* decided to change the leadership of the party and, during its regular congress held on February 20-22, 1998, the movement adopted a moderate and pragmatic stance towards collaboration with the government.

In January 1998, an initial dialogue with the Royal Palace resulted in the nomination of a socialist delegate to the presidency of the Lower Chamber with the support of *al-Kutla* parties, the Islamists and part of the Centre parties. Despite its lack of a stable majority in parliament, in February 1998, the king entrusted the USFP leader, Abderrahman Yusufi – whose party held the largest number of seats in the lower chamber – with the task of forming a new government. By March 1998, a new government had been formed, admittedly with some difficulty, and over 40 ministers were appointed. Most were socialists, some had been nominated by the king and others belonged to *al-Kutla* bloc, together with representatives from the RNI and the MNP. The process of forming the cabinet was complex. On the one hand, the Palace imposed constraints, retaining its prerogative over certain portfolios which it considered affected the monarchy. On the other hand, the parliamentary process required a coalition government which could rely on the support of the majority in the lower chamber. Negotiations between the parties were complicated, each being conscious of its importance – whether real or symbolic – and, as a result, these discussions took place in secret. This resulted in the formation of a hybrid government, comprising many interests, some of which represented the *Makhzen* and guaranteed the *status quo*, while others symbolized political change. The various portfolios were shared amongst seven parties and in some cases, the ministers and secretaries of states of a particular ministry belonged to different parties.

The Palace also insisted that some key ministries should remain in the hands of their previous incumbents. Thus, Abdellatif Filali remained in the foreign ministry, Driss Basri in the interior ministry, Omar Azziman in the justice portfolio and Abdelqader M'Daghri Alaoui in the religious affairs ministry. It was the renewal of Driss Basri's mandate, however, which was the most contentious. Indeed, since his nomination as interior minister in 1979, Driss Basri had been the opposition's *bête noire*. Nevertheless, he had been responsible for implementing the constitutional reforms the government had undertaken during the years leading to the 1997 elections. The renewal of his mandate – which was mitigated by the transfer of the national and regional development section to another ministry – was seen as an attempt by the Palace to keep an eye on the new government and to retain control of the sensitive issue over the Sahara.

The USFP obtained thirteen portfolios, including the most important ministries dealing with economics (Finance and Agriculture) and social affairs (Employment and Housing). However, strategic ministries controlling sectors where urgent reforms were needed, such as Administration, Justice and Education, remained outside the party's control. *Istiqlal* obtained six important economic portfolios (including Energy, Public Works, Planning and Privatization), one social portfolio (Health) and one political portfolio (Communications). The RNI, which had been strengthened by the elections – it was now the third most important political group in parliament and had come second in the local elections – became a key part of the coalition government because of its political weight and its liberal outlook. After much political wrangling, it finally obtained six ministerial posts, though this did not placate party militants who criticized their leader for failing to obtain posts that truly reflected the party's political weight, having accepted minor ministries instead. The PPS/PRP won three portfolios (including one important one, Education), as did the MNP, while the FFD got two and the PSD one, all of them of minor importance. In essence, therefore, economic and social ministerial responsibilities were allocated to the USFP and its allies, in accordance with their political weight and negotiating ability, whilst security, foreign relations and the question of the Sahara remained in the hands of ministers directly responsible to the King. As a result, the new government was neither smooth continuity nor a complete break with the past, it was rather the expression of an agreement on the constitution of a new team, itself the result of a clever intermixture of interests with a delicate balance of power that may be difficult to preserve.

Its formation, however, demonstrated that the increasing risk of internal destabilization because of the economic crisis, social tension and political deadlock and the necessity for Hassan II to ensure a smooth transition process for his successor eventually opened the way to political change in Morocco. Furthermore, Morocco's attempts to consolidate its bilateral relations with the European Union, together with the lessons drawn from the Algerian experience, also played a role in encouraging political change. Nevertheless, the November–December 1997 elections did not provide the opposition with the triumph it had expected, so that political transition did not occur as a direct result of the electoral process. Indeed, the electoral system ensured a clear balance among the three main political blocs – the opposition and the two blocs traditionally in power (the Right and the Centre) – without any bloc enjoying a clear majority in either chamber. None the less, institutional reform in Morocco, with the new climate of consensus over the political structure as its key element, despite the potential instability, has had positive benefits. The imperatives of consensus between old and new forces – the *Makhzen* and the opposition – mean that political reform has become the symbol of a reconciliation between the monarchy and the opposition, as well as a reflection of royal will, rather than a victory at the ballot box. The endlessly complex alchemy of political reform in Morocco required that political transition be imposed from the top, before it could itself prepare the ground for political change to be stimulated from below.

The Tunisian State

In economic and social terms, Tunisia should be the best prepared of all Maghreb states to face democratic transition because of its economic success, its higher standard-of-living and its declining birth rate. All of these are important aspects of socio-economic development that are not present in neighbouring North African countries. The 'new era', which followed Habib Bourguiba's removal from office on 1 November 1987, seemed to herald the beginning of open political dialogue between the leadership and the opposition in Tunisia. This was encapsulated in the National Pact in November 1988.[20] However, dialogue, together with the controlled and restricted attempt to integrate Tunisia's Islamist movement into the formal political life was gradually superseded by a strategy based on its eradication from the political arena. Legal opposition parties were co-opted in order to obtain their approval of the regime's security policy against the Islamist movement.[21]

A new national consensus based on co-operation against the 'Islamist threat' forced the opposition to play by the rules set by the regime, which limited political liberalization so that opposition parties only had a minority presence in parliament. Although the May 1995 local elections effectively ended the consensus created by the government, they occurred at a time when the opposition had already been weakened. This was especially true of the MDS (*Mouvement Démocratique Socialiste*) which had, by then, lost its symbolic capacity to counterbalance the party in power.[22] In fact, the regime's appeal for consensus was presented to political parties as a request for moderation and caution so that they would support the regime against the 'Islamist threat'. The state went on to stress the necessity of this support as a guarantee of national stability. This also meant support for its security policy, considered as an absolute priority by the government and as the only way of ensuring the country's economic prosperity and progress. Unanimity became the condition *sine qua non* to ensure that 'Tunisia would not become Algeria' and the challenges of security and stability – always of great concern in Europe – were placed at the heart of the system.

Reference to the crisis in Algeria became a useful instrument of governmental policy. It acted as a foil to divert criticism and was brandished as justification for the government's repression of the Islamist movement and of its opposition to rapid political liberalization, which would have made the transition towards democracy possible in the near future. This official discourse was all the more easily accepted by Tunisian society as the regime possessed two important policy assets. Firstly, Tunisia's economic results were good – with a 4.6 per cent average annual growth rate, a moderate 4.7 per cent annual inflation rate, a low level of foreign debt, and increased living standards.[23] Secondly, the success of the government's broad social policy was reflected in President Ben Ali's popularity – Tunisia devotes 18 per cent of its budget to the social sector, 75 per cent of the population are home owners and regional development has been given a boost. The government compounded this success by developmental measures in severely depressed areas, progress in education, and measures in favour of women. Women's issues are an essential strategic asset on the international stage if a state wishes to project itself as a modern entity faced with the threat of Islamism. They also help in any official attempt to attract domestic westernized sectors of public opinion which otherwise might be highly critical of the regime's authoritarianism and its discriminatory practices.

All these factors have conspired to ensure that the Tunisian government enjoys the support of both the underprivileged and privileged sectors of society. In fact, the latter effectively constitute a new political class, made up of businessmen, managers and members of the professions who occupy key positions in the system. This class is presented as the epitome of modernity, with its international cultural and economic contacts. It also has the ability to face in two directions at the same time, depending on whether it acts as part of an emerging civil society or as a isolated group which tolerates repression in exchange for regime protection from its rival elite – the Islamist movement. Nothing in the current Tunisian political scene indicates that this *status quo* will be modified in the near or medium-term future. The regime seems to be confident that it can maintain its control over the country through its rigid security structures, its economic success, a measure of social progress and the way in which it manipulates popular fear of Islamism. It is convinced of its stability and sees no need to initiate political reform that would create more open consensus. Instead, it uses the economy as a legitimizing tool. Yet, there remains a valid question mark over the future evolution of a society where, by virtue of their socio-economic development, the middle class and the professions are becoming stronger and will soon aspire to more political participation and to genuine representation.

Political Reform and Violence in Algeria

Over the past ten years, political change has been repeatedly sought in Algeria – so far without conspicuous success, even if political violence has significantly diminished in recent years. Between 13 March 1993, when the High State Council initiated a 'political dialogue with the opposition and associations', and the *Conférence de l'Entente* in September 1996, when a National Consensus Programme[24] was approved for the third time in three years, political dialogue was attempted on several occasions but failed on each occasion because each attempt failed to include all political groups.[25] The consensus achieved in January 1995 by the members of the Sant' Egidio Accord, the so-called Rome Platform, could have led to a wider dialogue, for example. The democratic formula it contained was agreed by various political groups (Islamist, Berber, secular and social-democrats) and presented to the regime. It argued for a culture of consensus as opposed to one of centralized decision-making. Unfortunately, neither the Algerian state nor the international community seized the opportunity it offered.

The importance of the Sant' Egidio Accord is emphasized by the way in which it divides political initiatives in Algeria since 1992 into two phases. The first phase was characterized by an essentially military strategy and Algeria's political life was officially presented as a struggle between the regime and the Islamists. The issues of the legality of institutions and political participation remained secondary considerations. The January 1995 Platform represented a political challenge for the Algerian regime, not because the project had real chances of success – the regime, by refusing to participate in the Rome meetings, had from the outset vitiated the proposal because it was based on dialogue and national reconciliation – but because it showed that there were non-Islamist political forces in Algeria which were willing to include the FIS in a non-exclusive political transition process in to order to reach a peaceful solution. After the regime had rejected this form of dialogue, it sought a political alternative that aimed both to please the international community and to rupture the solidarity of the parties involved in the Rome Platform. The parties involved included groups with opinions ranging from a 'possibilist' scenario – which would have involved participating in the political game, even if the rules were restrictive – to the maximalists who saw group unity as a key strategy, whether or not they thereby excluded participation.

The regime's main counter-initiative to the Rome Platform was the November 1995 presidential election. This marked the beginning of a post-Chadli Benjedid political and institutional process – somewhat delayed, it was true, since the previous president had resigned at the start of 1992 – which culminated with the 28 November 1996 referendum on constitutional reform. The presidential election was successful in so far as, officially, there was a high turn-out. This was attributed to the fact that the Algerian government had convinced voters that participation was the only alternative to violence and the only hope for national reconciliation, an ideal that was never realized. In fact, instead of initiating a new process, the election simply gave the Algerian military regime new credibility in the eyes of the international community. The military were able to shake off the negative image which had lingered since the army-backed coup had interrupted the January 1992 general elections, it reinstated the old single political party, the FLN, in its role as the government party alongside a new movement, the RND (*Rassemblement Nationale Démocratique*), it consolidated *Hamas* (the major legalized moderate Islamist movement, now known as the HMI) by helping it win over the FIS's (*Front Islamique du Salut*, Algeria's Islamist movement which was denied its victory in the 1991–92 general elections by the army-backed coup) original constituency and, finally, it helped to isolate Aït Ahmed's FFS (*Front des Forces Socialistes*, the major secularist party with a strong base in Algeria's Berber community).

The subsequent constitutional reform, which destroyed the spirit of the liberal constitution of 1989, reorganized the institutional structure in such a way that it was subordinated to the interests of the regime. The legal and political framework created by the new constitution enables the president to rule by decree in situations where this was not previously allowed such as during periods of parliamentary recess. Furthermore, the president's powers have been extended and he is now able to nominate magistrates, provincial governors and the central bank governor. His new veto power has become particularly important since the president can virtually exercise it over parliament. Indeed, the National Assembly, transformed into a Lower Chamber, has to share legislative power with a new upper chamber (the National Council), which is elected by indirect suffrage and is made up of groups close to the regime.[26] Furthermore, in order to be approved, laws must be supported by three-quarters of the National Council, thus giving this body a virtual veto in its own right over the activities of the directly elected lower chamber of the National Assembly. Now that this reform is in place, parliament is no longer politically viable, for deputies only act as tribunes, rather than being true legislators. The new constitution makes no mention of role of the army, it does not acknowledge Berber linguistic claims and it proclaims Islam as the official religion of the state, although parties cannot be based on religious political platforms. In other words, the state imposes restrictions on citizens to which it does not subject itself. The reform has ensured that legislative elections can no longer be other than politically safe – a pluralist exercise in which parliamentary political influence has been neutralized, the opposition weakened and the main opponent, the FIS, eliminated.

Three months prior to the elections planned for 5 June 1997, the Algerian 'revolutionary family' which supports the government and which is made up of the War Veterans Association, the Sons of Martyrs of the Revolution, the ALN Veterans and the General Union of Algerian Workers (UGTA) rebuilt itself into a new party, the *Rassemblement National Démocratique* (RND). The new movement was created to revive the image of the FLN which had been severely tarnished by its longevity and by demands for political liberalization from its young militants. Neither the RND's blurred and ambiguous political message – 'to build a strong, confident and serene Algeria ... without disowning its patrimony' – nor the fact that it had only just been formed prevented it from obtaining 40.78 per cent of seats in the legislative elections, in addition to the FLN's 64 seats. The opposition parties in favour of dialogue with the FIS and of its political integration faced the elections in some disarray. The FFS was criticized by some of its own members who believed that its electoral boycott only served to marginalize the party and to exclude it from active social participation. Eventually, the party decided to participate in the elections in order for the party to survive politically, as did Louisa Hanoun's left-wing *Parti des Travailleurs* (PT), in order to acquire a public platform with the few seats (19 for the FFS and four for the PT) they won, even though the parliament had been almost entirely emasculated by constitutional reform. Other parties took a different approach. Among the parties opposed to the government but not to the army, the Berberist RCD (*Rassemblement Culturelle* Démocratique) obtained 19 seats, which provided the regime with a 'modernist' alibi and attracted social groups who felt threatened by Islamism. On the other side of the political divide, the 69 *Hamas* deputies (which had, by then, changed its name to the HMI – *Harakat li'l-Mujtama' is-Silm* in order to avoid the restriction over parties based on religious platforms) provided the regime with a channel of communication with the social groups who support the Islamists.

In political terms, the military regime used *Hamas* and the extremist clandestine Islamist group, the GIA (*Groupe Islamique Armé*) to weaken and divide the FIS and its own clandestine armed faction, the *Armée Islamique du Salut* (AIS). In authorizing an increased role for *Hamas* – regarded as a moderate Islamist group and was actually allowed to hold several ministerial portfolios – the regime hoped that the party would absorb Islamist supporters as well as those in the FIS hierarchy who had been disappointed with the party's inability to succeed in the struggle with the regime. *Hamas* and its leader, Mahfoud Nahnah, represented a constructive opposition, possibly even one which might compromise with the regime. As mentioned above, it already participated in government and was bound to play a considerable role in the social and political arena by absorbing the malaise which emanated from large sectors of the population who had previously identified with the FIS. In reality, *Hamas* was expected to be able to weaken the guerilla warfare within society, particularly around the capital, Algiers, waged by spontaneous, autonomous and anarchic armed groups, made up of young unemployed men who regard themselves as the victims of repression and have therefore decided to protect themselves. The security forces had been singularly unsuccessful in countering their activities. Nevertheless, *Hamas* does not seem destined to play a key role in politics. The rewards it is offered by the regime seem to be in the social and cultural spheres and as guardians of tradition. In accordance with the traditional pattern of relations between the state and Islam, therefore, the party will be entrusted with the Islamization of society, so long as it accepts the political *status quo*.

Since they appeared in 1992, the GIA has been a major source of competition for the FIS and has forced it out from the hegemonic position it had held within the Islamist movement until the 1992 coup. The prominence given in the media to GIA terrorism has tended to ignore the FIS's condemnations of these activities, well as the dissensions between the AIS and the GIA, which are particularly pronounced when the FIS initiates a new political dialogue or when the AIS criticizes the *fatwas* and excommunications pronounced by the GIA in its bulletin, *al-Ansar*. Indeed, the regime has ensured that the FIS cannot now come to power in its present form, if ever. In 1992 the FIS relied on the support of three million voters, it benefited from political legitimacy and was influential in the private commercial sector. All this was lost, however, as the movement buckled under political and military pressure from the regime, which also enjoyed support from abroad. On the other hand, the army failed to destroy the Islamist guerilla movement, despite its enormous political, economic and military resources, and it would be a mistake to assume that the FIS has lost its popularity, even if Algerians recognize that it is no longer capable of challenging the regime's hegemony.

117

The regime has also been very successful at convincing international opinion of its point of view. International economic organizations do not wish to see Algeria, a large, oil-rich North African state fall into the hands of extremist religious factions. They worry at the prospects of losing what they regard as valid interlocutors for economic dialogue and have, as a result, offered unprecedented economic support for the Algerian state, provided that IMF structural adjustment objectives are met. This is a request with which Algeria has rigorously complied. Yet, financial aid alone cannot prevent a social crisis and the situation worsens on a daily basis. According to the 1997 UN World Report on Development, Algeria is 73rd of 101 developing countries studied, a statistic that demonstrates that a gradual process of pauperization of the Algerian population is now taking place, even though Algeria's macro-economic statistics have improved. In reality, the improvement in macro-economic indices[27] was linked to external factors and was by no means universal, as the statistics demonstrate:

- There have been significant fluctuations in oil prices and oil production has risen as a result of foreign investment. Petrochemical production declined by 12 per cent in 1997.

- agricultural production rose in 1997, mainly because of exceptional weather conditions in 1996).

- Land privatization is uncontrolled in the absence of the rule-of-law – which explains why land became a crucial factor in the war in the Mitija region in 1998.

- Industrial output dropped by 8.5 per cent in 1997 – against 0.5 per cent in 1995.

- Imports dropped in 1997 because of the government's strenuous efforts to reduce them and the decline in the population's purchasing power.

Overall, the Algerian economy's dependence on the oil industry has increased – it represented 93.11 per cent of exports in 1997 – and state revenues derived from oil and gas have risen without there being any productive improvement in the economy overall. Thus, the Algerian economic model which is dependent on oil rent has been reinforced, giving rise to a brief macro-economic improvement which reflects a momentary stabilization of the economy devoid of any real structural progress. In short, Algerian economic policy has consisted of drastic reductions of imports and state expenditure in order to free financial resources to pay off external debt. This has translated into enormous economic pressure on the population as would normally be unacceptable under normal conditions. This, in turn, has led to a severe degradation in the social and economic situation of the Algerian population.

The IMF's substantial financial support for Algeria has largely gone to correcting the overall financial situation, given the enormous budgetary and public deficits, together with Algeria's external debt. Funds have also been needed to finance the war (the security budget rose by 150 per cent in 1995) but virtually no state funds have been used for education, health or housing. Out of 1,350 public enterprises considered viable for privatization, only 26 were actually sold by the end of 1998.

While begging and unemployment have increased dramatically – unemployment affects approximately 30 per cent of the labour-force as a whole, but involves 75 per cent of the economically active population in the 16-to-24 age range[28] – public housing provision was reduced by 70 per cent between 1995 and 1996; health standards are deteriorating and contagious illnesses and malnutrition[29] have reappeared. In reality, the only economic reforms that have been carried out to date have imposed severe constraints in the form of price increases, wage freezes, the dismantling of public enterprises and massive redundancies. What is more, the process of militarization of society has intensified, with an increase in the size of the security forces, the civil militias and paramilitary groups[30] as well as in the number of Islamist armed groups, despite the presidential amnesty offered in 1999. The entrenchment of violence into social structures and the gradual militarization of society have caused major social change as well.

The 1999 Presidential Election

The presidential election of 15 April 1999, which was earlier than intended under the constitution, was the consequence of the resignation of the then president of the republic, Liamine Zeroual, who in September 1998 announced his wish to give up the leadership of the state. This resignation was the expression of the conflict unleashed within the core of the regime, where palace struggles during the months of August and September 1998 had forced Zeroual to withdraw. The overt target was the group represented by Zeroual and his chief minister and advisor Mohammed Betchine, inasmuch as those who attacked them did not reveal themselves in public, using instead the 'independent' Algerian press which, in fact, is for the most part controlled by one or other clan.[31] The only satisfactory explanation of the gradual denouncing of the fraudulence of the electoral process through which he had been elected, which was deliberately orchestrated by political groups discreetly allied to one of the clans in the power elite and in opposition to the presidency's own clan is that this was quite deliberately designed to weaken him. Finally, in the early months of 1998 a virulent press campaign was unleashed against the president and his chief advisor, rendering public the turbulent business affairs of the latter, which led to the resignation of Zeroual and the early convening of elections later on in the year.

119

The source of the confrontation, related exclusively to the internal relations of the groups which make up the real power structures, arose from the attempt of Zeroual and his advisor to affirm their autonomy (arming militias in their favour and ensuring their control over certain economic channels) with respect to the army and the security services, directed by the head of the chiefs of staff, General Mohammed Lamari and the General Toufik Mediene respectively. This also happened at a moment in which two very relevant events took place: the end of the three-year agreement with the IMF, and the contacts that the president's circles maintained with the leadership of the FIS. In July 1997, the liberation of Abbasi Madani made clear that contacts already existed between the political circles of the presidency and the top echelons of the FIS, which appears to have given rise to a kind of rivalry between the presidency of the republic and the chiefs of staff. The latter did not want Liamine Zeroual to reap the benefits of the success of negotiations with the FIS, thus reinforcing his position *vis-à-vis* the high military command. As a result, the latter short-circuited the aforementioned negotiations by concluding directly with the armed wing of the FIS, the Islamic Salvation Army (AIS), an unlimited cease-fire agreement. How and under what conditions they succeeded in arriving at this truce, which the AIS has subsequently maintained, is part of the information which has never seen the light of day.

The political reasons for why the AIS opted for a unilateral cease-fire arose from the need to mark their distance from violence committed against civilians, to defend themselves against the amalgam made with the ambiguous and manipulated GIA, and to try and demonstrate who were the real authors of violence in Algeria. In a strange coincidence, all this process took place after the first and most repugnant of massacres to be publicly known, which exercised an intolerable psychological weight on the FIS, despite their repeated condemnations and denunciations of this violence.

Thus, on 23 September 1997, the AIS announced through a communiqué of its leader, Madani Mezrag, the cessation of hostilities:

> To the Muslim Algerian people, in order to dismantle the plans of those who await the opportunity to damage Algeria and the Algerians, and in order to open the doors to the sincere and committed children of Algeria to a just and legitimate solution, the national leader of the AIS orders all company leaders under his command to suspend all combat operations from October 1, 1997, and to make an appeal to all groups faithful to the interests of the nation and its religion to unite with this decision with the aim of unveiling the enemy who hides behind these abominable massacres and to isolate the residual criminals of the perverse extremists of the GIA and those who hide behind them.[32]

Their incapacity to break down the psychological barriers which blocked their credibility as a legitimate political opposition abroad led the leaders of the FIS to evolve clearly in favour of the unilateral and total cessation of armed struggle with the aim of depriving the regime of the alibi which had served them until then of achieving eight years of dirty war, thanks to which they had dominated the population, terrifying them and guaranteeing themselves extensive external support despite growing repression and totalitarianism.[33]

This situation made it ever more clear that the political game in Algeria was dominated by clan interests, fed by a nomenclature prepared to do anything to protect itself and maintain its privileges even if undermined by jealousies and internal struggles. The 'Islamist-security' dimension, until then used ceaselessly to hide the reality of the Algerian crisis was not the real crux of the war but rather corruption money and the control of income. Thus, the line of fracture between the clans was neither religious nor even political, but rather the access to big 'business' which, in addition to being derived from the hydrocarbon escort, had, thanks to the savage liberalization process unleashed under the tutelage of the IMF, been extended to include an import market worth more than $10 million annually.

In parallel, society, dominated by an enormous youth generation, suffers from an unemployment rate of more than 30 per cent (three out of four youths are unemployed, 40 per cent of Algerians live below the poverty line, 600,000 jobs have been lost in two years, giving rise to a wave of suicides, the price of milk is inaccessible for the most deprived families, there are 180,000 war orphans and an explosive mortality rate with illnesses such as tuberculosis on the rise. Only the climate of terror engendered by the violence under which this society lives has spared it from social explosion. A violence and terror, which to a large degree are derived from the existence of numerous armed militias, paid for by the state.

Given the maximum publicity to the violent actions of the most radical (at the same time hiding the politically correct behaviour of the FIS and its proposals for dialogue towards a political settlement of the conflict), choosing victims for media reasons (as if only 'modern' women and westernized elites have died), and counting on the personal support of a number of the leaders of so-called 'lay' political parties (RCD and Ettahadi) and a battery of 'feminists' formed *ad hoc* who have monopolized media visibility in Europe, particularly in France, the Algerian military regime has dedicated itself to creating and expanding information sources designed to 'dehumanize' what was once a powerful movement of political opposition, capable of alternating in power, with which important sectors of civil society identified and which entered into conflict with the regime in 1992 when the latter reacted against the sharing of power in order to protect its political, and above all, economic privileges. Certain of the incapacity of the west to understand that Islamism is a movement which challenges authoritarian regimes, of which this is its main dimension, the regime has constructed a 'culturist' theory (based essentially on classic visions of Islamic fanaticism, the incompatibility between Islam and democracy, the impossible modernity of Islam ...) which hides the real sociological dimensions of war and blocks its analysis in objective terms.

In this way, it has been possible to ignore the violence committed by the state and by the various armed civilians paid for by the state, as well as all attempts to investigate the situation in neutral or international manner, and when the opacity of Algerian information has reached outsiders, not by accident, images of rural massacres, they have accepted explanations which insult the intelligence: that, for example, these massacres are irrational and barbarous acts undertaken by supposed and unknown 'madmen of God', when it is obvious that these actions clearly come within the type of strategy followed by military groups faced by guerrilla movements (exactly as in El Salvador, Guatemala or Chiapas, where, it is true, the absence of Islam allows outsiders to be more clear-sighted).

The Candidates and the Campaign

The crisis which provoked the presidential electoral process of April 1999 had the qualitative importance not only of revealing the internal contradictions of a power both fragmented and dominated by personal interests, but also of the lack of functionality of the institutions of state. The 'Zeroual case' made clear the weakness of institutions in place since 1995, which had only been created for tactical ends: to devalue the project of the Rome Platform born in January 1995,[34] divide the signatories of the latter and as an alternative, feign a 'democratising desire' of the Algerian regime.

Another factor relevant to the 1999 presidential elections was that initially, there was no candidate who represented the consensus of the army, which signified an important fissure within the army which the candidates for the opposition tried to take advantage of in order to occupy the public forum and relaunch a process which included the possibility of real political change. The high military command had always taken major historical decisions by consensus in order to assure the continuity of the system (through the designation of Chedli Benjedid to the presidency in 1979, for example, the supervised democratization of 1989, the *coup d'état* of 1992, the presidential candidature of Zeroual in 1995, etc.), which they had been unable, or unwilling, to achieve this time This new situation was what inspired the other candidates to come forward and the FIS, for the first time since 1992 not to call for a boycott of the electoral process. On 4 April, the representation of the FIS abroad called for the vote to be given to Ahmed Taleb Ibrahimi, who even though not an Islamist, was considered 'the most apt to regroup Algerians and the most suitable to pull the country out of crisis' even though this was 'not to side against other candidates whom we respect' including in this Abdelaziz Bouteflika.

Throughout the campaign, it was shown that three candidates – Ait Ahmed, Mouloud Hamrouche and Taleb Ibrahimi – from among the seven who stood were the main representatives of the dominant political currents in Algerian society:[35]

(1) Ait Ahmed, the leader of the FFS, represented Algerian social democracy (he is a member of the Socialist International), Mouloud Hamrouche represents the sector known as that of the 'reformers', that is to say, those who having arisen from the system and the FLN, initiated the process of reform from 1989 which enjoyed an ephemeral existence. (that is, from 1989 to June 1990). The 'reformers' denounced the *coup d'état* of 1992, signed the Rome Platform and were distanced from the FLN in January 1996 in favour of Boualem Benhamouda, the regime thus 'retrieving' the FLN of old.

(2) Taleb Ibrahimi also came from the system (he was Minster of Culture and Foreign Affairs), but since 1992 he had denounced the military strategy of suspending the elections of January 1991 and since then defended a political solution and the integration of the FIS within the political system. He could also count with the charisma which came from his family's links with the Association of Oulemas of Ben Badis.

(3) The army candidate, Abdelaziz Bouteflika, a political leader from the period of Boumedienne for whom he was Foreign Minister, seemed to represent a more substantial figure than his predecessor, even though nothing indicated that his margin for manoeuvre would go any further than the designs of 'those who decide' in Algeria. Once his candidature was confirmed as that of the regime, all those linked to the regime closed rank tin his support: the RND, the FLN, the main central trade union, the UGTA and the 'constructive' opposition of the regime: Hamas and al-Nahda openly and the RCD less explictly.[36]

Perhaps the most relevant factor of this particular election was the unitary dynamic which was generated among the six candidates competing against Abdelaziz Bouteflika, which was concretized in their common denunciation of electoral fraud and their withdrawal one day before the elections to delegitimize the candidate 'predestined' to succeed, even before considering the manipulations taking place in some mobile electoral colleges and abroad, where the election took place one day earlier. The results not only gave an absolute majority to Bouteflika, but also humiliated the other six candidates who achieved only 25 per cent of all the votes cast, given that their withdrawal was not taken into account (under the assumption that the electoral law did not foresee such and eventuality) and the elections went ahead with the voting papers of all seven candidates.

According to the official results, Abdelaziz Bouteflika emerged as the winner in all the wilayas of this first, and only electoral round. Thus on 16 April, Bouteflika accepted his presidential responsibilities and denounced 'the manoeuvres destined to disturb the electors and to discredit the elections in international opinion' and considered that 'the Algerian people have expressed themselves clearly and democratically'. He also declared that for the moment, there would be no change of government nor anticipated legislative elections (the four parties which supported him controlled 80 per cent of parliamentary seats).

Bouteflika and 'Peace of Arms'

Once installed in the presidency, Abdelaziz Bouteflika , regardless o international opinion and insofar as the opposition tried to organize themselves while their protest demonstrations were prohibited, the regime was creating for the middle of June a growing *mise en scène* through the announcement, with great media attention, of several events: the communiqué of the cease-fire with the armed wing of the FIS, the announcement by the new Algerian president of a projected law on the 'Concorde Civil' for the rehabilitation of the members of the aforementioned guerrilla forces, and the publication of a letter from Abbasi Madani blessing these initiatives, in order, as the symbolic date of the 5 July anniversary of independence approached, achieve its height with the release of more than a thousand Algerians imprisoned – for the most part arbitrarily for their supposed proximity to the Islamist movement – all of which presented as an outcome of peace for the Algerian society suffering under civil war since 1992.

Was there really something new in this process or was it really meant to bring to the credit of the new president of the republic a situation, which in fact had existed in an undercover fashion since 1997, awaiting the appropriate moment to present it to the benefit of the regime? Could this process be considered as the start of political change or of a new survival strategy for those in power to maintain the status quo, permitting them to control the income and Algerian society with the blessing of the international community?

The law of 'civil concord' which has formed a key axis on which President Bouteflika has based his process of reconciliation is in reality no more than a revised version of the so-called law of '*rahma*' (clemency) which has existed since 1995 for those Islamists prepared to give up their arms.

Equally, it remains within the realm of policing and security without comprising any type of political agreement: it is of a purely penal nature, directed a criminals with the use of any political qualification, including silence over acts of torture, abductions, disappearances, of which there have been many in recent years in Algeria. Further, the members of the committees called on to apply the law of the 'Civil Concorde' represents the executive above the judiciary, with a larger representation from among the police and security forces.

As such, the current Algerian process contains a number of shadowy aspects and provokes a number, among which stand out the lack of transparency and the absence of a political dimension, made clearly the total marginalization of the political parties (including the FIS itself, given that the process is not the result of a political negotiation between the Algerian government and the leaders of the FIS, but a cease-fire between the army and the guerrilla forces of the AIS and an act of clemency on the part of the president of the republic towards some of them).[37] In other words, it is no more than a pardon for some of those accused of acts of terrorism without modifying in any way the arbitrary and authoritarian legal and military framework which has converted the regime into a military dictatorship. However, a national political reconciliation within a democratic framework, which has been discussed and signed by all, does not appear to enter into the current project of the Algerian regime. The opposite in fact appears to be the case, that is to say, with this law of 'civil concord' and this framework for peace 'made to measure' the leadership requirements of the president, the real powers in Algeria have avoided once again the demands of a genuinely political solution, achieved though a national congress for peace to include all parties, including the FIS and which would open a process of democratization and structural reform of the economic and political model.

Further, day by day it is a process which has despised and ignored political society, just at a moment when after the presidential elections in April there was a unitary dynamic between the leaders of the opposition who withdraw on the grounds of electoral fraud and started a process of organising and mobilising Algerian society with a certain future. In front of this, the political dimension appears now to have been limited to those benefits which accrued to the person of Bouteflika and to the regime. That is, to compensate for the lack of legitimacy of the electoral process in which Abdelaziz Boutelflika was elected head of state, obfuscate the voices of the real opposition in the country, whitewash the image of the regime, above all overseas, following a presidential electoral campaign in which the central theme was not the 'Islamist-security' dimension but the corruption of the regime and its responsibility for the violence, and silence voices which for some time have been denouncing the situation of human rights in Algeria. And all this without any sharing of power, and no offer of juridical nor political or institutional reform.

A referendum on peace does not necessarily create peace, and the liberation of 2,300 Islamist detainees, although it does constitute an indubitable distension, was no more than a belated parallel disarming of the AIS in 1997. Thus, an agreement between the Algerian authorities and the AIS, about which ordinary Algerians are ignorant of all details, is not sufficient to resolve a conflict which is not so much military as political. Proof of this is that violence has not completely abated in Algeria, among other reasons because there are many groups which hold arms in Algeria (the disarming of 200,000 civilians does not seem to form part of the process) and open repression, the desire for vengeance and atrocious poverty favour the constitution of a lumpen mass of all types of terrorism. If to this is added the threat of the president to bring down a 'merciless punishment' on those who had not surrendered their arms by its deadline of January 2000,[38] the mechanism of repression and vengeance might well be set in train again.[39]

And so this process rather indicates that, with nothing to indicate that anything is about to change, that the concept of peace that the Algerian authorities appear to hold is that of 'peace of arms', but not a political peace, which demands a moral and ethical dimension and norms and transparent rules respected by all. Thus it will be difficult to resolve the enormous economic and political problems which Algeria suffers, without forgetting that they were at the origin of the war and that the war was a tribal form of violence against a citizenry which does not cease to express its need for peace.

NOTES

1. The *Istiqlal*, led by Muhammed Boucetta, represents the nationalist right wing whose discourse relies heavily on Islam as one of the fundamental elements of its socio-political programme. As the former nationalist movement, it supported the Royal Palace in the early 1960s and was reintegrated into the government between 1977 and 1984. From the 1990s, however, it became firmly entrenched in the opposition when it became a member of the Democratic Bloc. The USFP, led by Abderrahman Yusufi, is a social democrat type of party and has been the most active party in the Moroccan political arena despite its increasing internal divisions – between the moderate wing and the younger and more radical grass-roots on the one hand and between those in favour of attracting Islamist groups and those who oppose it on the other. To the left of the USFP is the *Parti du Progrès et du Socialisme* (Party of Progress and Socialism, PPS) the former communist party, legalized in 1974 and led by Ali Yata, and a small Marxist group, the *Organisation de l'Action Démocratique et Populaire* (Organization for Democratic and Popular Action, OADP), legalized in 1984. A recent split within this group led to the creation of the *Parti Socialiste Démocratique* (Democratic Socialist Party, PSD). Finally, the small left-wing group *Ila-l-Amam* (Forward) and the extreme Islamist movements remain illegal.
2. Until the latest reforms, the Moroccan parliament consisted of a single Chamber of Representatives, two-thirds of whom were elected by universal suffrage and the remaining

third was indirectly elected among the members of chambers of commerce and industry, chambers of agriculture and artisans, trade unions and local councils. The traditional function of indirectly elected deputies was to amend the popular vote, thus reinforcing the number of loyalist deputies. This is why the opposition has always demanded that the whole Chamber be directly elected.

3. *Al-maghreb*, 17 Oct. 1995. According to this report, education reform is essential for Morocco for the period following structural adjustment. It will guarantee sustained growth and enable the population to participate in development. The elimination of illiteracy is the cornerstone of modernized and increased productivity and is necessary for new methods and innovative techniques to be developed. Similarly, the next priority must be the development of good primary education and secondary education. This explains why there has been an emphasis on education, housing and health in the budget towards the end of the 1990s. The king himself, in a speech delivered on 3 March 1997, announced the creation of a commission for education reform under his authority 'with the mission of assessing the present state of education and vocational training and to provide a detailed diagnosis' (*Libération*, 4 July 1997).

4. Article 3 of the constitution, which excludes the existence of the single party state, provides the basis for political pluralism. This provision reflected the Palace's interest in atomising the National Movement represented by the *Istiqlal* – which had led the anti-colonial struggle – thus preventing it from becoming a powerful single party after independence, for this threatened to weaken the monarchy, or even lead to its abolition, as was the case in Tunisia.

5. This Arabic term, which originally meant 'warehouse', is generally used to refer to the Royal Palace and the state apparatus.

6. The creation, in 1996, of an Association of Unemployed Graduates is tangible proof of the social consequences of this situation. This association numbers 130,000 members and has organized demonstrations and sit-ins.

7. *Jeune Afrique*, No.1863, 1996, p.12.

8. An exhaustive analysis of Morocco's economic and financial situation can be found in Beatrice Hibou's essay *Les enjeux de l'ouverture au Maroc. Dissidence économique et contrôle politique* (The challenges of economic openness in Morocco. Economic dissidence and political control), Les Etudes du CERI, Paris, 1996.

9. The participants in this dialogue were Abderrahman Lahjouji, the president of the employer's confederation (CGEM), Noubir al-Amaoui, the leader of the *Confédération Démocratique du Travail* (Labour Democratic Confederation, CDT), Abderrazak Afilal, leader of the *Union Générale des Travailleurs Marocains* (General Union of Moroccan Workers, UGTM), linked to the *Istiqlal* and the Interior Minister, Driss Basri, who represented the government. The agreement stated that a follow-up committee should meet every six months. It is estimated today, that out of nine million workers, approximately 500,000 belong to 17 trade unions, including the three main unions which signed the social pact.

10. The declaration made public the agreement over 'essential questions', including the drawing up of new electoral rolls, the preparation of a new electoral code and the creation of a national monitoring commission. Furthermore, the government undertook 'to prevent illegal administrative interference in the elections and abuse of power', *Libération*, 1–2 March 1997.

11. *al-Tawhid wa-l-Tajdid* was the result of the union between two Islamist groups, the most important of which, *al-Islah wa-l-Tajdid* (Reform and Renovation), was led by Abdellillah Benkirane who declared in an interview to the French newspaper *Libération* on 6 February 1997: 'We make no secret of the fact that we have closer relations with the *Istiqlal* than with other parties. Our respective visions and positions are close. This party is perhaps the closest to us as far as future challenges are concerned'.

12. The movement's application to obtain legal status in 1992, under the name *Hizb al-Tajdid al-Watani* (Party for National Renovation), was rejected but this did not stop it from publishing a newspaper, *al-Rayya* (The Standard). However, this moderate Islamist group has always had good relations with the regime, unlike *al-'Adl wa-l-Ihsan* (Justice and Charity), the group led by Abdessalam Yassin who was jailed in the 1970s and subsequently kept under house arrest. This movement, according to its spokesman, Fathallah Arsalan, aims for

political recognition and participation in the political process, but it is still far from achieving this goal.

13. *La Nouvelle Tribune*, 1–7 Aug. 1996.
14. Besides the two main parties, the *Istiqlal* and the USFP, the PPS and the OADP are also part of *al-Kutla*.
15. These are political groups which play the role of state parties opposed to the nationalist political forces. They represent the elite and are parliamentary corporations rather than parties. They were all created just before elections around the figure of the then prime minister. Thus, the *Mouvement Populaire* (Mouvement for the People, MP) was founded in 1957 in order to control Berbers through patronage networks and the *Parti Démocratique Constitutionnel* (Constitutional Democratic Party, PCD) was formed in order to weaken the *Istiqlal* in the wake of independence. Later, the regime recruited supporters amongst 'independents' in order to obtain a majority in government in the shape of a political party. Thus, independent deputies were brought together in 1978 under the umbrella of the *Regroupement National des Indépendents* (Independents National Front, RNI), led by the prime minister, Ahmed Osman. The RNI's scission then led to the creation of the *Parti National Démocratique* (National Democratic Party, PND) because of the 1984 general elections. A year earlier, the interior minister, Reda Guedira, had founded the *Union Constitutionnelle* (Constitutional Union, UC), led by Prime Minister Maati Bouabib, in order to participate in the 1983 local elections. The ideology of these groups is a combination of 'Hassanism', liberalism and market economy and spans the whole political spectrum from radicals to moderates. *Al-Wifaq* is made up of the UC, the PND and the MP.
16. There have been many discordant voices on this matter, including that of Muhammad Sassi, the secretary general for *Jeunesse Ittihadiyya* (United Youth, USFP), which is close to Amaoui. In an interview with Maghreb *al-Yaum* (25 June 1997), he declared that the alliance with *Istiqlal* was a mistake and that the USFP must focus on 'building a great left-wing party' during its congress.
17. *Le Matin du Sahara*, 7 May 1997.
18. The rift between the 'labour' trend (led by the head of the group of affiliated trade unions linked with the party, Noubir Amaoui, and its historical leader, Fqih Basri) and the 'social-democrat' wing (led by the director of the party organ, *Libération*, Muhammad al-Yazghi) widened throughout 1996 and the gap was only bridged through the efforts of party general secretary, Abderrahman Yusufi. Conflict was re-ignited during the debate on political reform and in particular on the question of whether the consensus proposed by the regime should be accepted. Amaoui, against all expectations – especially amongst young socialists – decided not to participate in the party's executive committee which was expected to decide whether or not to support the reforms, and this probably constituted the decisive factor in the USFP's decision in favour of the reforms. However, Amaoui put all his energy and charisma into the struggle for the CDT leadership, which took place during the third CDT National Congress. He exhorted the congress to exclude the 'Yazghists' from trade union leadership and to incorporate the groups *Nahj Dimuqrati* (Democratic Way), created by previous members of *Ila-l-Amam* and the *Parti de l'Avant-Garde* (Avant-Garde Party, PAG). By leaving the USFP's executive committee, Amaoui showed that the Congress had been a progressive development in the evolution of trade union independence, that is to say the autonomy of a large portion of the grass-roots, much to the party's dislike.
19. *La Vie Economique*, 20 June 1997.
20. The Tunisian National Pact, signed on the anniversary of President Ben cAli's coming to power, took the shape of an historic agreement amongst all political forces in the country on a series of general democratic principles, which underpinned the new era launched by the deposition of President Bourguiba. The fact that the Islamist movement *al-Nahda* was invited to participate in the drafting and signing of this pact suggested that the Islamists might be integrated into the institutional political system.
21. Nevertheless, the Tunisian Islamist movement, represented by *al-Nahda*, the party led by Rashid Ghannushi, adopted a legal position founded on democratic principles (which originally caused some defections within the membership).
22. These elections revealed a gradual weakening of the legal opposition caused by internal

crises and possibly also because its complacency towards the regime had discredited it. Furthermore, it became evident that the political system had not in fact been broadened, as the opposition had hoped would be the case, as a reward for its 'good behaviour'. The MDS only ran in 32 of the 257 constituencies and it proved unable to provide the necessary 60 candidates to run in the capital. The *Alliance Démocratique* (Democratic Alliance, formed by the *Ettajdid*, the MUP and the UDU) only ran in 16 constituencies and the PLS in one. The RCD, however, was present in every constituency and was only challenged in 50 of them. *La Presse*, 22 May 1994.

23. 1996 general report on development, *La Presse*, 10 Dec. 1996.
24. The signatories of this platform were the FFS, the FIS, the MDA, the PT, *al-Nahda* and the Algerian League for Human Rights
25. Neither the FIS, the FFS nor the FLN participated in this dialogue.
26. Two thirds of National Council members are elected by indirect suffrage and secret ballot by the members of local and *wilayas* popular assemblies. The last third is nominated by the president from national scientific, cultural, professional, economic and social personalities. Journal Officiel (JORA), 8 Dec. 1996.
27. In 1997GNP was set to increase by five per cent (against four per cent in 1996); inflation was to fall to 9 per cent (against 18 per cent in 1996) and, for the first time in ten years, there was a favourable trade balance of $4.2 million in 1996. These figures can be explained by the rise in oil prices and the immediate effects of repeated external debt rescheduling. Indeed, the collapse in oil prices in 1999 produced precisely the reverse effect, thus confirming Algeria's oil dependent state.
28. Over 250,000 young people arrive on the labour market every year; 70 percent of the population is under 30 and, according to the World Bank, Algeria needs investments worth $25 billion in order to create enough jobs. See World Bank Report, *Claiming the Future: Choosing Prosperity in the Middle East and North Africa*, Washington, DC, 1995, p.80.
29. National Economic and Social Council Report quoted in Libertés, 28 Oct. 97.
30. The strategy of the Algerian military, unable to control the continuous defection of regular troops to the guerillas, has been to gradually adopt a tactic which consists in delegating public order in rural areas to local civilian militias which literally occupy the areas and carry out *razzias* against the Islamist *maquis*. Their brutality unleashes even greater violence, often against peasant populations, and contributes to the spiral of militarization of the Algerian society.
31. Nothing further from independent, the Algerian press would be better defined as public and private. The only newspaper which could be described as independent, *La Nation*, under the direction of Salima Ghezali was, after several temporary closures, made definitively illegal in December 1996. In reality, the Algerian press has been the instrument of the struggles between clans, who settle scores through a press linked, directly or indirectly, to one or another sector. When a clan crosses the 'red line', before things get out of control, it often receives 'messages' through the medium of the press. The battle for the presidential election, a consequence itself of a crisis within the system, gave a good example of this.
32. The terms of the accord relating to this truce with the Algerian generals have never been known, only that there is some information about the existence of 'areas of peace' that the army has guaranteed in the zones controlled by the AIS. Thus, the degree including the victims of the ‚national tragedy', as much Islamists as non-Islamists have been linked by some observers as one of the consequences of these transactions. However, the radical opposition mounted by the families of the victims of terrorism (Islamist, of course) blocked the implementation of a plan which would have recognized victims from both sides.
33. See Gema Martín Muñoz, *El Estado Arab. Crisis de legimidad y contestación islamista*, Barcelona: Bellaterra, 1999.
34. In the form of a democratic pact which, as a national contract put forward a declaration of principles on which to base the pacification of the country and a peaceful transition, the Rome Platform brought together the FIS and other parties and non-Islamist political representatives (the FFS of Ait Ahmed, the FLN led then by its 'reforming' wing, the Workers' Party of Louisa Hannoune, the Islamist party of al-Nahda, the Algerian Human Rights League, led by Ben Yahia). It represented a political challenge to the Algerian regime

129

not because it signified a proposal with real possibilities for success (given that the regime, merely by rejecting it would short-circuit the Rome proposal, based as it was on dialogue and national reconciliation), but because it demonstrated that the official representation of the conflict did not sit well with reality, making clear that the problem was one of the democratization of the system and that other, non-Islamist forces, together with the FIS, sought peace through a democratic transition with no political exclusions.

35. The candidates were: Abdelaziz Bouteflika, Ait Ahmed, Ahmed Taleb Ibrahimi, Mouloud Hamrouche, Abdallah Djaballah (the former leader of the party al-Nahda who, contrary to the rapprochement of his party to the regime, gave up his position to create a new formation, whilst al-Nahda remained under the leadership of Lahbib Adami), Yousef al-Khattib, of the old nationalist guard, prestigious head of 'Wilaya IV' during the War of Liberation, and Mokhdad Sifi, prime minister between April 1994 and December 1995 who surprized many by gaining the 75,000 signatures needed to present his candidature.

36. On 8 April 1999, the leaders of Hamas (Mahfoud Nahnah), of the FLN (Boualem Benhamouda), the RND (Ahmed Ouyahia) and al-Nahda (Lahbib Adami) signed a common political declaration supporting the candidature of Abdelaziz Bouteflika.

37. In fact, the proposed 'concorde civile' put forward by the Algerian president has not gained the general consensus in the party: Ali Belhadj has kept silent and Abdlekader Hachani – later assassinated in November 1999 – along with other FIS leaders expressed very harsh criticisms of it.

38. At the end of 1999, according official figures, several thousand Islamists had submitted to the law, but non-official sources put the figure at no more than 300, which signifies a presidential failure.

39. José Garçon, 'Le Mystère Bouteflika' in *Politique Internationale*, 4e trimestre 1999.

Security Issues in the Mediterranean

Towards a New WMD Agenda in the Euro-Mediterranean Partnership: An Arab Perspective

MOHAMMED EL-SAYED SELIM

The Euro-Mediterranean (Euro-Med) world, a term which we use to refer to member-states in the Euro-Mediterranean Partnership (EMP), is one of the most dangerous arenas for the development, deployment, and proliferation of Weapons of Mass Destruction (WMD), and their delivery systems. Britain and France are 'legitimate' nuclear powers under the nuclear Non-Proliferation Treaty (NPT), and they possess a highly developed nuclear arsenal. Eleven of the member-states of the European Union (EU) are members in the North Atlantic Treaty Organization (NATO). As such, they are protected by NATO's nuclear umbrella, and some of them are arenas for the deployment of NATO's air-delivered nuclear warheads.[1] In the Middle East, Israel has 100–200 nuclear warheads. The Vanunu revelations, Thomas Hirsch's book on Israel's nuclear capabilities, and the confirmations by different Israeli officials have made it quite clear that Israel has introduced the nuclear factor into the Middle Eastern politics.[2] No other non-European member of the EMP is even close to Israel's nuclear capability. Iran's nuclear capabilities are still in their infancy and it will be a number of years before the Islamic Republic may be in a position to realize its nuclear aspirations. Algeria has a 15-megawatts nuclear research reactor near Ain-Oussera which was placed in 1991 under the inspection of the International Atomic Energy Agency (IAEA). Syria and Egypt are not known to have any significant nuclear facilities and the Iraqi nuclear programme has been crippled.[3]

As far as other forms of WMD are concerned, the US Office of Technology Assessment has confirmed that Israel, Libya, Syria, Iraq, and Egypt possess chemical weapons.[4] It is also widely believed that these countries have biological weapons. Most of them have the capability to deliver their WMD, but the range and accuracy of Israel's delivery systems are widely acknowledged to be superior to those of any non-European actor. Whereas Israel is working towards the achievement of a protective anti-missile system, other Middle Eastern actors are not. Further, some WMD-possessing states in the EMP are not parties to the global regimes to eliminate or prevent their proliferation. Israel is not a party to the NPT and many Middle Eastern actors, mainly Egypt, Syria, Iran and Libya are yet to accept the Biological Weapons Convention (BWC), and the Chemical Weapons Convention (CWC). None of them, except Israel, have endorsed the Missile Technology Control Regime (MTCR).

Cognizant of the potentially hazardous consequences of the deployment and proliferation of WMD, the parties to the Barcelona Declaration undertook to promote regional security by acting in favour of nuclear, biological, and chemical non-proliferation, through adherence to non-proliferation regimes, and arms control and disarmament agreements, such as the NPT, the BWC, the CWC, and the Comprehensive Test Ban Treaty (CTBT), as well as regional agreements such as weapons free zones. They also pledged to fulfil in good faith their commitments under arms control, disarmament, and non-proliferation conventions. Realizing the security threats inherent in the Middle East in particular, they undertook to establish a verifiable Middle Eastern zone free of weapons of mass destruction, nuclear, biological, and chemical and their delivery systems.

Notwithstanding these general undertakings, the parties of the EMP are in deep disagreement over virtually all the issues involved. They differ on the objective of the entire enterprise, in terms of whether this involves the removal of WMD or simply their non-proliferation. They also differ regarding the mutuality of the commitments and the geographical universe in which they should take place. Whereas some actors perceive themselves as being outside the scope of the projected system for the removal or non-proliferation of WMD, others advocate a pan-Euro-Med commitment. Finally, they disagree on the modalities of dealing with the question of WMD, such as the linkages between peace settlements and the arms control process.

The objectives of this comment are to delineate the main issues involved in the question of WMD within the EMP framework, identify the main approaches advocated by different parties, and suggest certain modalities for dealing with the issue. The intention is not to defend the Arab approaches to the issue, but to identify a policy framework based on explicitly-stated assumptions, goals, and concepts, and to draw from it certain inferences concerning future directions of the EMP in the area of WMD. Neither is the concern to present a master plan for dealing with the question of WMD, but rather to suggest a possible agenda for action which addresses itself to the security concerns of all actors in the EMP.

Problematics

The issue of WMD within the framework of the EMP poses major problems which make it difficult to achieve the objectives spelled out in the Barcelona Declaration and which also call for an innovative approach to deal with them. These problems can be categorized as problems related to the characteristics and perceived utility of WMD, problems centered around the diversity of regional sub-systems in the Euro-Med universe, problems related to the strategic connections between these sub-systems and adjacent sub-systems, and finally problems related to the strategic disequilibrium in the EMP in the area of WMD.

(1) WMD are characterized by their accessibility, transferability, usability, and ability to inflict unacceptable losses. Chemical and biological weapons are relatively easy to manufacture and stockpile, using low-level technology at low cost. They can be produced for civilian purposes and transferred to military ones at short notice. Further, certain WMD systems can be used with insufficient preliminary warning, and the attacker may remain unidentified, particularly in the case of biological weapons. Contrary to the widely-held belief that WMD serve only as a deterrent and as last resort weapon, they can actually be employed in situations that fall short of total war waged for absolute annihilation or survival. Certain categories of WMD, including nuclear weapons, lend themselves readily to tactical uses especially if the attacker perceives that there is no deterrent. The accessibility of WMD and their use as tactical weapons have increased the temptation to develop, deploy, and use or threaten to use them in conflict situations, especially when they are perceived as an ultimate security insurance, given their ability to inflict tremendous losses which can result in the elimination of entire communities. Taken together, these characteristics complicate the task of persuading states to remove their WMD, especially since removing these weapons is almost as costly and complicated as developing them.

(2) The EMP is a highly diversified entity. It comprises a variety of sub-systems such as the Middle East, North Africa, the Balkans, Southern Europe and Northern Europe. Each sub-system has its own dynamics, problems, and conflicts. These sub-systems are different in terms of their levels of economic development, political stability, regional integration, and, more importantly, they have different commitments under the global regime for the control of nuclear weapons. Despite their diversities these sub-systems are interrelated. Security threats and arrangements in one sub-system necessarily spill over other sub-systems. This combination of diversity and interconnectedness calls for an approach which takes into

135

consideration the particular problems of each sub-system and the universality of commitments under any security arrangement. Such formula requires building not only inter-state agreement but also inter-region consensus. The task of reconciling diversities with commonalties, and particularism with universalism is clearly a formidable one.

(3)   There are strong geo-strategic connections between the Euro-Med world and adjacent regions at different levels which are both geographical and functional. Most Euro-Med actors have strong strategic linkages with powers outside the EMP. The European partners and Turkey are members in NATO, which necessarily brings NATO into the picture. NATO's nuclear strategy takes into account both national European nuclear deterrents and global arms control. One cannot discuss the future of nuclear weapons within the framework of the EMP without taking these linkages into account. Furthermore, although the USA is not an EMP partner, its role in the issue of WMD in the EMP cannot be ignored. It has a strong military presence in the Mediterranean and has been fully supporting the Israeli nuclear programme.[5]

In addition, the Euro-Med system is also connected with adjacent sub-systems, such as the Arabian Gulf, and Southern Asia. Controlling WMD in the Euro-Med system must take into account that such sub-systems may be ridden with WMD. Israel may feel threatened if its nuclear weapons have been eliminated while South Asian actors keep theirs. These actors are under no Euro-Med obligations to remove their nuclear arsenals. The issue of WMD in the EMP is also being dealt with in other forums, such as the Middle Eastern multilateral negotiations (Arms Control and Regional Security Working Group, ACRS), the Organization for Security and Co-operation in Europe (OSCE), and the American-Russian arms control negotiations. Attempts within the EMP to create regimes for the control of WMD could duplicate or complicate negotiations in these forums.

(4)   The strategic structure of the EMP regarding WMD represents, in our judgment, the most serious obstacle to the control of those particularly deadly weapons. Whereas the two nuclear European members in the EMP and Israel have developed elaborate arsenals of nuclear weapons, including efficient delivery systems, and – although complying with treaties calling for their removal – they may still possess other kinds of WMD, whilst other EMP actors cannot match these capabilities. Some of those actors do not possess nuclear and other WMD in the first place, and those who possess the latter do not have the capability to deter a first strike or to launch a deadly first or second strike. Building on its

extensive capability to wage a first nuclear strike with its long-range delivery systems, as well as on its satellite reconnaissance assets, Israel is in a position to wage a non-conventional war, yet remain relatively immune from counter attacks.

As a result of all these factors, the structure of the EMP is characterized by a high level of strategic disequilibrium. There are no historical precedents for the control of WMD under these conditions. Historically, the issue of WMD was dealt with under one of three conditions: military defeat, strategic collapse, and strategic equilibrium. The first case scenario is well represented by Iraq. The Iraqi arsenal of WMD was only removed after the military defeat of Iraq in the Second Gulf War in 1991. Iraq was forced to accept the unilateral removal of its WMD under the threat of military action including missile attacks by the Americans. The second historical precedent occurred when Kazakhstan, the Ukraine, and Belarus, former Soviet republics, agreed to remove their nuclear weapons after their independence as a result of the collapse of the Soviet Union in 1991. Although these republics were inclined to retain their nuclear capabilities, domestic economic hardships and Western pressure persuaded them to remove them. Rooted in a strategic collapse, the nuclear disarmament of South Africa was more or less similar to the experience of the former Soviet republics. The collapsing apartheid regime was coerced to de-nuclearize before the black majority take-over. The third historical model in which WMD were removed was the American–Soviet agreements during the cold war to reduce nuclear capabilities. Such agreements were made possible when the two superpowers reached a situation of strategic equilibrium and a relationship of balance of terror. Fear of mutual destruction convinced the Americans and the Soviets that a reduction of their WMD was in their best interest.

The strategic structure of the EMP is quite different to these historical models. As we have seen, the main distinguishing characteristic of the EMP is the strategic disequilibrium between the partners. Under this condition, it is extremely difficult to remove or control the proliferation of WMD. Countries possessing WMD do not feel obliged to give up what they already have simply because this will reduce their strategic superiority in an international system characterized by anarchy and security dilemmas. Meanwhile, perceptions of security threats will always motivate non-WMD powers to strive to possess such weapons in order to reach a situation of equilibrium which could enable them to engage positively with others. The task of persuading the haves to give up what they have and the have-nots not to pursue the path of the haves, is certainly not an easy one to achieve.

In this comment, we shall try to develop some ideas which could help the Euro-Med partners to deal with these problematics. In order to achieve this objective, we will briefly review the main issues involved and the various approaches advocated by EMP actors to deal with them. We now present a policy framework for dealing with the WMD and infer from it a set of policy recommendations which could present a viable approach to the control of WMD in the Euro-Med world.

Control of WMD in the EMP: Issues and Approaches

Because the Euro-Med world consists of multiple actors with different capabilities, commitments, and legitimacies in relationship with WMD, the issue of the control of WMP entails a number of different issues. Although these issues are interconnected, each has its own history, and dynamics. For the purpose of our argument, the most important issues are the control of WMD in the Arab-Israeli context and the issue of the nuclear capabilities of France and the UK in the EMP as well as the linkages between the EU and NATO. A brief review of these issues and the approaches advocated by different actors to deal with them may be useful before we turn to the task of identifying possible future policy options.

WMD within the Arab–Israeli Context

The issue of WMD was only put on the agenda of Arab-Israeli negotiations seriously after the second Gulf crisis (1990–91) which had unveiled Iraq's arsenal of WMD.6 The issue was included in the Middle East peace negotiations both because of the declarations and proposals of the USA, France, and the permanent members of the Security Council, and through the deliberations of Middle Eastern actors within the ACRS. It became increasingly clear that there were two main approaches to the control of WMD in the Middle East – the 'non-proliferation and selective elimination' approach and the 'comprehensive elimination' alternative. The two approaches differed in their views of the relationship between different forms of WMD, the universality of the commitments involved, and the timetable for the elimination of WMD.

The first approach was represented by the US arms control proposals of 1991 and 1993, the French arms control plan of 1991, the 1991 declaration of the permanent members of the UN Security Council, and Israeli proposals. The May 1991 arms control in the Middle East proposal submitted by former President Bush called for a freeze on the acquisition, production, and testing of all surface-to-surface ballistic missiles in the Middle East and restrictions on export licenses for the technology involved with a view to their ultimate elimination.[7] The proposal also called for the establishment of a verifiable ban on the acquisition and production of separated plutonium, enriched uranium, and other elements used in nuclear weapons, the accession of all Middle

Eastern countries to the NPT, and the placing of all nuclear facilities under the safeguards of the International Atomic Energy Agency (IAEA). Middle Eastern countries were also persuaded to join the BWC and the CWC.[8] These conventions call for the total elimination of biological and chemical weapons. The Bush proposal was criticized on grounds that it did not specify a timetable for the elimination of nuclear weapons thereby leaving countries which already possessed them with an advantage over those who would be denied access to them.

It also focused on the export of missile technology, leaving local capabilities to manufacture them intact. Israel, being the only Middle Eastern countries with indigenous missile-production capabilities, would be under no obligation to remove them. Further, the application of the American proposals resulted in keeping Israel as the only nuclear power in the Middle East for an unlimited period of time. Whereas the Arabs would be committed to remove their biological and chemical weapons, Israel would be under no obligation to eliminate its nuclear arsenal even if it joined the NPT, for the mandate of the NPT does not include nuclear weapons stockpiled in the basement! Despite these criticisms, President Clinton reiterated similar proposals in his statement before the United Nations General Assembly in September 1993. Addressing the issue from a global framework, Clinton suggested banning the production of plutonium and highly-enriched uranium for the purpose of producing nuclear devices. He also suggested reaching more restrictive regional measures in areas ridden with instability and the threat of nuclear proliferation. According to Avner Cohen, Israel's present nuclear capabilities would not be affected by the Clinton proposal.[9]

The French proposal for arms control in the Middle East announced by former President Mitterrand in May 1991 and the Declaration issued by the permanent members of the United Nations Security Council in July 1991 on the issue of WMD in the Middle East subscribed to the same philosophy. The Mitterrand proposal called for the 'banning' of chemical and biological weapons, the 'reduction' of nuclear weapons, and monitoring missile technology with a view to limiting their use for military purposes. Likewise, the 1991 Declaration of the permanent members of the Security Council asserted that their goal was to ban WMD in the Middle East. In order to achieve this objective, they suggested a freeze on the acquisition of surface-to-surface missiles as a prelude to their removal and a ban on the production and export of materials which could be used in producing nuclear weapons. It also called on Middle Eastern countries to place their nuclear activities under the regular inspection of the IAEA. The selectivity of both the Mitterrand and the permanent members proposals must not be overlooked. The Mitterrand approach called for the removal of some categories of WMD and the reduction of others. It happens that the ones to be removed are the only ones possessed by some Arab states and the ones to be reduced are the only ones monopolized by Israel. Further, the freeze and inspection processes suggested by the permanent members will serve only to prevent the Arab countries from acquiring missile and nuclear technology, since IAEA inspection does not apply to nuclear stockpiles.

The Israeli approach is in line with these proposals. Israel agrees in principle on the de-nuclearization of the Middle East. However, such step should be taken only after peace treaties have been reached with 'all' Middle Eastern countries, and confidence-building and confidence-and-security-building measures have been incrementally introduced. Meanwhile, all Middle Eastern countries should subscribe to the BWC and the CWC and a ban on the exportation of missile technology to the Middle East should be imposed.[10] Operationally, this means that Israel will be turned into the only power possessing nuclear weapons and missiles in the Middle East for an unlimited period of time.

The second approach was mainly advocated by the Egyptians and to a lesser extent by the Syrians. The crux of the Egyptian approach to WMD in the Arab–Israeli context is the simultaneous elimination of all categories of WMD. This means that the Arabs and the Israelis will join all global regimes for the control of WMD at the same time and that Israel will place its nuclear arsenal under international control as a prelude to its destruction. In this context, Egypt links its accession to the CWC to Israel's endorsement of the NPT and its de-nuclearization within a specified framework. Further, the Egyptians favour the adhesion of all actors to the verification measures of the IAEA. The Israelis consider these measures as inadequate and advocate the establishment of a regional verification and inspection regime similar to the one created by the Latin Americans in the 1967 Tlatelolco Treaty establishing a nuclear-free zone in Latin America. The Egyptians call for a ban on the transfer and local production of WMD and their ingredients. They argue that a ban on the transfer of WMD technology only will work in Israel's favour because it locally manufactures a considerable portion of its needs in WMD. They also prefer to begin the process of removing all forms of WMD from the Middle East without necessarily waiting for the completion of the peace process.

Removing such weapons, in their judgment, would provide a strong momentum to the peace process.[11] However, the Egyptians are not clear over their perception of Iranian and Turkish commitments towards the suggested arms control regime. They seem to favour an Arab–Israeli regime for the elimination of WMD that would leave aside Iran and Turkey. As for the Syrians, although they advocate the comprehensive elimination of WMD, they agree with the Israelis that any arms control regime must be preceded by an Arab–Israeli political settlement. The first step in the control of WMD should be an Israeli commitment to 'no-first use' of its nuclear weapons. This will be the first step in the process of their inclusion into the projected arms control regime. However, ballistic missiles should not be included in that regime because they are a stabilizing factor, given Israel's air superiority. Certain measures could be introduced to minimize the risk of their use, such as pre-notification of missile experiments.[12]

WMD in the European Context

The issue of the possession of nuclear weapons by France and the UK in the EMP has been a subject of debate only within the framework of East–West arms control negotiations. As these countries enter into a security partnership with their Mediterranean neighbours, the issue of WMD deployed in the European theatre will have to be discussed within the EMP as well. The European approach toward this issue has been enunciated in the London Declaration issued on 6 July 1990 by the Heads of State and Government of NATO countries with respect to both national deterrents and their coordination within NATO's strategic planning.

The Declaration emphasizes that nuclear weapons 'will continue to fulfill an essential role in the overall strategy of the Alliance to prevent war by ensuring that there are no circumstances in which nuclear retaliation in response to military action may be discounted'.[13] The former British foreign secretary, Douglas Hurd, also asserted that his country would not dismantle its nuclear deterrent as 'new threats have developed in a thoroughly disorderly world'. The 1995 edition of the *NATO Handbook* affirmed that 'the maintenance of an appropriate mix of nuclear and conventional forces based in Europe will be required for the foreseeable future'. It went on to argue that the fundamental purpose of NATO's nuclear power is 'to preserve peace and prevent war or any kind of coercion'.[14] Along with other EU partners, Britain and France subscribe to the principle of the universal removal of biological and chemical weapons, the non-proliferation of nuclear weapons and missile technology. The Arab partners would prefer to see the Mediterranean as an area free of WMD. This would include the removal of the nuclear warheads from European territory, and a firmer British and French commitment to fulfill their obligations under the NPT, such as the gradual reduction of their nuclear capabilities and the transfer of nuclear technology to developing countries for peaceful purposes.

A Policy Framework for the Control of WMD in the EMP

The problematics and contending approaches just outlined call for the identification of a policy framework in response, from which specific policy options may be inferred. Our suggested policy framework has two main dimensions, conceptual, and structural. Proposals for the control or removal of WMD must be based on explicitly stated assumptions, goals, and concepts. If these assumptions, goals, and concepts are acceptable, we can then infer from them certain policy options. Such proposals must also draw upon the existing knowledge and historical experience of arms control and the conditions under which it could contribute to peace. The second dimension of our policy framework relates to the structural arrangements for the control of WMD, especially the choice between a pan-Euro-Med system or sub-regional systems and the nature of the linkages between them. The two dimensions will be reviewed respectively.

The Conceptual Dimensions of the Control of WMD

The end of the cold war and the threat of a global nuclear confrontation, the rise of global interdependence, and the primacy of socio-economic issues should have logically led to the decline of the need to develop and stockpile WMD. Despite the indefinite extension of the NPT, and the establishment of a global regime for the removal of chemical weapons under the CWC, it seems that WMD will remain as a major component of international politics throughout the twenty-first century. Nuclear powers have vowed to keep their nuclear arsenals and are engaging in activities designed to ensure their indefinite monopoly of these weapons. Non-nuclear powers are also trying to develop nuclear options or less expensive non-conventional weapons. Most countries still view WMD as an ultimate instrument of security and political coercion. They develop and possess WMD to achieve and reinforce security, as defined by them, and (unless they are subject to conditions of military defeat or political collapse) they will only remove them if such removal will achieve the same objective. Consequently, a viable approach toward the control of WMD is one which brings about security for all the parties. The viability of such approach can only be properly judged from this perspective. An approach which jeopardizes the security of the parties or of some of them, or achieves the security of some to the detriment of the others is not likely to endure. It logically follows that the issue of the control of WMD must be discussed within a security-for-all framework. If such framework is accepted, then the next question to be resolved is the conditions under which the control of WMD would promote the security of all. If such conditions are identified, then we could proceed to draw policy recommendations from them.

The functions of WMD have been conceptualized differently by two main schools of thought; liberal and realist. The liberal school argues that WMD are a threat *par excellence* to national and international security because they are inherently de-stabilizing. The possession by one actor of WMD in a conflict situation motivates others to do likewise, which results in the proliferation of these particularly deadly weapons. A country which develops

WMD in order to achieve security will ultimately be threatened by them. The production and use of the American nuclear bomb in the 1940s persuaded the Soviets to produce their own nuclear weapons, China's development of the nuclear bomb in 1964 obliged India to develop its own, which, in turn, motivated Pakistan to go nuclear, and the Arabs began to consider the nuclear option after it became clear that Israel had developed its nuclear bomb. In all these cases the original producer of the bomb ended up as a target of the same weapon. Further, the availability of WMD to one actor represents a strong motivation for their use, even if such use is not absolutely necessary, especially if the attacker perceive there is no deterrent to such use.[15] The USA used the nuclear bomb twice against the Japanese in the final days of the Second World War although it was known that it would have been possible to defeat Japan with conventional means, albeit at high human cost. Consequently, the elimination of WMD is crucial to achieve security for both possessing and non-possessing states. The liberal argument is partially reflected in the Barcelona Declaration's emphasis on the non-proliferation of WMD and the establishment of a nuclear-free zone in the Middle East. The assumption is that nuclear weapons are a threat to all actors. In the Middle Eastern context, Yazid Sayigh has argued that WMD are a destabilizing factor, especially in the absence of an Arab-Israeli peace settlement, and given geographical proximity, small national territorial spaces and population size in the area. He also asserts that Israeli non-conventional weapons have 'underpinned past refusal to contemplate certain political and territorial concessions, and then encouraged a manipulative approach to regional politics. Out of a strategy of superiority come notions of political domination'.[16]

The realist school, which is widely accepted by most analysts and politicians, contends that WMD perform a stabilizing function in inter-state relations because they create a credible deterrence. After all, the cold war did not escalate into a third world war, despite the bi-polarity of the international system, because of the introduction of the nuclear factor. Consequently the best insurance against the use of nuclear weapons is to maintain the capability to use them. Kenneth Waltz, a widely respected International Relations theorist, has argued that

> Nuclear weapons may lessen the intensity as well as the frequency of wars among their possessors. For fear of escalation, nuclear states do not want to fight long or hard over important interests, indeed they do not want to fight al all. Minor nuclear states have even better reasons than major ones to accommodate one another.[17]

Adrian-Price also contends that:

> Nuclear weapons have an indispensable deterrent function. Given their

enormous destructive power, they render the notion of war as a continuation of politics by other means totally absurd. No configuration of conventional forces can fulfil this deterrent function.[18]

Further, Gerald Segal and other authors have asserted that it is difficult to dismiss the utility of nuclear weapons in a world in which nuclear proliferation is likely to continue. They went on to argue that a British nuclear capability is the most likely way that Britain could retain its independence through a policy of deterrence.[19]

In the Arab–Israeli context, Avner Cohen argued that Israel's WMD have served to deter Arab attack on Israel and achieved their objective of maintaining security and regional stability.[20] WMD are not only a policy insurance for national security, but also a safeguard mechanism for regional stability and peace, the realists argue. Such stabilizing functions can only be fulfilled when the contending parties are in a situation of equilibrium. In this situation, the incentive to use WMD will disappear for fear of retaliation. Philip Sabin has succinctly made this argument in his analysis of the restraints on the use of WMD when he writes:

> The pattern of nuclear, biological, and chemical (NBC) warfare over the past eighty years suggests that the most important disincentive to use these weapons has been fear that the enemy would respond in kind. Most instances of NBC use have been against opponents incapable of effective retaliation, whereas in the conflicts, such as the Second World War and the 1991 Gulf War, chemical weapons have been held back, despite being available to both parties.[21]

In the Arab–Israeli context, Shai Feldman developed a similar view arguing that an Arab–Israeli nuclear deterrence would be effective, stable, and credible.[22] Adel Safty also advocated a nuclear option for Egypt on grounds that it would reduce the risk of future wars between Egypt and Israel by ensuring that no political or ideological difference could lead to a military confrontation and would place serious restrictions on the strategy of escalation used by the Israelis in 1956 and 1967. He went on to argue that 'there is no reason why nuclear deterrence, which worked between nuclear powers, cannot work between Egypt and Israel'.[23] Also, General Gur argued that WMD could result in regional stability if there is an Arab-Israeli balance of terror, whereas the Arabs and the Israelis would find it difficult to accept the destruction expected as a result of their use.[24]

An examination of the liberal and realist arguments reveals that, although they differ in their perception of the utility of WMD, they agree that these weapons will have a negative impact on global and regional security only when they are unevenly distributed among the conflicting parties. They also agree that WMD are likely to be dysfunctional to regional security if the regional environment is ridden with conflicts in which territorial and statehood issues are at stake. The conclusion to be drawn is that the impact of WMD on security depends on their distribution, and the context within which they are being considered.

WMD serve as a regional security guarantee when they are evenly distributed among conflicting parties. By even distribution we mean the possession by all actors of WMD capable of delivering a deadly second-strike to the enemy. This is the situation which characterized superpower relations during the cold war and Indo-Pakistani relations since the 1970s. If one actor enjoys a monopoly over WMD, there will be a great motivation to use or threaten to use them to blackmail or compel others to act in preferred ways. The USA used the nuclear bomb against the Japanese in the final days of the Second World War, but did not use them against the Soviet-backed Viet Kong during the Vietnam War in the 1960s and 1970s, and the Iraqis used chemical weapons against the Iranians during the Iraqi–Iranian war (1980–88), but they did not use them against invading Western coalition forces during the Second Gulf War (1990–91). The common denominator amongst these cases is that the attacker used WMD only when he perceived no deterrent and refrained from using them when the adversary was perceived as capable of delivering a similar response.

Israel has actually used its nuclear arsenal during the October 1973 War as a means of compulsion. This has occurred when nuclear-tipped missiles were put on alert and deployed in their firing position to compel the United States to accelerate its aerial re-supply effort, although the war was being fought on Arab territories and the survival of Israel was not at stake. As a group of scientists from the Massachusetts Institute of Technology recently put it, 'one sided possession of nuclear weapons confers such a great military advantage that it has implicitly meant the coercion of the have-nots', a form of 'nuclear imperialism'.[25] In short, one can conclude that uneven distribution of WMD is the worst scenario in which their use, or the threat of their use, could be encouraged.

It could be argued that the use of WMD will also depend on the nature of the political regime. Democratic regimes are not likely to use WMD even if they were available to them. But because authoritarian regimes are adventurous and perceive no domestic constraints on the ability to go to war, they are more likely to use WMD if they are at their disposal. Consequently, the nuclear bomb will be safe in the hands of Britain, France, and Israel, but will be a dangerous weapon in the hands of Iraq, Syria, or Iran. In his analysis of Arab–Israeli nuclear capabilities, Uri Bar Joseph has argued that, because some Arab leaders are irrational, a nuclear bomb in their possession will be extremely dangerous and for this reason Israel must retain its nuclear capacity.[26] We are not sure whether there is a relationship between the nature of the political regime and its propensity to use WMD. All political regimes are likely to use WMD depending on the deterrence relationship with their adversaries. After all, one must not forget that the nuclear bomb was used for the first time by a democracy. This was because, as we have just argued, the attacker perceived no deterrent. Furthermore, the Saddam Hussein authoritarian regime did not use WMD against the United Nations coalition forces, although it was losing the war and facing total military defeat, because the regime was aware of the deterrent capabilities of these forces.

Strategic disequilibrium is not the only variable which could lead parties to consider WMD. The use of WMD also depends on the issues in whose context WMD use is being assessed. WMD are more likely to be used if the issues at stake are major political issues – especially those related to the control of disputed territories, national identity and statehood – and in the context of relations characterized by profoundly socio-cultural and protracted conflicts. Conversely, they are less likely to be considered or used when the issues at stake are mainly technical or ideological in nature. Major political issues and protracted conflicts create deep goal incompatibilities which could result in the WMD-possessing power to consider using them to break the political impasse. This explains the differential outcomes which might result from two relationships characterized by strategic disequilibrium. WMD are not likely to be used in disequilibrated relations such as Euro-Arab relations or American–Canadian relations, because of the technical nature of the issues in the former and the overall positive context of the latter. However, they have been considered in the Middle Eastern context because of the intensity of territorial and identity conflicts there.

It logically follows that the reinforcement of regional stability and peace in the Euro-Med universe depends on the pursuit of a strategy of equilibrium between conflicting parties, especially if regional relations are dominated by major political issues. A strategy which brings in or perpetuates disequilibrium is likely to result in the same outcome it was supposed to avoid. Yet we have seen that the Western and Israeli approaches focus mainly on perpetuating Arab-Israeli disequilibrium by insisting on eliminating only some categories of WMD, thus leaving Israel as the only nuclear power in the Middle East for an undefined period of time. In the absence of an Arab deterrent, this will result in Israel using or threatening to use its nuclear capabilities to dictate a political settlement.

The strategy of equilibrium has two main implications for the control of WMD. The first implication is that a strategy of non-proliferation will not necessarily serve the cause of regional stability and peace, especially in regions ridden with conflicts related to territory and statehood and in which one actor monopolizes certain categories of WMD. In this case, a non-proliferation strategy will be a prescription for hegemony and protracted conflict rather than peace. When the non-proliferation strategy was introduced in 1968, within the framework of the NPT, the global system was a bipolar one and there was a strategic equilibrium between the superpowers. Despite their diverse political loyalties, most states accepted this concept because they were sure that the bipolar equilibrium provided a reasonable safeguard against the use of the nuclear bomb by any of the 'legitimate' nuclear powers. We have seen earlier that the structure of the EMP is quite different from the global structure under which the non-proliferation strategy was introduced. Under these conditions, a non-proliferation strategy will not bring about stability, especially in the Middle East which is characterized by disequilibrium in the context of basic conflicts over territories. This is essentially because that strategy will not result in a stable deterrence.[27] Criticizing the strategy of non-proliferation does not necessarily mean abandoning it, but rather recognizing the conditions under which the strategy has worked in the past and beginning to introduce it in the EMP only when such conditions are present.

The second major implication of the strategy of equilibrium is to approach the issue from the wider concept of linkages. The core linkages in the EMP are those between different categories of WMD, between WMD and conventional weapons, between arms transfers and local production of arms, between different actors in the Euro-Med universe, between the Euro-Med universe and adjacent regional sub-systems, between regional and extra-regional actors, and between the issue of WMD and the political resolution of conflicts within the EMP. The worst scenario for the future of WMD in the EMP is to remove one category of WMD and retain the other, especially if these weapons are not equally possessed by all the actors. As we have seen, this could result in perpetuating regional disequilibrium and hegemony. A more rational and far-sighted approach is to address all non-conventional weapons including their delivery systems either through a maximalist strategy of removing them or a minimalist strategy of retaining them. The policy implication of this approach is that if biological and chemical weapons are to be removed then nuclear weapons must also be removed.

Secondly, 'the barrier between WMD and conventional and non-conventional weapons is rapidly eroding. New conventional weapons are expected to have a revolutionary impact on the future battlefield.'[28] Removing WMD without regard to the conventional balance of power is not likely to result in stability if that balance is in a state of disequilibrium. One may recall that, during the post-Second World War decade, Western nuclear superiority represented the main deterrent against Soviet conventional superiority in the European theatre. The removal of Western nuclear weapons, leaving the Soviets as the only conventional power in Europe, was inconceivable.

Likewise, removing WMD from the Middle East, whilst leaving Israel's qualitatively superior conventional arsenal intact, will only result in the reinforcement of disequilibrium and hence instability. Approaches to remove WMD should proceed in parallel with approaches to control conventional weapons. This element was acknowledged by the Barcelona Declaration when it affirmed that the parties 'will consider steps to prevent the proliferation of nuclear, chemical, and biological weapons as well as excessive accumulation of conventional weapons'. Nevertheless, the Declaration did not link progress on the removal of WMD with progress on the control of conventional weapons. It also put more emphasis on the non-proliferation of WMD than on the control of conventional weapons. References to the former are more detailed, emphatic, and precise, than those to the latter.

Thirdly, most proposals on arms control in the Middle East have approached the issue from the angle of restricting arms 'transfers'. As the Arabs import most of their weapons while Israel manufactures most of its arms needs, such control will only help to reinforce Arab-Israeli disequilibrium. Hence, a control on the transfers of WMD components should proceed in parallel with control on the local production of those materials.

Fourthly, the reciprocity and mutuality of commitments of all Euro-Med partners are crucial if a meaningful progress is to be achieved. Exempting certain actors from these commitments, as envisaged by the Bush proposal, is not likely to be accepted by other actors, as it will create new sources of threat.

Fifthly, it is only logical to expect that some Euro-Med actors, such as Israel, would reject the removal of their WMD as long as some extra-regional powers are still armed with these weapons. Perhaps the main non-Euro-Med actor whose WMD capabilities may represent a threat to some Middle Eastern actors is Iran. Although we believe that Iran's strategic thrust is not towards the Middle East, but rather towards the Arabian Gulf and Central Asia, the Iranian factor must be taken into consideration when assessing the status of WMD in the EMP. This will require engaging positively with Iran so that it would accept the same controls on WMD as applied in the EMP. However, the strategic outreach of the EMP cannot extend as far as Pakistan, as Israel has proposed. The inclusion of Pakistan will bring India and China, and eventually all the nuclear powers, into the picture – which would mean that no control over WMD in the Euro-Med context is possible.

Finally, progress on control must be linked with progress on the resolution of political issues which led to the stockpiling of WMD in the first place. WMD are outcomes rather than causes of conflicts. The contradiction of interests and the perception of injuries and grievances of some of the contending parties motivate them to develop these deadly weapons.

Madariaga has eloquently argued in 1937 that 'nations don't distrust each other because they are armed. They are armed because they distrust each other'.[29] Elsewhere, this author has argued that Middle Eastern arms races are consequences of regional conflicts, not the other way around.[30] If this is the case, then an emphasis on the control of WMD without reference to the unresolved political issues will lead to the wrong strategies. An arms control regime based upon unresolved conflicts and perceived injustices is not likely to lead to peace. As a result, control of WMD should be linked to any relevant peace process that is in progress. Agreements on the control of WMD must be entrenched into the peace treaties. In this case, such agreements will provide security guarantees and serve to solidify the peace process. The argument that one actor should be allowed to keep its nuclear arsenal even though peace agreements have been reached contradicts the logic of equilibrium. It could be agreed that all parties will be permitted to keep their WMD, until total confidence between the parties has been achieved and maintained. This would be a more practical approach but would mean that the peace process itself would then still be incomplete.[31]

Accepting these linkages does not necessarily imply that Euro-Med actors should proceed simultaneously in all dimensions, or make progress in one dimension conditional on progress in others. It means that all parties should acknowledge the centrality and vitality of these linkages for the establishment of a durable regime for the control of WMD, and that they should set an action agenda postulated on them and on the overall concept of strategic equilibrium. Such linkages will have a heuristic value in identifying priorities and feasible courses of action.

The Structural Dimensions of the Control of WMD

Having argued for a policy framework based on the concepts of security, equilibrium, and linkages, the next question to be addressed is whether or not we can speak meaningfully of a pan-Euro-Med regime for the control of WMD, or whether we should establish sub-system regimes, each of which suits the characteristics and needs of a specific sub-system. We have seen earlier that the Euro-Med universe is a diverse region with a wide range of highly differentiated sub-regions. Such diversity has made some analysts sceptical about the notion of a pan-Euro-Med regime. Further, the deficiencies of global regimes for the control of WMD, such as the NPT and the BWC, have led some actors to advocate a sub-regional approach. For example, Israel prefers a Middle Eastern regime for the control of WMD.

Despite the diversity of the Euro-Med universe, one can identify certain elements which call for a pan-Euro-Med approach to the question of WMD. The security environments in the Euro-Med sub-regions are highly interdependent. Political instabilities and economic uncertainties in the Middle East, North Africa, and the Balkan are likely to influence European long-term security concerns, and the emerging forms of chauvinism, economic exclusivism and protectionism in Europe will create new security threats in other regions. The deployment of WMD and their long-range delivery systems around the Mediterranean is a security concern for all the partners. Consequently, a Euro-Med approach has considerable merit as a means of identifying common sources of threat and new forms of inter-relationships. Further, from a pragmatic viewpoint, the EMP cannot remain oblivious to the threats posed by WMD. The socio-economic partnership will remain fragile as long as it does not recognize the threats that result. For example, the expansion of new export routes for oil and gas across the Maghreb, and across the Mediterranean, and the opening of new transport links between Turkey, Iran, and Central Asia with possible links to Europe, could be jeopardized as a result of the deployment of WMD. Finally, a Euro-Med approach could complement other approaches, offer fresh ideas, and provide alternatives to stalemated sub-regional frameworks.[32]

In our judgment, these forms of interdependence call for a pan-Euro-Med approach, but do not necessarily mean the establishment of a pan-Euro-Med regime for the control of WMD. Whereas a pan-Euro-Med approach refers to a set of concepts and principles universally accepted by the actors as a framework for dealing with the question of WMD, a pan-Euro-Med regime means a set of institutional arrangements and operational mechanisms empowered to take specific steps to control WMD. The asymmetrical perceptions of sources of threat in the Euro-Med world, and the inter-linkages between most of the actors and extra-regional ones reduce the feasibility of a Euro-Med regime, similar to the one envisaged by the NPT or the CWC. The EMP could function as a facilitator of communication among the partners with a view of developing a set of ideas and concepts universally agreed upon, and on which sub-regional negotiations, and regimes could be based. It could also serve as the initiator of commitments to join all global regimes for the control of WMD, as a prelude to establish sub-regional ones. Finally, the EMP could take the initiative to reform present global regimes for the control of WMD so as they would become better instruments for achieving security for all.

For example, the BWC lacks a mechanism for verification of compliance. The MTCR is yet to be formalized and globalized. It is not based on a treaty or a convention, and it focuses on banning the 'transfer' of ballistic-missile technology to proscribed as well as potentially proscribed states, leaving domestic manufacture of such technology outside its scope. No wonder the MTCR is the only global regime accepted by Israel as it denies missile technology to its rivals, but retains its own.

A New Euro-Med Agenda for Action

Euro-Med approaches to the issue of WMD must be based on the premise of achieving security for all through a strategy of equilibrium and linkages. Given the present disequilibrium, and the hegemonic tendencies the latter has already brought into the Middle East, we believe that the starting point in this strategy is the role of the European Union. The EU is the initiator and most powerful partner in the EMP. Under conditions of strategic disequilibrium, the role of the EU is crucial in setting precedents for the control of WMD and persuading other WMD hegemons to do likewise. A credible and effective EU role could proceed along four main lines of action, namely:

- a conceptual adjustment of the strategies of non-proliferation and confidence-building measures (CBMs);

- an active pursuit of a strategy of global nuclear disarmament under the NPT regime;

- an active role in the peace processes in different regions in the EMP;

- and a positive engagement in providing security guarantees to non-EU partners after the removal of their WMD.

The most crucial element in the EU role is a conceptual one. The strategy of non-proliferation needs to be placed within the wider framework of strategic equilibrium. A strategy of non-proliferation (or counter-proliferation as advocated by Les Aspin, former United States Secretary of Defense in 1993) could result in disequilibrium and instability. In this case, the strategy would be counter-productive. The EU can pursue a strategy of non-proliferation to the extent it would not jeopardize regional equilibrium or reinforce present forms of disequilibrium. Likewise, the emphasis of the EU on introducing CBMs will not necessarily help to achieve breakthroughs in the area of the control of WMD. This is essentially because the strategic requirements for the successful application of the concept of CBMs in Europe when it was introduced in the 1970s, are not present in other areas of the Mediterranean. Europe started applying the concept of CBMs when it reached a point of strategic equilibrium with the Soviet Union and all parties had agreed on the stabilization of present borders. Both conditions do not exist in other regions, especially in the Middle East. These regions are characterized by strategic disequilibrium and acute territorial claims. Being a *status quo*-oriented concept, at least in its early versions, CBMs will result in the reinforcement of present forms of disequilibrium rather than rectifying them. However, this does not necessarily mean that we should abandon the concept of CBMs in approaching the question of WMD. Rather, the concept should be adapted to the requirements of an effective control of these weapons.[33]

The second main dimension in the EU role is the initiation of specific steps towards reducing the present stockpiles of WMD in Europe with a view to their ultimate removal. We have seen that the European powers have vowed to keep their nuclear weapons because new threats have developed. We are not sure whether the handling of these new threats requires a nuclear deterrent, but we are sure that, with this logic, there is no way the EU can convince others of the importance of giving up their WMD or refraining from developing them unless the EU itself makes moves towards the global de-legitimization of WMD. An Egyptian scholar has taken issue with this approach arguing that 'if nuclear weapons play an important role in preventing war ... why could this inexorable logic not apply between other regional nuclear powers?'[34] It is important for the EU to take operational steps toward implementing British and French commitments under the article 6 of the NPT. According to this article 'each of the parties undertakes to pursue negotiations in good faith on effective measures relating to cessation of nuclear arms race at an early date and to nuclear disarmament, and to a treaty on general and complete disarmament under strict and effective international control'.

During the 1990s, NATO took major steps towards the reduction of the nuclear arsenal in Europe. The overall NATO stockpile of sub-strategic nuclear weapons in Europe has been reduced to about one-fifth of the level of the 1990 stockpile, and it has already been decided, under the START II Treaty signed in 1993, that multiple warhead intercontinental ballistic missiles will be eliminated and strategic nuclear stockpiles will be reduced by two-thirds. These are extremely positive steps towards creating a safer Europe and convincing others to do likewise. However, considerable nuclear weapons still remain in Europe and in the hands of the Americans and Russians, whilst the nuclear powers in Europe are determined to retain these weapons. We believe that the EU would better serve the cause of the Euro-Med security if it called for the convening of a conference of the five nuclear powers to begin the process of the de-legitimization and elimination of nuclear weapons. This would provide a powerful stimulus to the process of eliminating WMD from the EMP.

The third dimension of the proposed role for the EU is its active involvement in promoting the peaceful resolution of outstanding regional conflicts, such as the Arab–Israeli conflict, and the Turkish–Greek conflict – although the latter already seems on the way towards resolution. Such involvement will alter the way in which the elements of security are perceived and managed by regional actors, especially in relationship with the utility of WMD. Furthermore, in parallel with these processes, which are expected to be long-term in nature, the EU should be prepared to provide negative and positive security guarantees to non-European partners once they endorse the principle of the elimination of their WMD. So far, the nuclear powers have been reluctant to give positive security assurances, because some of the most obvious states against which the assurances will have to be given are allies.[35]

In the Middle East, the power politics paradigm is still alive and well. Forces of strategic disequilibrium are constraining any serious move on the question of WMD. Without an active European role, Middle Eastern actors are not likely to engage in serious negotiation. In this respect, there are three possible options which could be considered by the negotiating actors, all of which satisfy the criteria of equilibrium and security for all.

(1) The first option is an agreement among Arabs, Turks, and Israelis on the elimination of WMD without undue delay and before reaching final settlements of the outstanding issues between them. The parties would join all global regimes for the control of WMD and destroy existing stockpiles of WMD under Euro-Med supervision. NATO will provide security guarantees for non-NATO members. In the meantime, political negotiations will proceed between Arabs and Israelis, and between Arabs and Turks to reach political agreements with active EU participation.

(2) The second option is an agreement between the same actors to eliminate their WMD within the framework of peace settlements. In this case, no actor will be required to join any global regime for the control of WMD until peace agreements have been reached and implemented. The Arabs will not be asked to join the CWC, and the Israelis will not be persuaded to accede to the NPT. Political negotiations will proceed in earnest and the final status of WMD will be entrenched into the peace agreements and implemented in parallel to these agreements. The EU will also halt its differential treatment of various Euro-Med actors regarding their access to WMD, until peace agreements are reached.

(3) The final option is that the parties will postpone the removal of WMD until after peace agreements have been reached, secured, and solidified. The parties will not begin negotiations until after the peace agreements. They will reach an agreement on the removal of their WMD to be implemented at a later date in a specified time frame.

Within these options the accession of all the parties to the global regimes could be supplemented with sub-regional verification regimes, and the EU or NATO could provide security guarantees once the final status of the territorial issues has been decided. Further, the crucial linkages between arms transfers and the local production of arms, and between WMD and conventional weapons should be firmly secured. Combinations of these options are also feasible provided that they create balanced commitments and power relationships.

Although we advocate the immediate removal of WMD from the Middle East through the pursuit of the first option, we believe that the second option is more practical, given the present Syrian and Israeli approaches. Israel and Syria are not likely to accept the reduction or removal of their WMD as long as the present political impasse persists. Once genuine momentum is restored to the Middle East peace process, the parties will be in a better position to talk seriously about their WMD. Until such a time, it would not be feasible to ask the Syrians to accede to the CWC and destroy their non-nuclear WMD without asking the Israelis to accede to the NPT and eliminate their nuclear weapons as well. However, we believe that Israel's accession to the NPT would provide a strong CBM in the Middle Eastern context. Such a measure would put Israel on a par with the Arabs as far as the NPT is concerned. It would not jeopardize Israel's security as it would not be required to destroy its nuclear arsenal, but only to cease the production of nuclear bombs. However it would drastically change the context of Arab–Israeli relations, and create a better environment for engaging in serious negotiations on the issues of the occupied territories and WMD. Egypt has recently joined the Pelindaba Treaty which declares Africa to be a nuclear-free zone – and Israel should reciprocate by joining the NPT.

Conclusion

Despite the forces of globalization and interdependence, and the reduction of the European nuclear arsenal, the EMP is a prime arena for the stockpiling and deployment of WMD. Euro-Med actors still view these weapons as an ultimate security guarantee, and whoever develops them first strives to prevent others from pursuing a similar course of action. However, the actors pledged in the 1995 Barcelona Declaration to incorporate the question of WMD into the Euro-Med projected security arrangements through a strategy of non-proliferation and establishing a nuclear-free zone in the Middle East.

In this comment, we have attempted to present policy recommendations and scenarios for dealing with the issue of WMD in the Euro-Med world. We have argued that controlling WMD in this universe confronts certain formidable problems, such as the diversity of regional sub-systems, the geographical and functional connections between the Euro-Med universe and adjacent regions, the strategic disequilibrium which characterizes the EMP, and the basic disagreements among the parties on virtually all the issues involved. These problems make the issue of WMD in the EMP unique. Because there are no historical models to draw upon, we have to begin by identifying a policy framework from which certain strategies could be drawn.

We have argued that a viable approach for the control of WMD is one based on two main postulates: (i) achieving security for all the conflicting parties by preventing them from using or threatening to use WMD; and (ii) acknowledging the conditions under which WMD are more or less likely to be used or considered as a viable option. Our review of the literature has shown that WMD are likely to be used or perceived as a useful instrument of coercion if power relations are characterized by strategic disequilibrium in the area of WMD, and in relationship with major political issues. We have concluded that a strategy which brings about equilibrium is more likely to achieve the objectives of stability and peace. A strategy of equilibrium has two main implications for the control of WMD, namely: (i) the assessment of the strategies of non-proliferation and CBMs from the perspective of their impact on regional equilibrium; and (ii) approaching the question of the control of WMD from the wider framework of the linkages between different elements involved – such as the linkages between different forms of WMD, between WMD and conventional weapons, between arms transfers and local production of WMD, between the Euro-Med universe and adjacent regions, and between the issue of WMD and the peace processes. The acknowledgment of these linkages and their overall impact on strategic equilibrium will have a heuristic value in identifying priorities and feasible courses of action.

At the policy level, we have argued that the EU is in a position to set the Euro-Med agenda in the direction of controlling WMD with a view to their total removal. Given a strategy of equilibrium, especially between the non-European partners in the EMP, the EU could then proceed towards the conceptual adjustment of the strategies of non-proliferation and CBMs, the active pursuit of global nuclear disarmament under the NPT regime, the activation of the Euro-Med peace processes, and the positive engagement in regional security guarantees. At the Middle Eastern level, we have suggested three policy options, all postulated on the concepts of equilibrium and linkages. We have advocated the option of removing all WMD from the Middle East within the framework of peace settlements between Arabs, Israelis, and Turks. Until such time, the major thrust of any EU approach would be to guarantee stability through a strategy of equilibrium, which would mean that all regional powers will maintain similar relationships with global regimes for the control of WMD.

NOTES

1. For a review of British and French strategic nuclear forces, see IISS, *The Military Balance 1996/97*, London: Oxford University Press, 1996, pp.53, 73–5.

2. For a review of Israel's nuclear capabilities, see S.H. Hersh, *The Samson Option*, London: Faber & Faber, 1991.
3. Leonard Spector, 'Nuclear Proliferation in the Middle East: The Next Chapter Begins', in E. Karsh, M. Navias and P. Sabin (eds.), *Non-Conventional Weapons Proliferation in the Middle East*, Oxford: Clarendon Press, 1993, pp.145–8.
4. SIPRI, *SIPRI Yearbook, 1992, World Armaments and Disarmament*, Oxford: Oxford University Press, 1992, pp.161–2; SIPRI, *SIPRI Yearbook, 1994, World Armaments and Disarmament*, Oxford: Oxford University Press, 1994, p.316; J. Robinson, 'Chemical Weapons Proliferation in the Middle East,' in Karsh, Navias and Sabin, op. cit., pp.69–98.
5. W. Burrows and R. Windrem, *Critical Mass*, New York: 1994, asserted that 'although Washington denied Israel off-the-shelter nuclear weapons, it did almost everything else possible to ensure that the Israelis developed exactly what they needed', p.309.
6. Before that, it was known that Israel was the only power with actual nuclear capabilities. However, the USA and Israel rejected the Egyptian request to put the issue on the agenda of the Camp David negotiations in the Middle East in 1978; see W. Quandt, *Camp David: Peacemaking and Politics*, Washington, DC: Brookings Institution, 1986, pp.356–60.
7. The Bush proposal excluded Turkey from the geographical domain of its projected arms control regime, which means that Turkey would be permitted to keep any WMD it might have. As a result, it would enjoy a position of superiority in relationship with Syria and Iraq, countries which have considerable disagreements with Turkey.
8. *Facts on File World News Digest*, 1991, pp. 390-391, and SIPRI, *SIPRI Yearbook*, 1992, op. cit., pp.161–7.
9. Avner Cohen, *Towards a New Middle East: Re-thinking the Nuclear Question*, Abu-Dhabi: The Emirates Center for Strategic Studies and Research, 1996, p.46 (in Arabic).
10. For a review of the Israeli approach, see Interview with Isaac Rabin, *Al-Ahram* (Cairo), 13 July 1994; Eytan Bentsur, 'Israel's Vision on the Goals and Principles of the Regional Security and Arms Control Process', in Fred Tanner (ed.), *Arms Control, Confidence-Building and Security Co-operation in the Mediterranean, North Africa, and the Middle East*, Valletta: University of Malta, 1994, pp.69–75; Savita Bande, 'Israel and the Nuclear Non-Proliferation Regime', *Strategic Analysis* (New Delhi), 15/4, April 1993, pp.147–60.
11. Speech by Foreign Minister Amr Moussa at the NPT Review Conference on 20 April 1995, *Al-Ahram*, 21 April 1995; Mohammed El-Sayed Selim, 'Egypt and the Middle Eastern Nuclear Issue', *Strategic Analysis*, 18/10, Jan. 1996, pp.1381–98; Hossam Aly, 'Prospects for Arms Control in the Middle East: A View from Egypt,' in T. Couloumbis and T. Dokos (eds.), *Arms Control and Security in the Middle East and the CIS Republics*, Athens: The Hellenic Foundation for European and Foreign Policy, 1995, pp.165–80. For a review of the Arab and Israeli approaches, see Gerald Steinberg, 'Middle East Arms Control and Regional Security', *Survival*, 36/1, Sept. 1994, pp.126–41.
12. Mohammed Diab, 'Regional Arms Control in the Arab–Israeli Conflict: A Syrian Viewpoint', *Review of Palestinian Studies (Majallat al-Dirasat al-Filistinya)*, 18, Spring 1994, pp38–52 (in Arabic).
13. See the 'London Declaration', *Survival*, Sept.–Oct. 1990, pp.469–72.
14. *NATO Handbook*, Brussels: NATO Office of Information and Press, Oct. 1995, pp.41–2.
15. M. Bundy, W. Crowe Jr. and S. Drell, 'Reducing Nuclear Danger', *Foreign Affairs*, 72/2, Spring 1993, p.141.
16. Yezid Sayigh, 'Middle Eastern Stability and the Proliferation of Weapons of Mass Destruction', in Karsh, Navias and Sabin, op. cit., pp.179–80, 190–91. This view was also advocated by two Egyptian former Generals: Mamdouh Atiyya, and S. Selim, *Chemical and Biological Weapons in the Contemporary World*, Kuwait: Soad al-Sabbah Publishing House, 1992, pp.11–51 (in Arabic).
17. Kenneth Waltz, 'Towards Nuclear Peace', in D. Brite, M. Intriligator and A. Wick (eds.), *Strategies for Managing Nuclear Proliferation*, Lexington, DC: Heath, 1983, pp.132–3.
18. Adrian Hyde-Price, *European Security Beyond the Cold War: Four Scenarios for the Year 2000*, London: The Royal Institute for International Affairs, 1991, p.177.
19. G. Segal et al., *Nuclear War and Nuclear Peace*, London: Macmillan Press, 1988, p.155.
20. Cohen, op. cit., p.19.

21. Philip Sabin, 'Restraints on Chemical, Biological, and Nuclear Weapons: Some Lessons from History', in Karsh, Navias and Sabin, op. cit., p.13.
22. Shai Feldman, *Israeli Nuclear Deterrence: A Strategy for the 1980s*, New York: Columbia University Press, 1982, pp.71–83.
23. Adel Safty, 'Proliferation, Balance of Power, and Nuclear Deterrence: Should Egypt Pursue a Nuclear Option?', *International Studies* (New Delhi), 33/1, 1996, p.32.
24. Quoted in Khalil Shikaki, 'The Nuclearization Debates: The Cases of Israel and Egypt', *Journal of Palestine Studies*, 14/10, Summer 1985, pp.77–91.
25. Wiesner B. Jerome *et al.*, 'Ending Overkill', *Bulletin of the Atomic Scientists*, March 1993, pp.12–23.
26. Uri Bar Joseph, 'The Hidden Debate: The Formation of Nuclear Doctrines in the Middle East', *Journal of Strategic Studies*, 5/2, June 1982, pp.210–22.
27. Some analysts have argued that 'deterrence stability will be strengthened by proliferation': G. Quester, 'Nuclear Proliferation and Stability' in Brite, Intriligator and Wick, op. cit., p.115. A former Egyptian General has also suggested that one option for the Middle Eastern states is to possess a specific numbers of non-conventional weapons by permission. Quoted in Sayigh, op. cit., p.198.
28. S. Neuman, 'Controlling the Arms Trade: Prospects for the Future', in Karsh, Navias and Sabin, op. cit., p.279.
29. Quoted in Barbara Tuchman, *The Alternative to Arms Control*, Los Angeles: Center for International and Strategic Studies, University of California, 1982, p.13.
30. Mohammed El-Sayed Selim, 'Reconceptualizing the Arms Control Process in the Middle East: Towards a New Framework', *Pakistan Horizon* (Karachi), 49/4, Oct. 1996, p.29.
31. This linkage was advocated by Sabin when he argued that 'the ideal outcome remains NBC disarmament as part of the Middle East peace process', Sabin, op. cit., p.30. It was also recommended by Hans Blakes, Director-General of IAEA. He maintained that any peace agreement in the Middle East must include a clause on nuclear disarmament: interview with *Al-Ahram*, 27 July 1994. A former Egyptian General also maintained that arms control in the Middle East without a peace settlement will be counter-productive. Othman Kamel, 'Arms Control in the Middle East', in *Challenges to the Arab World under the Global Transformations*, Paris: Center for Euro-Arab Studies, 1994, p.309 (in Arabic). On the other hand, Kemp advocated de-linking the peace process from the process of eliminating WMD in the Middle East. He argued that 'once there is peace between Israel and its neighbors, it will become much more practical to discuss regimes to eliminate weapons of mass destruction and their means of production': J. Kemp, 'Arms Control and the Arab–Israeli Peace Process,' in Karsh, Navias and Sabin, op. cit., p.258.
32. Our arguments for a Euro-Med approach draw upon Ian Lesser's valuable paper, *New Dimensions of Mediterranean Security*, RAND, Santa Monica, CA, 1996 (mimeo).
33. W. Hopkinson suggested that a 'dose of confidence and security-building measures, which might be the precursor of weightier developments, would be welcome': 'Arms Control and Supplier Restraints: A UK View,' in Karsh, Navias and Sabin, op. cit., p.238. Kemp also argued that Israel should unilaterally open its Dimona nuclear reactor to inspection in return for Arab commitments not to acquire nuclear weapons. He considered this to be a confidence-building measure: Kemp, ibid., p.250. Kemp's suggestion results in keeping Israel as the only nuclear power as it does not deal with the Israeli nuclear bombs in the basement.
34. Safty, op. cit., p.23.
35. SIPRI, *SIPRI Yearbook, 1994*, op. cit., p.613.

8

Weapons of Mass Destruction and Euro-Mediterranean Policies of Arms Control: An Israeli Perspective

MARK A. HELLER

In security affairs, as in architecture, form should follow function. If the opposite approach is adopted, if function is forced to fit the mould of existing form or structure, the result is likely to be irrelevant, at best, and perhaps even counterproductive. If this logic is correct, then even if some commonality of concerns in the Euro-Mediterranean Partnership (EMP) area is posited for security purposes – a position that does not easily stand up to close scrutiny – EMP policies on arms control and limitations can be fully appropriate only to security problems that are characteristic of that area but that neither impinge on nor are impinged upon by security problems of other regions. Otherwise, such policies will reflect the reverse logic: of a structure or institution in search of a function, or an actor in search of a role.

This implies a rather limited range of possibilities, since there are very few issues that fall precisely in the Euro-Mediterranean niche between truly global problems, on the one hand, and more traditional regional security complexes, on the other. That is why the major focus of security cooperation in the EMP is expected to be on what is often called 'soft security' or 'the new security agenda'. What is true with respect to 'hard security' in the conventional context is equally true in the context of weapons of mass destruction and long-range delivery systems.

The existence and possible proliferation of such weapons within the EMP are undoubtedly matters of concern, indeed, of perceived threats, for EMP states. But they are at present neither specific nor unique to this context. For one thing, no Euro-Mediterranean regime can ignore the United States, which is a non-regional power but maintains large military forces, including non-conventional weapons, in the area. For another, no Euro-Mediterranean regime can fully accommodate the entire range of members' security

158

concerns. As a general principle, states view arms control as an instrument of national security rather than as an ideological desideratum, and they will formulate their approach to possible EMP arms control policies through the prism of their own security concerns and threat perceptions. This is particularly evident in the case of those, like Israel, whose 'security space' extends beyond the EMP area. The purpose of this paper is to review the varieties of arms control that might be applicable to weapons of mass destruction (WMD), to provide an Israeli perspective on this issue, and to suggest some modest but potentially significant EMP contributions.

Varieties of Arms Control

The basic objective of cooperative security is to enhance security by reducing the risk of war, not in an absolute sense, but rather relative to the traditional methods of unilateral force buildups and/or alliances. As a major component of co-operative security, arms control seeks, through co-operative measures between potential adversaries, to provide a more effective and reliable alternative to 'self-help'. Other considerations, normally of an international or domestic political nature, also enter into calculations about the advisability of arms control measures. But where military threats are significant, the security factor is almost always paramount.

Of these threats, the most prominent is the possibility of *purposeful, surprise attack by an adversary force*. Ordinarily, states try to deter or defend against such possibilities by building their own forces and/or allying with other forces in such a way as to deny any initial success to a putative attacker or at least to ensure that retaliation will be so painful that it will outweigh the value of any putative gains in the mind of the adversary.

The imperfections of traditional defence posture are too well known to require much elaboration. Suffice it to say that deterrence is not always a viable response to the problem of purposeful attack, either because asymmetries in resources are too great, because the political credibility behind deterrent threats is lacking, or because the adversary's calculus is not the same as the defender's, given different sensitivities to costs or perceptions of interests, domestic political constraints or miscommunication.

And even when self-help through defense or deterrence is viable, it may introduce a second type of insecurity: *crisis instability*. In an atmosphere of rising tension due to disputes of a political or other nature, states may take certain actions (such as warnings, force buildups or new dispositions) which, though of a defensive or anticipatory character, may easily be interpreted on the other side as indicators of offensive intentions. Such actions often create pressure for anticipatory or preemptive measures. This is a generic problem of escalation dynamics, well documented in analyses of the outbreak of the

First World War, but it is exacerbated by the introduction of technologies, such as surface-to-surface missiles, that permit very little advance warning of imminent use and, as yet, virtually no effective passive defense (thereby creating very strong incentives for decision-makers, in crisis situations, to neutralize them before they can be launched).

The demonstrated inability of traditional security policies to eliminate such insecurities explains the intellectual appeal of cooperative security as well as the inclination of states to consider cooperative security, including arms control, as a possible alternative. It is because of this that they agree to explore the possibility that voluntary, agreed limitations on military capabilities may provide a more efficient and/or cost-effective means of threat reduction than can military buildups limited only by a state's demographic, economic and technological resources.

For analytical purposes, arms control measures can be divided into three categories. The first is *declaratory*. Declaratory measures involve statements of non-aggressive intent, more specifically, declarations of commitment to the non-violent resolution of disputes. Parties declare that their military forces are for defensive purposes and undertake a policy of 'no first use' of part or all of their order-of-battle. Such measures have been the focus of doctrinal debates in the past, particularly in the East–West context during the cold war, when specific attitudes were shaped by asymmetrical force structures and capabilities; the Soviet Union, which enjoyed a numerical preponderance in the conventional balance-of-power in Europe, tended to stress the notion of 'no first use' of nuclear weapons, while NATO advocated a declaratory policy of 'no first use' of any force, at all. Declaratory arms control relates to intentions, rather than to capabilities, and while declarations of intent are valuable measures of reassurance in and of themselves, they can never really reduce insecurities, since they are never completely credible. In order to inspire greater confidence, they need to be reinforced by observable behaviour that actually limits capabilities to act in ways that declarations have renounced.

This brings us to the second category – *operational* arms control. Operational arms control may be compared to the 'software' or 'operating systems' of military forces. Without actually reducing theoretical capacities, it nevertheless reduces the ability to pose certain threats to others by placing limitations on the location of forces and on how they are maintained and managed on a routine basis. Perhaps the most prominent example of operational arms control is demilitarized or limited-forces zones, which keep armed forces away from border areas and therefore reduce their capacity to launch a successful surprise attack. Other examples include limitations on the type, size and frequency of military exercises and requirements for pre-notification of authorized exercises.

The third category is *structural* arms control, which can be compared to the 'hardware' of military forces. Structural arms control places material limitations on capabilities, by constraining the amounts and/or types of forces and equipment that states maintain. In some cases, it may promote the same objective of constraining the capacity to launch a surprise attack by addressing the configuration of military forces, and particularly the internal balance between 'short-warning' capabilities (for example, standing forces) and 'long-warning' capabilities (for example, reserve forces). In extreme cases, like the 1986 Intermediate-range Nuclear Force (INF) Treaty in Europe, arms control can even provide for the elimination of an entire class of forces or weapons systems.

Because structural arms control deals with material matters, there is a tendency to think that only it is 'real', and that the other categories fall under the less rigorous rubric of 'confidence-building measures' (CBMs) or 'confidence-and-security-building measures' (CSBMs). But the important question is not the distinction between the means, but rather the extent to which the different means are able to contribute to the common overall purpose, which is to reduce insecurities.

The theoretical advantages of cooperative security policies are not in dispute; it is the feasibility of particular measures in particular circumstances that raises serious questions. One question has to do with their credibility. How reliable are they? In both operational and structural arms control, as in declaratory arms control, the objective of reducing threats (real and perceived) can only be promoted if agreed restraints are accompanied by agreed verification and transparency measures. These enable the parties to confirm through reliable means that actions by other parties actually conform to their assumed obligations. With respect to declaratory arms control, such measures basically examine the extent to which the mass media, educational and military curricula and socialization, and training programs, doctrines and plans actually complement declarations of non-aggressive intent. In the operational and structural realms, they range from more pervasive monitoring procedures (for example, aerial reconnaissance and the posting of observers at maneuvers or in limited-forces zones) to the most intrusive on-site inspections of military and industrial facilities.

But even if the problem of verification can be satisfactorily solved, attitudes toward specific operational and structural arms control proposals, like those toward declaratory arms control, are normally conditioned by specific contextual considerations of threats and capabilities. It is rare that all the parties involved will view a particular proposal in an equally favorable light, since their own security posture is unlikely to be affected in an equal manner. In this sense, universal elimination agreements, like the INF Treaty, are exceptions in the history of arms control. The more normal pattern is for states to stress different types of limitations in the hope of constraining adversary capabilities more than their own (such as the Western emphasis on tank armies during all the years of East-West negotiations on conventional arms limitations in Europe). And even when there are agreed global ceilings, as in the SALT-I Treaty, these often permit tradeoffs or flexible mixes within the global ceiling that address each side's particular concerns or rigidities. Such considerations also inform Israeli perspectives on arms control.

Israeli Perspectives on WMD Arms Control

Israel's approach to arms control as a vehicle for threat reduction is conditioned by its perceived threat environment, which is multi-dimensional and regional. For this reason, Israel has always been skeptical about selective arms control emphases on those asymmetries that seem to work in its favor, especially in the nuclear field; these imply a potentially detrimental impact on its overall security posture. And for this same reason, it has always had reservations about global regimes that disregard the specific regional context. A regional context such as the EMP, which partly overlaps but is not fully congruent with Israel's regional threat environment, will only go part way toward addressing the inadequacies of global limitation and verification regimes, as revealed most starkly by the Non-Proliferation Treaty/International Atomic Energy Authority (NPT/IAEA) experience in Iraq.

Israel's security posture is essentially a function of its permanent quantitative inferiority in military manpower, conventional arsenals and strategic depth *vis-à-vis* a varying array of past, current or potential adversaries. For many years, these asymmetries left it vulnerable to conventional offensives by its immediate neighbors, and particularly to surprise attacks by standing forces that might produce substantial, perhaps even crippling gains before its own largely reservist army could be mobilized. More recently, this threat has been compounded by the acquisition of ground-to-ground missiles and unconventional weapons development programs by neighbors and by more remote but hostile states such as Iraq, Iran and Libya. For the most part, Israel has responded to these threats by developing a deterrent posture based on an offensive operational doctrine grounded in escalation dominance. The threat of escalation could be horizontal (preempting or carrying the battle quickly into enemy territory) and/or vertical (compensating for numerical inferiority by applying more effective or destructive maneuver and firepower).

In either case, it depended on a qualitative advantage to achieve this capability. In neither case were WMD, including nuclear weapons, invoked as part of the deterrent and they did not, in fact, deter conventional military attacks against Israel. Instead, they hovered in a doctrine of ambiguity, presumably as an instrument of last resort against some kind of conventional collapse or against non-conventional attack.

Concerns of the first sort have been partially alleviated by the Middle East peace process, which helps to reduce the probable extent of an Arab military coalition; the second threat is somewhat mitigated by the constraints imposed on Iraqi WMD and missile programmes since the Gulf War. But the peace process is itself both partial and incomplete – partial in the sense that important elements remain entirely outside (and, inddeed, hostile to it); incomplete in the sense that even some of the existing tracks have not yet culminated in peace agreements, much less in the kind of adjustments in military posture and security relations that would eliminate Israel's need to rely on traditional elements of threat reduction. This is unlikely to happen until all major elements in the Middle East (including those outside the EMP) enter into peaceful relations with Israel, adopt some credible declaratory, operational and structural limitations on the capabilities most threatening to Israel (including in the conventional field), and begin to elaborate all-encompassing regional security structures – the Middle East does not yet have even rudimentary region-wide organizations like the Organization of American States (OAS) or the Organization of African Unity (OAU) – that entrench the notion of normal, regularized interactions. As for the second concern, it is sustained by the fact that the United Nations Special Commission (UNSCOM) inspections regime has collapsed and the assumption that sanctions on Iraq will not be maintained indefinitely, perhaps not even until the regime in that country has been transformed, and by the indications of WMD and long-range missile development or procurement programs by Iran.

Israel's basic perspective with respect to WMD arms control, especially of a structural nature, can therefore be summarized as follows: Israel favors the idea of a Weapons of Mass Destruction Free Zone (WMDFZ), provided that it is elaborated in the appropriate context, that is, in the relevant zone (the Middle East threat environment), in the relevant conditions (a comprehensive security regime), and in the relevant political climate (of peace).

Implications for EMP Policies

The ultimate aspiration of EMP policies, including those on WMD, should be to help replace traditional defense postures with a comprehensive regional security system within the context of stable peace. Ideally this would mean, if not the implementation of the prophetic injunction to turn swords into plowshares and spears into pruning hooks, then at least of some approximation of what once seemed only a slightly-less utopian prospect in Western Europe: of a Belgium not living in fear of a more heavily-armed

Germany and a Germany not living in fear of a nuclear-armed France. But this aspiration cannot possibly be realized in the near term, if at all, and if major structural arms control elements of such a system are posited as near-term objectives, there is little that the EMP can realistically do to bring them about, not only because the endogenous prerequisites for such a system are lacking, but also because the construction of such a system is inconceivable without the active involvement of the United States.

However, if arms control is viewed as a part of longer-term confidence-building process, with some value in its own right, then EMP can make a modest but significant contribution to security in the Middle East and the Euro-Mediterranean region as a whole.

(1) The first is to support the Arab-Israeli peace process, both in terms of political and material support for the existing tracks and in terms of encouragement of positive involvement by parties currently outside the process.

(2) The second is to consider expansion of EMP so that it overlaps more fully with the Middle East threat environment. If this happens, then any regional measures on material limitations will, at least from Israel's perspective, apply to the pertinent region. In practice, this means soliciting the involvement of Libya, Iran, Iraq and the Gulf States in discussions of possible agreements on CSBM/arms control measures. This would admittedly dilute the Euro-Mediterranean character of the partnership, but the alternative is to exclude major elements from Israel's threat environment, thereby rendering the notion of self-restraint on material military capacities altogether irrelevant.

(3) Meanwhile, EMP should encourage a variety of CSBMs of a declaratory and perhaps operational nature. The former category can include a commitment to the ultimate aim of a Euro-Mediterranean region free of weapons of mass destruction, along with elements of a 'Code of Conduct' intended to provide verbal reassurances about non-belligerent intentions – a necessary first step inn advance of more ambitious measures. The main component of such a Code would be the commitment to abstain from the first use of force and to resolve conflicts by peaceful means.

Operational measures should include some practical reassurances to back up the declaratory elements, particularly by adopting practices and procedures that enhance transparency in military activities and constrain the capacity of states to launch an effective surprise attack. The following are some examples of the types of measures that should be considered:

(a) creation of limited-forces or demilitarized zones along borders;
(b) creation of aerial intelligence regimes involving a combination of national reconnaissance activity (with satellites and/or prenotified manned flights) and third-party overflights;
(c) prenotification of military maneuvers and exchanges of observers;
(d) exchanges of visits by military delegations and of curricula of military command colleges;
(e) establishment of direct military-to-military communications links at a level (perhaps Chiefs of Operations) high enough to be of significance when ambiguity or uncertainty about operations create anxieties;
(f) establishment of mechanisms for regular consultation about extra-regional threats or threats from non-state actors; and
(g) publication of data about military budgets and arms transfers.

Such measures are of a general nature, and are applicable to all types of weapons systems. In addition, it is possible to envisage certain 'precursor' measures that begin to address the specific question of WMD and delivery systems. For example, the destabilizing effect of missiles, particularly in pre-crisis or crisis situations, may be somewhat mitigated by an undertaking to provide pre-notification of missile test-flights and to test them only on non-threatening trajectories.

Measures of this sort, while much more modest than sweeping structural arms control agreements, are feasible even before a comprehensive regional security is in place, precisely because they help reduce threat perceptions without actually compromising defense capabilities. Indeed, one of their attractions is that they can be initiated on a bilateral or sub-regional basis, thus laying the building blocks for future expansion to other countries, rather than having to wait for the adherence of all relevant actors. Such measures are valuable because they help to build confidence, prevent or manage crises, and create an atmosphere conducive to the consideration of more ambitious steps. While they do not constitute the wide-ranging arms control regime appropriate to a comprehensive regional security system, they can help encourage a process that may ultimately make that possible.

(4) Additionally, the EMP can consider some EMP-specific supply-side controls, by agreeing to refrain from intra-EMP WMD and missile-technology transfers. The history of supply-side arms control is not encouraging, and many of the most important supply sources of weapons and delivery systems (especially missiles) are outside the EMP area. Nevertheless, an EMP measure of this sort might help constrain proliferation. Perhaps just as important would be tighter control on 'dual-use' technologies and components or precursors, in order to reduce the

risk that non-state actors will acquire the ability to develop or assemble WMD.

A Note on Sequencing

Some of these measures, and others, were under consideration in the context of the Middle East in the Arms Control and Regional Security multilateral working group (ACRS). ACRS, however, was suspended in 1995 and shows no signs of being reconvened. Despite the lack of congruence between the geographical focus of ACRS and EMP, EMP can partially fill the gap, while extending the effort to manage or reduce tensions to other parts of the Mediterranean. Pending the resumption of ACRS talks, the existence of some alternative forum to promote the general process of mutual familiarization and confidence-building, even if it amounts to little more than seminar diplomacy, is a matter of some urgency.

The question of the order in which these measures are adopted is less critical. All are part of the same general process of confidence-building, and the promotion of a culture of security cooperation based on greater confidence is widely acknowledged to be an essential prerequisite of more far-reaching structural arms control agreements in the future. The question of complete trust is, of course, irrelevant; if it existed, co-operative security and arms control would be possible but not necessary. What is important is to begin gradually to build trust, so that what is necessary becomes gradually more possible.

Consequently, the list of measures proposed here is not intended to imply any chronological ordering. Indeed, any rigid notions of proper sequencing are misplaced, and what should prevail instead is a pragmatic approach that essentially implies a willingness to pursue whatever CSBMs are possible, whenever possible, without making the adoption of some measures contingent on the adoption of others.

In short, it is important to recognize that the process itself is important: the promotion of greater familiarity and mutual openness and the incremental institution of modest measures can pave the way for structural arrangements that now seem visionary but may eventually become practical at some point down the road.

9

Arms Control in the Mediterranean Area: A European Perspective

PASCAL BONIFACE

The issue of weapons of mass destruction (WMD) in the Mediterranean area raises a dual problem of definition:

- First, the range of weapons involved need to be defined. In the 1950s, the terminology used was NBC weapons (nuclear, biological and chemical weapons). Terminology has changed with military technology, however, and the more common term is now weapons-of-mass-destruction (WMD), a more comprehensive term. In addition to nuclear, chemical and biological weapons, this usually covers the devices which may be used to carry such weapons, including ballistic missiles, even though these carriers can be, and usually are, equipped with conventional munitions. It seems, however, illogical to place nuclear weapons and other weapons into the same category, as the former are deterrents and the latter are weapons intended for use. None the less, this conventional approach to definition will be maintained in this discussion, firstly because it forms the basis for today's strategic debate, and secondly because as regards nuclear weapons in the region, the essential issue of debate is whether these weapons are, in fact, intended for use or merely as a deterrent.

- The second part of the definitional problem, which is more difficult to resolve, is of a geographical nature. To take only the countries participating in the Euro-Mediterranean Partnership (EMP) into consideration would be to oversimplify the matter. This would leave out countries that, in the eyes of many of the parties involved, form an integral part of the regional strategic equation, and often constitute an undeniable threat to their security. Israel could not conceive of a system of arms control that did not include Iran and Iraq. Indeed, these two countries feature high on the list of security concerns of other Euro-Mediterranean countries too, even though they are not, strictly speaking, included in the area. The Euro-Mediterranean area, specified in the Barcelona Process, is meaningful on a political, diplomatic and economic level, but not in strategic terms. Libya poses an altogether different type of problem. Paradoxically, the very reasons for which it was not included in the Barcelona Process originally are those which make its integration into an overall regional security system indispensable. Therefore, for this discussion to be relevant in terms of analysis at a strategic level, it must take into account a wider area than just that defined by the Euro-Mediterranean partnership.

Official Nuclear States

Among European Union (EU) member states, two countries possess nuclear weapons and an explicit policy of deterrence. Although they are prepared to reduce their nuclear strength, they are far from ready to give up their status as nuclear-armed states, as recognised in the Non-Proliferation Treaty (NPT).

France possesses five nuclear missile launching submarines, one of which is a 'new generation' vessel. There are two submarines (sometimes three) at sea at all times, and four are operational. They are rotated, with a fifth vessel being out of operation for maintenance purposes at all times. Each operational submarine is capable of launching nuclear missiles and carries 16 M4 missiles equipped with six nuclear warheads, which gives France a submarine capacity of 384 warheads overall. By 2015, according to plan projections, France should have four nuclear missile submarines with three sets of M51 missiles, an overall total of 288 submarine-based nuclear warheads.

France also has three Mirage 2000 squadrons (45 aircraft in all) equipped with medium-range air-to-ground nuclear missiles (ASMP). The French navy's aircraft carriers have and additional two Super-Etendard squadrons equipped with ASMP missiles (36 aircraft). By 2008, these ASMP missiles will be replaced by a slightly longer-range missile, the ASMP-1. Including the aircraft in reserve, the number of aircraft equipped with nuclear warheads in France's possession is estimated to total 80 units. Added to the submarine forces, this gives a grand total of 464 nuclear warheads.

It should be noted that, since the beginning of the 1990s, France has considerably reduced its nuclear capacity – usually of its own accord and not as a result of any treaty obligation. The medium-range Hadès ground-based missiles were placed in reserve and then abandoned for good. The short-range Pluton missiles, which the Hadès missiles were supposed to replace, were withdrawn from service, as were the AN 52 gravitation bombs carried by

Jaguar aircraft. The planned number of new-generation nuclear missile launching submarines was reduced from six to four. France decided to sign the Non-Proliferation Treaty (NPT) and reduced the operational status for all its nuclear forces. It was the first state to declare a moratorium on nuclear testing, although this decision was reversed by President Chirac immediately after he came to power. However, after an initial set of nuclear tests, France launched a zero option with respect to the Comprehensive Test Ban Treaty (CTBT) (thus renouncing the low-power tests permitted under the initial draft of the treaty), shut down its fissile material production facilities at Pierrelate and Marcoule, closed the Mururoa site, and signed a treaty creating the nuclear-free zones of Rarotonga and Pelindaba. Finally, the ground missile site at the Plateau d'Albion (18 missiles) was closed.

This reduction was spurred by budgetary restrictions (since the overall budgetary deficit had to be reduced, the defence budget was reined in and, within it, the nuclear budget experienced the most important cutbacks) as well as strategic concerns (the overall level and nature of threat has lessened and it was necessary to participate in the general disarmament process to meet the expectations of the non-nuclear signatories of the NPT). Hence France now possesses two nuclear components only; submarine and air-borne weapons.

Great Britain possesses 288 nuclear warheads, distributed among 48 missiles on-board four submarines. In the new Trident missile (D5) programme, certain missiles may carry only one nuclear warhead rather than six, to act as an ultimate deterrent, rather than being assigned to strategic retaliation missions. Soon, Great Britain will no longer have ground or air-borne weapons, and will therefore only possess one nuclear component, with a maximum capacity of 288 nuclear warheads.

The French strategy of 'dissuasion' (deterrence) can be described in fairly simple terms. Its objective is to deter all aggression towards or major threat to France's national territory, thus transforming it into a sanctuary, or to France's vital interests. The latter, unlike the former, are not defined in geographical but in political terms. However, they are not explicitly defined in advance so as to confuse and deter a potential adversary. The French concept of deterrence is based on a concept of essential deterrence – that is to say that France considers that it does not need as many nuclear weapons as other countries may possess in order to wield a deterrent influence over them – and since France does not have the means to retain a large number of weapons anyway, it has made virtue out of necessity in this type of policy formulation! Under this concept of deterrence by 'the weak towards the strong', nuclear weapons have an equalising function, so that the principle of 'the more the better' becomes redundant. In short, the French concept of nuclear strategy is purely deterrent in nature. François Mitterrand often repeated the phrase that nuclear weapons are not made to win wars, but to avoid them. The French concept of deterrence is also known under the rubric of 'touts azimuts', meaning that French nuclear weapons are not directed against any one specific country, for their sole function is to protect the national sanctuary and vital national interests, regardless of whom the potential aggressor may be.

> According to France's Ministry of Defence 1994 *White Paper on Defence:* The French concept of 'dissuasion' will continue to be defined as the will and ability to intimidate an adversary to such an extent that they are deterred from threatening our vital interests, regardless of who they are, what levels of damage they are prepared to suffer and what they stand to gain ... our deterrence system must be reserved for protecting our vital interests, whatever the origin and form of the threat. There is no need to give too specific a definition of these interests, which are subject to interpretation of the most senior officials of state. Nonetheless, in essence, they consist in the free exercise of our sovereignty and the integrity of our national territory, its dependencies, its air space and surrounding waters.[1]

Great Britain has not deemed it necessary to describe its doctrine in such detail. However, in general terms, British strategy is comparable to that of France. In December 1995, at a symposium organised by the Institut de Relations Internationales et Stratégiques (IRIS), Sir Christopher Mallaby, Her Majesty's Ambassador to France, gave a very detailed presentation of Britain's deterrence doctrine.[2] He argued that Great Britain will maintain its nuclear force at the minimum level required to act as a deterrent. The nuclear 'button' is the Prime Minister's responsibility and he/she has sole decision-making power based on his/her appraisal of the nation's vital interests. Great Britain makes its decision alone; there is no double-key system or right to veto in association with the United States. In both countries, there is a consensus in favour of maintaining a nuclear policy. French public opinion's support for the 'dissuasion' doctrine remains strong: 61 per cent consider that France could not guarantee its defence without the 'force de dissuasion', 28 per cent hold the opposite opinion, 21 per cent feel that it should be strengthened further, and 32 per cent feel that it should be maintained in a state of operational readiness. For 39 per cent the existing strength should be maintained, and 23 per cent feel that it is time to begin reducing it.[3]

In 1997, within one month of each other, Great Britain and France – on 1 May and 1 June respectively – experienced an electoral move of the political spectrum to the left. This did not, however, alter attitudes towards the nuclear issue. The Labour Party, for its part, had learned its lesson in the 1980s, when its position was seen by public opinion to be too extreme and contributed towards its inability to regain power. Now, however, as far as defence doctrine is concerned, the pacifist path has been abandoned. In its programme entitled

'A Fresh Start for Britain', Labour swears continued allegiance to the prospect of a nuclear-free world, but specifies that disarmament must be a mutual, balanced and verifiable process. Labour is in favour of multilateral disarmament, a radical change since the 1980s when it wanted Great Britain to lead the way on unilateral disarmament.

In France, during the 1995 presidential election campaign, Lionel Jospin's programme included the statement that: 'The nuclear 'force de dissuasion', supported by the submarine fleet, must remain the pillar of our defence system, guaranteeing our independence.' The opposition of the Socialist Party to the renewed nuclear testing was not because it was against deterrence, but rather because it considered that nuclear tests were not essential for France to maintain a deterrence force, and that such action could only serve to arouse public hostility toward nuclear issues. France therefore continues to follow a policy of strictly essential deterrence; of minimal 'dissuasion'.[4]

The joint Green Party-Socialist Party declaration, signed in January 1997, was careful not to call for the renunciation of nuclear weapons, calling instead for action to reduce armaments, to fight against nuclear proliferation and to eliminate weapons of mass destruction (WMD). The electoral alliance of the Socialist Party with two other parties (the Greens and the Communists) hostile to nuclear dissuasion, which is now in government, will not provoke any changes in French strategy. A policy of minimal deterrence (in conjunction with an active policy towards disarmament, as is currently the case) does not harm communist or ecologist sensitivities to the point of preventing them from supporting or even participating in the government. This consensus is made up of four elements:

• the maintenance of a policy of deterrence;

• the rejection of nuclear war;

• the need to create a link between French nuclear power and European defence; and

• the establishment of a link between deterrence and nuclear disarmament.

At the beginning of the 1990s, however, there was a great risk that France would abandon the policy of dissuasion to adopt a combat-oriented nuclear doctrine. It was based on a mixture of fear over nuclear weapons proliferation, combined with the perception of a threat from the South. This launched the debate in France on the possibility of changing the strategic nuclear doctrine. Some argued in favour of a switch from the 'weak to the strong' doctrine to one of the 'strong to the weak', or even the 'strong to the crazy', in the sense that potential adversaries were now seen as inherently weaker than France and also as inherently irrational in their external policy formation. According to this theory, France's deterrence doctrine, suitable for the East–West context of the cold war, was no longer suitable in a more dynamic strategic environment where the threats took many different forms and were more radical.

After the fall of the Berlin wall, and the Gulf War, the option of using tactical nuclear weapons for purely traditional military purposes was abandoned in favour of the option of miniaturised weapons for surgical strikes. This involved the ability to perform accurate strikes of limited effects on a chosen target without causing environmental damage. The argument was that it was impossible to deter the countries of the South with the same type of threat – heavy strikes on urban areas – which were used against the former Soviet Union. The advantage of developing nuclear weapons with reduced destructive effects would be that it would be easier to use such weapons.[5] The disadvantages, however, were exactly the same as before, namely that nuclear weapons would cease to be simply a deterrence mechanism, acquiring a combat role instead – something that France had always managed to avoid. The need for accurate weapons for surgical strikes must be reserved for conventional weapons alone. Only nuclear weapons can truly dissuade and deter, but that is all they may do.

With the introduction of the policy review leading up to a *White Paper on Defence* and the associated campaign for renewed nuclear testing, it looked as if those who wished to modify the strategic deterrence concept had won the endless struggle between the two perceptions of the role to be assigned to nuclear weapons. From 1992 to 1994, the call for a move towards 'more flexible' methods of deterrence inexorably gained popularity with politicians on both the right and the left of the political spectrum, and with security experts.[6] Nothing came of the iniative however, and the dangerous implications of these theories was finally revealed, particularly with respect to the nuclear testing debate. As a result, the *White Paper on Defence*, published in February 1994, contained the following passage: 'France has no known adversaries at the present time. Its strategy remains essentially defensive. The rejection of conventional and nuclear conflict which forms the basis for the doctrine of deterrence ('dissuasion') is still its inspiration. It remains one of the keystones of the indispensable national consensus in defence matters'.[7] It went on to state, even more clearly, that 'French strategy is one of deterrence, allowing no possible confusion between deterrence and use'.[8]

The matter was further clarified on 5 May 1994, in a presidential speech on deterrence, when François Mitterrand summed up the issue as follows:

> I am opposed to any inter-mixture of pre-strategic and tactical weapons. If we adopted a deterrent system of successive nuclear warning triggers, all we would be doing would be to adopt the notion of graduated response. Conversely, if there is only a single and final warning, there

can be no higher level of threat to a potential aggressor, for, after this, comes war ... I would be against any renewed risk of straying from this doctrine – as when I hear it suggested, for example, that we should use nuclear power against the weak or irrational to solve a problem beyond our national territory or our vital interests. Should we come around to the idea of surgical strikes (another term they use is to decapitate the threat) which could go so far as to lead to nuclear warfare?

The president was, in effect, confirming the stand he had taken during the Gulf War. He had, at the time and in accordance with French doctrine, refused to envisage using nuclear weapons in the conflict because neither the French sanctuary or France's vital interests were in danger. Indeed, during the subsequent presidential electoral campaign, the three main candidates supported a traditional vision of 'dissuasion' and there is, therefore, today once again a powerful national consensus in favour of maintaining a purely deterrent role for French nuclear weapons, excluding all possibilities of nuclear war.

An Unofficial Nuclear Country

One other country which participates in the Barcelona Process also possesses a nuclear force which is unofficial but widely acknowledged to exist – Israel. Yet, although Israel has never officially admitted to possessing nuclear weapons, thus pursuing a policy which Shimon Peres referred to as 'nuclear fog',[9] its refusal to sign the NPT, which was maintained during the period leading up to the 1995 Extension and Review Conference of the Treaty, was a further indication of its nuclear capabilities. It also possesses several ballistic missile carriers for its weapons, as is well-known throughout the region. Indeed, in 1995, Aly Maher El Sayed, the Egyptian ambassador to France, declared to the influential French daily, *Le Monde*, that 'The Jewish state currently holds ... more than one hundred nuclear warheads; furthermore it has completed a miniaturisation programme which enables it to make discriminating use of this weapon'.

Estimates of Israel's nuclear power always hover around a capacity of 100-to-200 nuclear weapons. Indeed, according to the revelations made by Mordechai Vanunu – since imprisoned in solitary confinement in Israel – to *The Sunday Times*, Israel has 200 nuclear weapons.[10] Seymour Hersh, the American journalist has subsequently claimed that Israel possesses hundreds of tactical nuclear weapons.[11] Interestingly, it should be noted that the Israeli nuclear programme – the only programme in the region to actually produce weapons, for other programmes have not had any outcomes – is never identified as a danger by Western powers. It is, of course, true that Israel does not aim its missiles at countries on the northern banks of the Mediterranean, although, during the cold war, it did target the southern part of the Soviet Union. However, the problem is that it is the existence of the Israeli nuclear arsenal which motivates and justifies other states in creating nuclear programmes in the region.

At Dimona, in the Negev desert, Israel possesses a heavy water research reactor and two uranium enrichment plants, as well as a plutonium reprocessing facility, none of which are covered by International Atomic Energy Authority (IAEA) guarantees. It also possesses half a dozen uranium processing facilities and a heavy water production plant which are no longer monitored by the IAEA.[12] In addition, Israel has F15, F16 and F4 aircraft capable of launching nuclear weapons and short-range missiles (MGM-51, Lance with a range of 130 km and a load capacity of 450 kg), as well as medium-range missiles Jericho 1 (500 kg, 500 km) and Jericho 2 (100 kg, 1500 km). Israel is also developing cruise missile programmes (200 and 400 km ranges).

In 1995, during negotiations to extend the life of the NPT, many countries, mainly Arab nations led by Egypt, were against extending it indefinitely because Israel continued to refuse to sign the treaty. Israel's stand on the NPT involves not signing it before having signed peace treaties with all Arab states. It would then support the establishment of a WMD-free zone in the Middle East. However, the fact that Israel possesses nuclear weapons and carriers which enable it to reach all the countries in the region remains the main obstacle to establishing such a zone.[13] It seems clear that Israel has no desire to give up its nuclear capabilities, for they are seen as the ultimate way of guaranteeing the existence of the Jewish state. Certainly, recent negative developments in the peace process and the hardening of the Israeli government's attitudes towards it push the prospect of real peace far into the future.

Furthermore, in the absence of any real pressure or threat of sanctions, the Israeli government has no reason to adopt a more open attitude. These nuclear capabilities have always been a major cause of concern for Israel's neighbours. They have never been seriously denounced by Western countries, including those which are most committed to non-proliferation of nuclear weapons. The attitude of countries outside the area is of capital importance on this matter. Although the United States has always vehemently condemned the unrealised nuclear ambitions of Arab states and Iran (even though these countries have signed the NPT), it has never criticised the Israeli programme which has real substance to it. The disarmament plan for the Near-East, presented by President Bush on 29 May 1991, sought to close down nuclear programmes in the region but left Israel's advantage there intact. In December 1993, Frank Wisner, American Under-Secretary of State for Defence, went so far as to declare that the threats overshadowing the Jewish state justified the fact that the latter retained nuclear weapons, even though his statement contradicted the objective of non-proliferation in the region. At the end of January 1995, John Holum, Director of the ACDA (US Arms Control and Disarmament Agency), indicated that Israel was not subject to significant pressure from America to sign the treaty because, whilst hoping that Israel would sign, the United States was aware of the special situation created by the refusal of several of its neighbours to accept its very existence.[14]

In February 1995, the Israeli daily, *Ha'aretz*, announced that Israel would be prepared to sign the treaty within two years of achieving global peace in the region. This report covered a verbal commitment made in Cairo by Shimon Peres, but it was not subsequently confirmed. The Israeli refusal to sign the NPT is justified by issues not covered by treaty and which can be manipulated to national advantage, as Iraq has demonstrated. These include factors such as such as the relative narrowness of national territory, the constant hostility of some states in the region, the balance of power which would be less favourable to Israel in conventional weapons matters and, finally, the proliferation of ballistic missiles and chemical weapons in the region. Eventually, the NPT was prolonged unconditionally for an indefinite period, but accompanied by a set of principles and objectives, which were not legally binding but were intended to encourage further progress towards disarmament. A resolution, proposed by Russia, the United States, the United Kingdom and France, called upon all countries not to delay signing the treaty, and also called on Middle Eastern countries to set up a zone free of nuclear, chemical and biological weapons, as well as of delivery means, in the region.

In any case, quite apart from political judgements on the policy of the Netanyahu government over the NPT, it must be noted that the objective situation did not encourage Israel to make concessions. Israel's nuclear monopoly in the Near East was effectively ratified by treaty when its Arab and Muslim neighbours signed the NPT for an unlimited period,[15] thus creating a profound strategic imbalance in the region. This type of imbalance did not exist elsewhere – in the arms control negotiations between the Soviet Union and the United States, or between India and Pakistan, or even Argentina and Brazil, for example. Israel's 'nuclear fog' policy however, precluded not only the possibility of setting up a system of arms control, but also the creation of any confidence-building measures, as when Israel refused a team of Egyptians the right to inspect its facilities. Nor were measures which did not affect Israeli nuclear strength but would have provided greater openness, such as public access to data on the number of nuclear weapons, were not permitted either.

A confidence-building measure can be defined as any exchange of information or any means for exchanging or allowing for the exchange of information on military policy and capacity, without necessarily imposing regulatory armament levels. This does not involve arms control measures or disarmament measures which would directly affect the size and level of readiness of arsenals. Confidence-building measures do not affect the existence, the size or expansion of such arsenals, but help to establish a better climate and level of trust which can subsequently lead to disarmament measures. Conversely, unbalanced situations, internal lack of will and lack of external pressure create stalemate.

Regional WMD Capabilities

What is the WMD situation in countries linked to the Euro-Mediterranean Partnership (EMP) area? Iraq is a special case as, until 1998, its WMD capability was closely monitored by the United Nations Special Commission (UNSCOM). This monitoring will be the subject of renewed Security Council attempts to revive the UNSCOM system, despite Iraqi opposition, and Iraq will presumably not be able to equip itself with this type of capability in the medium term. All monitoring and control regimes will be based on United Nations Security Council Resolution 687 (1990). Section C of Resolution 687 requires that Iraq comply unconditionally with the obligations in the 1923 War Protocol. It also requires that Iraq accept that its chemical and biological weapons, weapons research and development facilities, related support and manufacturing facilities, ballistic missiles with a range of more than 150 km and the facilities for repairing and manufacturing them, be destroyed, removed or neutralised under international supervision. Iraq must unconditionally accept not to acquire or develop nuclear weapons or materials which could be used to manufacture them, or their sub-systems and components, or the related research and development or supporting and manufacturing facilities. The original UNSCOM mechanism set up by the United Nations involves three different types of operation: on-site inspection and recording of data; the elimination of materials which could be used to manufacture nuclear weapons and the facilities constructed for this purpose, and inspection and control, all at the expense of the Iraqi government.

Iraq is not the only potential culprit, however. Iran has frequently been suspected of wishing to acquire nuclear weapons. However, no proof of an organised programme has ever been found, and IAEA inspections have proceeded normally. Quite apart from alarmist information disseminated by Israeli and American security and information services, which allege that Iran will very soon be in a position to obtain nuclear means, observers estimate that even if Iran had any real intention to develop nuclear weapons, an intention which remains to be proved, it would not be able to do so for at least ten years. As far as delivery systems are concerned, the situation is more complex, for Iran had several hundred Scud-B (300 km) and a hundred or so Scud-C (550 km) acquired through North Korea.[16] Reference is sometimes made to the help that China would provide to Iran to develop a 700-to-1000 km range missile. Mention is also made of the many programmes under development with Chinese and North-Korean co-operation (No Dong 1,500 km range, DF 25, 1,700 km range) although no specific date can be given as to when this type of equipment would become operational. On 27 March 1992, the Director of the CIA, Robert Gates, declared before the Armed Forces Committee of the Chamber of Representatives in Congress that the CIA estimated that 'Iran was trying to acquire nuclear military capability'. However, to date, no published proof exists to substantiate this statement.

What would be the real threat of a nuclear Iran? In all likelihood, Iran's main concern would be to protect itself permanently against external attack. Iran may wish to have a nuclear arsenal to protect both its regime and state against external threat without wishing to use such an arsenal to threaten the existing international order. Could the objective of the Iranian regime simply be to deter the Americans, the Iraqis or anyone else from attacking them, without any concomitant vision of hegemony?[17] Indeed, could Iran threaten other countries? This is unlikely as far as other nuclear countries and their allies are concerned, although it would be much more worrying for countries which do not possess a deterrent. When the United States attempted to thwart the sale of Russian nuclear power stations to Teheran (ironically enough, the proposed nuclear power stations were the same type as those that the United States itself wished to supply to North Korea) as part of the fight against proliferation, the Russians replied that these power stations did not lead to the bomb and that, in addition, Iran equipped with nuclear weapons did not threaten Russia in the slightest. The latter, happily equipped with its own nuclear forces is in a position to deter even a hint of Iranian aggression.

Iran also approached China to obtain new nuclear power stations but, for financial reasons, this project seems to have been abandoned. Teheran has an experimental reactor provided by the United States to the University of Teheran, as well as four small research reactors from China, two of which are at Esfahan and Kraj. Iran signed the NPT and a guarantee agreement with the IAEA came into force in May 1994. Since then, the IAEA inspectors have not found any proof of a weapons programme and congratulate Iran on its co-operation with the agency, which extends beyond the obligations of the treaty. In June 1997, Iran tested an air-sea missile which caused a flurry of protests from the United States. Although the fact of possessing this type of weapon means that Iran brings to bear more military weight in the Persian Gulf situation, it does not fundamentally alter the regional military balance and cannot be compared with the possession of WMD.

The situation in Libya is a quite different matter, for here perceptions have been allowed to overshadow the objective reality. As one commentator remarked: 'Few issues generate more apprehension in European policy circles than the proliferation of WMD in North Africa, where Libya is the leading regional proliferator'.[18] A comparison is often drawn between Colonel Qadhafi's statements denying that Libya possesses WMD and those proffered by Saddam Hussein just before the Gulf War. In essence, Libya is widely suspected of having clandestine chemical weapons manufacturing programmes and of not having abandoned Colonel Qadhafi's long-standing desire to acquire nuclear weapons. In the 1970s, the Libyan leader turned to the Chinese to ask for help in manufacturing a nuclear weapon. Interestingly enough, despite its public stand against the policy of nuclear non-proliferation – which it regarded as the result of the much criticized Soviet–American power condominium – Beijing did not respond to Libya's request, on the basis of the Maoist principle that 'One must be able to rely on one's own strength'. At the beginning of 1992, the international media hinted at a Libyan attempt to corrupt a top-level officer in the Russian Navy, in the hope of obtaining a nuclear weapon.[19] It would, however, be wise to take such claims with a grain of salt, for the media's Libyan nuclear claims more often than not arise from highly inaccurate information. It is difficult to believe that Libya could obtain nuclear weapons in the medium term, not least because the weapons embargo set up by United Nations Security Council Resolution 784 (1992) has considerably weakened the country's access to all kinds of weapons supplies. None the less, Libya does possess short-range missiles (SS-21 70 km, Scud-B 300 km) and medium-range Scud-Cs (550 km). It could also have a 950 km-range Al-Fatah missile under development.

Other countries in the region, such as Syria and Algeria which are seen as potential threats, are also suspected of WMD programmes. It is sometimes claimed that Syria holds bacteriological and chemical weapons. It would be capable of adapting neurotoxic agents to SS-21 (120 km range) and Scud-B (300 km) missiles. It also possesses Scud-C missiles (550 km) and CSS-6 missiles (600 km). Algeria caused much worry when it was discovered in 1991 that, with China's help, it was secretly constructing a research reactor at Ain Oussera. Since its discovery, this reactor has been placed under the watchful eye of the IAEA and Algeria has signed the non-proliferation treaty.

Real Risks, Exaggerated Threats

Matters must, however, be kept in proportion. It is hardly going to be possible to make a nuclear weapon in the national equivalent of the garden shed, unbeknownst to neighbouring states, with the help of a handful of recently qualified physicists.[20] Besides the requisite scientific knowledge which is, it is true, widespread today, and materials which are not as easy to procure on the black market as rumour would have it, the appropriate facilities are needed. In this connection, Iraq is often cited as an example of a country which has signed NPT while secretly continuing a nuclear programme. But, even here, it is important to consider the whole picture. Iraq spent colossal sums of money over ten years (equivalent to those spent by France on the Atomic Energy Commission's Military Applications Directorate), and employed 10,000 highly-qualified technicians from all fields within the nuclear industry, without ever actually being able to develop an atomic weapon. This experience demonstrates that, to succeed in such an endeavour, whilst absolute national priority must be given to the acquisition of nuclear capability, abundant financial resources and a sound technological basis are also essential – two factors which are not necessarily interrelated. The list of countries which meet all three conditions is much shorter than alarmist scenarios imply.

In short, a more accurate assessment of the risk environment would be that, 'For the moment, however, the most pressing war risks are south-south, and neighbours are the most likely first victims of war'.[21] The main risk is, in fact, that 'aggressive sanctuaries' do emerge. A country like Iran or Iraq would not threaten the European countries or the United States. However, the danger of threat articulation would be paramount for their less powerful neighbours who could not count on international help. It is clear that the outcome of the Kuwait crisis and of the subsequent Gulf War in 1990–91 would have been quite different had Saddam Hussein possessed nuclear weapons. In this case, the United Nations would have certainly condemned his acts as vigorously as it did at the time, but Operations *Desert Shield* and *Desert Storm* which led to the Second Gulf War and the victory of the anti-Iraq coalition would never have been undertaken.

This is not to suggest that proliferation is desirable, or that it would not have any effect on the state of international security. The arrival of a new country within the nuclear club would be a catastrophe in the eyes of the international community. From an objective standpoint, increased proliferation would cause international tensions to rise significantly and could even lead to preventive raids to destroy the proliferator's nuclear facilities, an action which could easily introduce a cycle of conflict in which the major powers would win easily. The longer-term consequences are much less clearly defined but the scars of these wars would disfigure the face of the world for a long time to come. Yet the situation is not completely unambiguous and, as long ago as 1968, Pierre Hassner commented that 'Nuclear weapons seem to encourage a kind of defensive nationalism marked by withdrawal, distrust and the desire for self-sufficiency; they seem to discourage offensive nationalism that involves conquest and expansionism'.

Country		Type of missile	Range	Current state
Egypt	Scud-100	ballistic missile	600 km	under development
	Badr 200/Vector	ballistic missile	850/1,000 km	eliminated
Iran	Scud-C	ballistic missile	600 km	in service
	Tondar-68	ballistic missile	1,000 km	under development
Iraq	Fahd	ballistic missile	500 km	banned by UN
	al-Hussein	ballistic missile	600 km	banned by UN
	al-Abbas	ballistic missile	900 km	banned by UN
	Badr 2000/Condor 2	ballistic missile	900 km	banned by UN
	al-Abed (Tammuz 1)	ballistic missile	2000 km	banned by UN
Israel	Jericho 1 (YA-1)	ballistic missile	480 km	in Service
	Jericho 2 (YA-3)	ballistic missile	1,450 km	in service
	Shavit	ballistic missile	7500 km	in service
Libya	al-Fatah	ballistic missile	950 km	under development
Syria	Scud-C	ballistic missile	600 km	in service
	M-9	ballistic missile	600 km	on order

Yet nuclear weapons or WMD alone are not enough; they must be delivered to their targets. What is the situation as far as weapons platforms are concerned? As regards carriers with a range of more than 500 km, the table below describes the situation for those countries which officially have no nuclear capacity. In essence, the monitoring of their weapons programmes has shown that around half-a-dozen countries south of the Mediterranean have ballistic capabilities. Naturally, this should be taken into account by European countries in evaluating the threats they may face, but the danger should certainly not be overestimated.

In the Western world, the proliferation of missiles is considered to be a means, given to the countries in the South, of striking right to the heart of the developed nations. More than 25 countries in the developing world now have ballistic missiles in their possession. In response to this development and to prevent further proliferation, developed countries have evolved an export control system, the Missile Technology Control Regime (MTCR). Yet, such proliferation is more often associated with the logic of regional rivalry than with a confrontation between North and South. If that is the case, although it is necessary to maintain a non-proliferation regime because prevention is always better than cure, constructing costly anti-missile defence systems, of the kind now being suggested to Europe by the United States, could be seen to be doubly unnecessary from a strategic point of view in two respects. Firstly, the threat of retaliation hanging over the potential aggressor will always be a greater guarantee than that of potential protection which is not necessarily going to function effectively and, secondly, the ballistic missile threat is often exaggerated.

William Perry, the American Secretary of Defence, declared before the Congress that the threat of ballistic missiles developed by Iraq, Iran and Libya would not arise for another ten years and he did not, therefore, see the need to rapidly develop new anti-missile systems.[23] In fact, at present, the ballistic missiles of the developing world do not constitute a real strategic threat. If all the weapons available were taken into consideration, they would represent three-to four-hundred missiles in total, most of them being Scud-B or Scud-C in type, with a range of 500 km. This is nothing compared to the four thousand V2 rockets that Nazi Germany launched against Great Britain without changing the course of the Second World War. The problem is, above all, psychological in nature. These missiles are more intimidating than any other kind of weapon, mainly because we are afraid of them, for popular perceptions overshadow reality. This is a common problem in threat perception. For example, the wave of terrorism which hit France in 1998 was spectacular but the number of fatalities and people injured as a result of it was minimal, compared to the losses caused by road accidents. It is true that subjective views, at certain times, create objective realities. However, it would be wise not to engage in self-fulfilling prophesies which help to exaggerate the danger. Those who most vehemently denounce a threat can end up helping to create it as a result of the fears they raise.

Regrettably, European states and now the United States have engaged in precisely this kind of exaggeration. On 20 February 1995 in Bonn, the United States, France, Germany and Italy signed a declaration of common intent to develop a ground-to-air defence system to replace the Hawk and Patriot systems. The MEADS project (Medium Extended Air Defence System) involved a missile with a range of 100 km, for a total investment of $40 billion (50 per cent from America, 20 per cent from France and Germany and 10 per cent from Italy). The aim was to provide defence against relatively primitive ballistic missiles by protecting either externally deployed military equipment, or national territory or, more exactly certain zones within it. On 6 September 1995 in a speech to the Institut des Hautes Etudes de la Défense Nationale, Alain Juppé declared that 'We now have less protection, particularly as regards more distant battlefields and the protection of national territory. We can justify the acquisition of antimissile systems for any theatre of operations to remedy this situation ... . There is nothing to indicate that new [nuclear] states would adopt a deterrence doctrine in nuclear matters'.

Yet, despite this alarmist talk, in 1997, France was to declare its withdrawal from the project. It has also, in common with its European partners this time, maintained its distance from American pressure for Europe to sign up to the proposed theatre-defence missile shield system that the United States decided to develop at the dawn of the new millennium. In reality, the 'South–South' risk is, in fact, much greater than the 'South–North' risk. The Middle East has long borne the threat of missile attacks. Ground-to-ground missiles were used during the Iran–Iraq war, the 1991 Gulf War and against Israel in 1973. During the Iran-Iraq war, Iraq launched 331 surface-to-surface Scud and modified Scud missiles against Iranian towns, and Iran responded by launching 86 missiles of the same type, together with 253 ground-to-ground Oghab missiles of a much shorter range (40 km).[24]

The problem of chemical weapons continues, however, to constitute a genuine element of concern within the overall regional strategic situation. It has acquired substance, largely as a result of Iraqi action, firstly against Iran, then against its own Kurdish population. Furthermore, the fear of Iraqi intentions in this regard during the Second Gulf War has meant that the pressure for chemical weapon disarmament has been stepped up. As Roberto Aliboni has pointed out, 'The countries in the region which possess chemical weapons and are capable of manufacturing them are Egypt, Iran, Iraq, Israel, Syria and maybe Libya'.[25] However, none of these countries has officially declared its possession of such weapons and the problem is complicated by the fact that several Arab nations have not signed the chemical weapons disarmament treaty because of Israel's failure to sign the non-proliferation treaty – an excellent example of interaction when different types of WMD are involved.

None the less, the link thus established between nuclear weapons and chemical weapons should cause some astonishment, for chemical weapons are not deterrent in nature, but are weapons intended for use. However, Arab countries clearly prefer to retain the chemical option, which is within their financial and technical reach, than the nuclear option, which often is not. Furthermore, such weapons are subject to less adverse pressure from the major powers, for chemical weapons, unlike nuclear weapons, are not directly associated with hegemony within the global hierarchy. The situation is currently that the agreement banning chemical weapons – which bans not only the use of these weapons (as did the Geneva protocol of 1923) but also their development, production and possession – was signed on 18 January 1993 in Paris and came into force in 1997, once it had been ratified by sixty countries. All the signatories undertook to destroy their chemical capabilities under international supervision.

The situation in the Middle East, however, is still profoundly unsatisfactory as far as these new treaty obligations are concerned, largely because of the tensions over Israel's nuclear capacity and because of the South-South chemical weapons threat as a result. All the countries in the strategic zone of the Mediterranean and the Middle East had signed the 1923 Geneva Protocol, although some of them have subsequently been accused of using chemical weapons. As far as the 1993 Treaty of Paris is concerned, it was signed but not ratified by Cyprus, Israel, Malta, Portugal, Somalia, Turkey and Iran. It was not signed by Egypt, Iraq, Libya, Syria and Lebanon. Iran is suspected of having produced mustard gas, chlorine and of having nerve gas capabilities. The Iranian stockpile of chemical weapons is estimated at 2,000 tons.[26] Libya is suspected of having constructed a chemical weapons factory near Rabat although Tripoli claims that this installation is a pharmaceutical manufacturing plant.

Strategic Debate and Mistaken Perspectives

Quite apart from the bilateral and multilateral Arab-Israeli strategic issues, it is clear that the notion of military balance is meaningless within the Mediterranean and Middle East region. The players differ too greatly between the North and the South, rigid or permanent coalitions do not exist and threat situations constantly change. It is extremely difficult to establish a balance of power between the countries along the southern shores of the Mediterranean. It is impossible to implement conflict prevention systems and models which were suitable for the European strategic theatre where the quest for balance was the priority of military and political leaders alike during the cold war from 1945 to 1991.

This fundamental imbalance between the North and South Mediterranean regions is not exclusively due to mutual fear. In reality, because of their military superiority, the countries in the North fuel the fears of those in the South. Even despite the increasingly marked reluctance of European countries to engage in external military operations[27] – the experiences of Bosnia and Kosovo not withstanding – the countries of the South fear military intervention which would cost them their sovereignty. In both cases, perceptions and subjective fears are much stronger than actual threats, but subjective perceptions, when they are too strong, can create objective tensions. Europe, indeed, is as prone to this error of judgement as are the countries of the Southern Mediterranean region. Thus, certain Western European 'experts' maintain the myth of a southern threat, thus conveniently replacing the Soviet threat which disappeared with *perestroika* and the fall of the Berlin wall. In short, cold war orphans have found a substitute adversary in order to justify their desired level of military spending. In an outstanding essay, Jean-Christophe Rufin criticised the situation as follows:

> The South! here is the new threat … articles, television and radio broadcasting, as well as books, announce and celebrate it and we pretend to have just discovered it. The confrontation between East and West is over. Confrontation between North and South arrives instead. Such symmetry is delightful to behold. Officers are painting their armour the colour of sand, aiming their missiles southwards and are studying the theory of the deterrence by the strong against the weak.[28]

François Cailleteau has pointed out that, 'The historical background to this approach – in particular for the French – is clear: it is a combination of the

Arab invasion of the 8th century and the Algerian War. The sociological background is equally clear: fear of demographic submersion and Islamic fanaticism'.[29] In 1995 Willy Claes, then Secretary General of NATO, made the unfortunate claim that 'Islamic fundamentalism is as dangerous as communism once was ... NATO can help to counteract the threat of Islamic extremism because it is much more than just a military alliance'.[30] It was a statement that cost him his job, but he voiced the views of an increasingly significant political class. Yet, is it really necessary to take the idea of a Southern threat seriously? Almost certainly this is not the case, for several reasons – including basic common sense, insofar as singling out a possible adversary in advance helps to create it. Stirring up the spectre of this threat in the Western world strengthens the conviction in the Arab and Muslim countries that no sustainable and equitable agreement is possible with the West. Furthermore, no meaningful comparison can be made between the South and the East. The Warsaw Pact was a perfectly cohesive and integrated system, being entirely controlled by the Soviet Union which provided 80 per cent of its military resources. In contrast, the Arab world is fragmented, and no one country seems to be in a position to assume leadership. The South is more intent on declaring war on itself, than on turning its attention to the West – and even if it wanted to, it is not in a position to do so. The difference in military strength between it and the West is considerable and is not likely to be reduced in the near future, even if certain Southern countries do equip themselves with ballistic missile resources. From this point of view, the Europeans have no need to fear, even if financial difficulties weigh heavily on military spending both north and south of the Mediterranean. Who are more suited to wield a threat: countries which, by draining a poor economy, could obtain the means to damage others, or those who today possess all the necessary means of retaliation, from naval blockade to nuclear annihilation, not to mention conventional bombs?

In any case, the term 'the South' is, in fact, used to designate only a small part of the developing world. Sub-Saharan Africa, for example, is not included and it is really only the Arab and Muslim countries that are involved, even though, for the sake of prudence or through cowardice, those who favour this theory prefer to use the imprecise general term. But even if only the Islamic countries are involved, the South is much less uniform than is often implied. It is hard to imagine Algeria and Morocco joining forces against France. It must not be forgotten that Turkey is a particularly loyal member of NATO. It is difficult to see what motivation Indonesia (the most highly-populated Muslim country in the world) might have for joining forces with Iran to combat the West! This type of anathema pronounced against the Muslim and Arab worlds will, in fact, only serve to strengthen their conviction that no equitable agreement is possible with the West and this, in turn, can only weaken the position of those – the majority at present – who promote openness and dialogue. This is, in short, the real danger of arguments of the kind put forward by Samuel Huntington in 1993 and which continues to cause repercussions in North–South relations.

In his article and in a later book, Samuel Huntington argued that a conflict between civilizations would be the last phase of the evolution of conflict in the modern world.[31] In the western world after the treaty of Westphalia, conflicts had been between princes, kings and emperors. After the French revolution they were between nations. In the twentieth century they were between ideologies (communism, national socialism and liberal democracy). The two world wars and the cold war were Western 'civil wars'. Today, in Huntington's view, is the era of the clash of civilizations. A civilization he defined as a cultural identity, which is defined both by objective elements – language, religion, history, customs and institutions – and by a subjective element – people identify with it. A civilization can cover several nations or one alone, as is the case with Japan. It can include many related civilizations, such as western civilization in Europe and North America, or Islamic civilisation with the Arabs, the Turks and Asiatic Muslims. Huntington defines eight distinct civilisations: Confucian, Japanese, Islamic, Hindu, Slav-orthodox, Latin American and African. He states that the differences between these civilizations, developed over several centuries, are fundamental, will not disappear overnight and are more dangerous than ideological clashes, because they do not allow for choice of identity – the question is no longer 'who are you for?' but 'who are you?'

Huntington predicts that the central axis of world politics will be the clash between the West and the rest of the world. While the objective of the cold war was to establish a stable strategic relationship between the United States and the Soviet Union, the objective now is to prevent non-western civilizations developing their military capabilities. He identifies a Confucian-Islamic connection, characterized by the export of North Korean and Chinese military equipment to Arab and Muslim countries, such as Algeria, Iraq, Libya, Iran and Syria, so they can obtain the technology required to redress the current balance of power with the West. The rational and thoughtful observer of international affairs should be beware of apparently enticing intellectual analyses, such as Huntington's. First, it should be noted that his prophesy does not correspond to contemporary reality and can lead to some bizarre conclusions. Paradoxically, for example, he could be accused of interpreting the Gulf War in the same way as Saddam Hussein who also saw his conflict with the Multinational Coalition as a war between civilizations,. Yet, the alliances involved were of a different nature entirely, as they involved both the West and the Arab world. Similarly, sales of Western weapons to Arab nations (greater in quantity than those from the People's Republic of

China and North Korea), should, according to Huntington, be interpreted as an 'Islamic-Christian bond'. In reality, in both cases they have nothing to do with civilisational problems but everything to do with commercial, strategic and industrial interests.

Huntington's thesis is merely an intellectually more sophisticated version of the theory of the Southern threat, and is victim of the same fundamental error of analysis – it does not correspond to reality, for most contemporary conflicts are now intra-state, not inter-state in nature. The thirty or so contemporary conflicts are civil wars involving populations and ethnic groups which may differ from each other, but which, generally speaking, belong to the same civilization. In any case, ultimately, Huntington's thesis has a disturbing deterministic streak, because it evokes a predestined history of unavoidable and eternal conflict. He also forgets that there is not *one* Islam, but many, as the war between Iraqi Arabs and Iranian Persians illustrated perfectly during the First Gulf War. Islam is multi-faceted between Shi'i and Sunni, each faction being divided into smaller groups, and also consists of different cultural sub-blocks, such as Turks, Arabs, Persians and Asiatic Muslims.

In a similar fashion, the thesis which argues for the essential irrationality of the leaders of countries in the South, has been used to justify the claim that the rules of deterrence which apply to countries in the North, will not apply in the South. This argument, which was even put forward in the 1960s to condition relations between France and China, is hardly more convincing than Huntington's thesis. It is based on a confusion of values with rationality. Iraq's Saddam Hussein or the Iranian leadership almost certainly have different values to Western leaders but they are not candidates for suicide! They can make mistakes in interpretation or analysis, as Saddam Hussain did in invading Kuwait – but, after all, America's President Kennedy and the Soviet Union's Leonid Brejnev made the same type of mistake in Vietnam and Afghanistan respectively – but he was able to avoid overstepping the point at which his authority and his regime would have been called into question.

The ideas encapsulated in slogans such as the Southern threat, the clash of civilisations, deterrence by the strong against the weak are essentially vague and dangerous theories sharing the common fault in analysis that arises from insufficient familiarity with national perceptions and strategic realities. One of the most useful confidence-building measures that could be implemented in the Mediterranean region would almost certainly be that of creating a joint strategic observatory or analysis centre for the countries of the area, where each country could establish how the threats are perceived and listen to and understand the analyses of its partners. It would be extremely useful to accurately understand reality in order to reduce the power of the imagination which could otherwise lead to real conflict. Indeed, it is astonishing for the impartial observer to note the current discrepancy between mutual, subjective and fearful perceptions of threats between the southern and northern banks of the Mediterranean, whilst being aware of the objective reality that there is no situation of conflict. It is worth repeating the point, made above, that the problem is that at some point, subjective fears, even if they have no objective foundation, can lead to real conflict. It would be interesting, for example, to examine Arab and Israeli views on this subject, for they should have extensive experience of it. Indeed, such an exercise might also illuminate their own vision of the threats they mutually and individually face and thus help to mitigate their head-to-head confrontation!

NOTES

1. *Livre blanc sur la Défense*, Paris: La Documentation française, 1994, p.82.
2. See 'Dissuasion britannique et dissuasion européenne', *Relations Internationales et Stratégiques*, 21, Spring 1996, pp.112–16.
3. Survey by Sofres, May 1996.
4. Pascal Boniface, *Repenser la Dissuasion nucléaire*, Paris, Editions de l'Aube, 1997, p.214.
5. 'Until now restricted to major anti-urban strategy, French doctrine has to change in favour of more selective capabilities directed against specific military forces or sensitive facilities. To do this, it must provide more accurate resources, difficult to intercept, very mobile and with reduced collateral effects'. Advice No.583 on the Finance Bill for 1994 (tome IV: Défense, Dissuasion Nucléaire) provided by the Right Hon. Jacques Baumel (Rassemblement pour la Republicain) on behalf of the Committee for National Defence and Armed Forces, Assemblée Nationale, Paris.
6. Pascal Boniface, *Contre le révisionnisme nucléaire*, Paris: Ellipses, 1994, p.126.
7. *Livre blanc sur la Défense*, op. cit., p.49.
8. Ibid., p.54
9. Quoted in Shai Feldman, 'L'extension du TNP et la maîtrise des armements nucléaires au Moyen-Orient', *Politique étrangère*, 3, 1995, p.616.
10. 'Revealed the Secrets of Israel's Nuclear Arsenal', *The Sunday Times*, London, 5 Oct. 1986.
11. *The Samson Option*, New York: Random House, 1991.
12. *Jane's Strategic Weapon Systems*, Couldson, UK: Jane's Information Group, Sept. 1996.
13. An Israeli analyst presented the capabilities of his country as a factor for peace which would not pose any problem to Arab nations. Avner Cohen, 'The Nuclear Issue in the Middle East', *Contemporary Security Policy*, 16/1, April 1995, p.53: 'Some Arabs, especially Palestinians, even perceive the Israeli undeclared nuclear deterrence as playing a positive and stabilising role in promoting the cause of Arab-Israeli peace, giving Israel the courage to make painful territorial concessions from a position of strength while knowing that it faced no existential threat'.
14. Feldman, op. cit., p.613.
15. Even though the unlimited extension of the non-proliferation treaty which took place in 1995 forbade the participating states to make use of the withdrawal clause in Article X, there is no doubt that, from the point of view of the Arab and Muslim countries of the Near and Middle East, the existence of Israel's nuclear capability would be considered as an event justifying the use of Article X.
16. Joseph Cirincione, Frank Von Hippel, *Ballistic Missile Defences on Perspectives*, Briefing paper No.9, Brussels: ISIS-Europe, Jan. 1997, p.2.
17. Shahram Chubin, 'Does Iran want Nuclear Weapons?', *Survival*, Spring 1995, pp.86–104.
18. Robert Waller, 'The Libyan Threat to the Mediterranean', *Jane's Intelligence Review*, 8/7, May 1996, pp.227–8.

19. Ibid., p.228.
20. Contrary to the claims of Jacques Attali for whom 'manufacturing a basic nuclear weapon is now within the grasp of any sophisticated country, or even non-state groups': *Economie de l'apocalypse*, Paris: Fayard, 1996, pp.37–8.
21. Ian O. Lesser and Ashley J. Tellis, *Proliferation Around the Mediterranean*, Santa Monica, CA: Rand Corporation, 1996, p.37.
22. Pierre Hassner, *La Violence et la paix. De la bombe atomique au nettoyage ethnique*, Paris: édition Esprit, 1995, p.121.
23. 'Perry Disputes Congress on Missile Fear', *International Herald Tribune*, 15 Feb. 1995.
24. IRIS, *L'Année Stratégique-Les Equilibres militaires*, Paris: IRIS-arléa, 1996, p.592.
25. Roberto Aliboni, *La sécurité européenne à travers la Méditerranée* (Cahiers de Chaillot, No.2), Paris: UEO, 1991, p.7.
26. SIPRI, *Sipri Yearbook 1996. Armaments, Disarmament and International Security*, New York: SIPRI/Oxford University Press, 1996, pp.663–4.
27. Pascal Boniface, 'The Changing Attitude Towards Military Intervention', *The International Spectator*, 32/2, pp.53–64.
28. Jean-Christophe Rufin, *L'Empire et les nouveaux barbares*, Paris: Editions Jean-Claude Lattes, 1991, pp.10–11.
29. François Cailleteau, 'Quelles menaces?', *Relations Internationales et Stratégiques*, 12, 1993, p.91.
30. *Nouvelles atlantiques*, No.2692, 8 Feb. 1995.
31. 'The Clash of Civilizations?', *Foreign Affairs*, 72/3, Summer 1993, pp.22–49.

10

The Euro-Mediterranean Security Partnership: Prospects for Arms Limitation and Confidence-Building

FRED TANNER

In its short life to date, the Euro-Mediterranean Partnership (EMP), rather like a roller-coaster, has experienced a number of ups and downs. The 1995 Barcelona Declaration optimistically aspired to the creation of a 'zone of peace and stability' in the Mediterranean region, in direct support for the formation of a free-trade zone and inter-cultural *rapprochement*. However, the rapid and steady deterioration of the Middle Eastern Peace Process in the second half of the 1990s has put much of the progress on hold. Even though the Barak government came to power in Israel in June 1999 with the promise of revitalizing the process, there still appear to be significant difficulties.

This study explores, in light of the results of the ministerial meetings in Malta in 1997 and in Stuttgart in 1999, the extent to which the Barcelona partners will be able to proceed in the domains of conventional arms limitations and confidence-building. With the escalation of violence among Barcelona partners in the Middle East, the platform for security cooperation has become very narrow. But the study advances the claim that there are niches where the EMP can still develop a basis for a future co-operative security regime.

After assessing the impact of the ministerial meetings upon security cooperation, the study looks at the achievements and limits to conventional arms control and militarily significant confidence-building measures in the Mediterranean region. In this context, the study examines the applicability of arms control to regions in transition and it considers what kinds of global and regional arms control-related arrangements are relevant to Euro-Med security co-operation. In its concluding section, the study explores the various domains of 'soft security' in which the EMP could meanwhile prepare the groundwork for the time when the political climate would permit more serious negotiations on arms control and confidence-and-security-building-measures (CSBMs) to resume.

Arms Control and Confidence-Building: Their Relevance to the Mediterranean

This section will look at how security co-operation in the area of arms control and confidence-building can be pursued within the Euro-Med Partnership in the aftermath of the EMP's Malta ministerial meeting in 1997. For this purpose, it is important to first briefly discuss the broader conceptual background of arms control in the period of the end of the cold war.

Current Thinking on Arms Control and Confidence-Building Measures

It is generally an accepted proposition that arms control represents a policy instrument through which states seek to improve their national security. Arms control in general terms has a structural impact on military holdings, an operational impact on military conduct, and a declaratory dimension in terms of transparency. In such a broad concept of arms control, the difference between armament control and confidence-building-measures (CBMs) is blurred. Constraining measures, for instance, can constitute either arms control or a CBM arrangement.

According to Hedley Bull, a classic analyst of arms control whose thinking is still relevant today, the objectives of arms control are to:

- reduce the likelihood of war;
- reduce the scope of violence of war if it occurs;
- reduce the political and economic costs; and
- uphold the moral obligation to combating the militarization of society.[1]

There are two partially conflicting schools of thought about arms control. In the *neo-realist* perspective, the main function of arms control is to redress and stabilise an existing balance of power. Co-operation among states is confined to the improvement (and not the elimination) of a deterrent relationship. In this sense, the purpose of seeking a strong military capability is not only for the objective of winning wars, but also for deterring aggression.

With the end of the cold war, the arms control concept has evolved from the management of military balances to the management of conflict. Robert Jervis convincingly argued that any theory of arms control 'must rest on a theory of the causes of war'.[2] According to Jervis, arms control assumes a greater role in conflict prevention and crisis stability under the conditions of a post-cold war setting. Geoffrey Kemp, in turn, has framed the questions of post-cold war armament control as a relationship between military technology and conflict.[3]

The *neo-liberal* approach sees in arms control a norm-building effort to facilitate the development of a common security regime, which, in turn, may be the precursor to a pluralistic security community.[4] Here, arms control is more a vehicle to shape perceptions of states and less an instrument to adjust their military capabilities. The neo-liberal thinking understands arms control as one avenue of co-operation among states that will lead to the removal of the security dilemma.

Thinking on arms control was substantially influenced by the emergence of regional arms control agreements and CBM-regimes. The bloc-to-bloc agreement on Conventional Forces in Europe (CFE), negotiated during the cold war and implemented with much difficulty during the post-cold war period, is the only example today of *regional structural armament control*. It limits the parties to certain ceilings in their major weapon systems stationed in the European area – defined as from the Atlantic to the Urals. The security bonus of CFE rests on the increased transparency and accountability of the armed forces.

There are, in turn, a larger number of formal and informal *regional CBM regimes* in force today. Such confidence-building-measures may be defined as any step that decreases tensions, or increases cooperation between states. The notion of confidence-building has been used for a large variety of purposes and they can be military, political, cultural, or economic in nature.[5] They all have in common the feature of being incremental, transparent and moderate in terms of their transaction costs.

Applicability Problems in the Euro-Mediterranean Partnership

How can security commitments take root in a region that is still characterized by a culture of adversial politics and the spectre of domestic violence? Cooperative measures such as arms control or CSBMs have an applicability problem with regard to the Euro-Mediterranean Partnership, as the designation of existential threats in several partner states may very well first be domestic and only subsequently external. In this sense, security cooperation in the Euro-Mediterranean Partnership can only progress to the extent that it does not compromise the internally propagated threat scenarios and enemy images of its partner states.

The internal/external security questions are rendered more complicated by geography and by rapid developments in the area of military technology. The short distances between respective borders and capitals, combined with the increasing range of power projection, tends to accentuate the effects of the security dilemma. Proximity tends to give offensive action the advantage over defence. For example, the lack of strategic depth and the vulnerable lines of communication, coupled with the fear of surprise attack require a number of military preparations, all of which are diametrically opposed to conflict prevention and confidence-building measures considered in the Euro-Mediterranean forum. Such military responses include the maintaining of forward defence posture with counter-strike capabilities, the high state of readiness of the armed forces, rapid deployment capabilities and the continuous upgrading of operational capabilities of armed forces.

Progress in military technology allows power to be projected over longer distances with greater accuracy: missiles and military aircraft have ever-longer ranges and improved guidance systems. The extended range of power projection increasingly determines regional security understanding. Israel's worst-case planning and counterstrike contingencies, for instance, include distant countries such as Libya, Iran, or even Pakistan, to the extent that their power projection could reach Israeli soil. Moreover, the possibility that rivals could deploy weapons of mass destruction has frustrated all efforts to obtain some normative control over evolving force postures in the region. For example, some states in the Mediterranean region officially consider chemical or biological weapons as legitimate force equalisers to Israel's nuclear capability.

With such multi-level threats to security and the widespread sense of vulnerability in the Mediterranean region, armament continues to be considered an essential instrument of survival. Most importantly, in some sub-regional settings the threat or use of force is still considered a necessary means to solve disputes. This is an important explanation for the fact that the region continues to find itself in an environment defined by excessive and destabilising arms build-ups. Given the multi-level threat scenarios, combined with sub-regional military rivalries and the continuous militarization of border areas, the application of classic arms control and militarily significant CSBMs in the Euro-Mediterranean region appears extremely urgent, but it is also a highly unrealistic objective at this point.

The acceptance that the major sources of instability in the Mediterranean are of domestic or regime-specific nature would greatly reduce the validity of neo-realist prescriptions to security co-operation and arms control. Indeed, the region lends itself more to a long-term political process to overcome the security dilemma, rather than to hard security measures aimed at deterrence stability. The conclusions of the Malta and Stuttgart ministerial meetings have indirectly confirmed these findings, as they do not venture into the realm of conventional arms control or military CSBMs. However, the Mediterranean Charter guidelines, issued after the Stuttgart meeting indicate the preparedness of the EMP partners to work towards creating *favourable conditions* of future negotiations on arms control and disarmament. For a better assessment of how far security co-operation after the Malta meeting can go – given the evidence it provided of the profound suspicions amongst EMP partners because of the hiatus in the Middle East peace process – it is important first to establish the existing *acquis* of arms control-related arrangements extending into part or all of the Mediterranean basin.

CSBM- and Arms Control Regimes in the Euro-Mediterranean Area

The Mediterranean region is not a vacuum with regard to multilateral or bilateral commitments in the fields of arms control and CSBMs. Security regimes, either in operation or as agreed blueprints, cover the various parts of the area. The EMP should not ignore these regimes for two important reasons. First, their existence will create appropriate conditions for a 'variable geometry' of security regimes, should the EMP arrangements take shape, since parties to the other regimes may have different agendas when it comes to security co-operation under the EMP framework. This will inevitably lead to potentially controversial debates about differentiated or graduated approaches to security co-operation in the region, such as voluntary sub-regional arrangements. Second, the existing regimes can serve the EMP as normative references, thereby helping to avoid protracted discussions or negotiations about the technical or definitional aspects of the commitments envisaged under an EMP-sponsored regime.

European CSBMs- and Arms Control Regimes

The Organisation for Security and Cooperation in Europe (OSCE) region extends deep into the Mediterranean. It includes the Northern Mediterranean states, the Balkans, Greece and Turkey as well as Malta and Cyprus. Activities and commitments under the OSCE's CSBM-regime include advanced notification of troop manoeuvres, observer participation, and restrictions in the number of military exercises. Other engagements under this CSBM-regime are the exchange of military data, the annual exchange of military budgets and verification and annual assessment procedures. The OSCE loosely cooperates with a number of Southern Mediterranean states through the contact group in Vienna and the holding of seminars on the OSCE experience in the field of confidence-building.[6]

The CFE Treaty, now under the auspices of the OSCE, commits 30 states to limit their heavy weapons on European territory in five categories.[7] The major achievements of CFE has been the creation of military stability and predictability in Central Europe, but not necessarily in the South, as a considerable part of the surplus weapons from NATO states have been 'cascaded' to the Eastern Mediterranean. NATO members Greece and Turkey received a most generous allowance for their future military holdings during the CFE negotiations. At the OSCE Istanbul summit in December 1999, a revised CFE agreement was finally accepted. It adjusted weapons entitlements to the post-cold war realities by removing the alliance-wide holding rules.

The implementation of the CFE and the CSBM arrangements created a *differentiated security regime* in Europe, where 30 parties were bound to a structural arms agreement while the remaining 25 states were not. Efforts to harmonize the security commitments were not very successful. The 1996 Lisbon Document requires 'complementarily between OSCE-wide and regional approaches' to arms control with the purpose of creating a 'web of interlocking and mutually reinforcing arms control obligations and commitments'.

Middle East Multilateral Track

The Multilateral Track of the Madrid Peace Process promotes through its Arms Control and Regional Security working group (ACRS) a pan-regional approach to arms control and security co-operation. ACRS includes Israel and its neighbours, as well as the Arab states from the Gulf and North Africa, thereby adding a wider regional dimension to the peace process. Syria and Lebanon chose not to participate. The ACRS working group had been meeting every six months since 1992, but it came to a standstill in 1995. It may now be revived again during the year 2000.

The achievements of ACRS in the Multilateral Track have taken place in four areas. First and foremost, progress was made in the area of *information exchange*. A plenary meeting in December 1994 agreed to establish a Regional Communication Network in Cairo; a temporary communication network began operation in The Hague in March 1995 and an itemised list of information topics was distributed.[8] Second, ACRS approved the creation of regional security centres in Amman, Tunis and Qatar. These centres would assume the function of conflict prevention centres in conjunction with the communication network. An expert meeting held in Amman in September 1995, agreed on a number of tasks for these centres.[9] Third, the Israeli–Jordanian Peace Treaty validated the legitimacy of the ACRS approach. The treaty explicitly refers to ACRS, stressing the need for a multilateral dimension to regional security. It commits the parties 'to create, in the Middle East, … a conference on security and co-operation in the Middle East (CSCME)'. It refers to ACRS as the forum through which a number of arms control-related objectives should be achieved.[10] The fourth achievement of ACRS is in the area of maritime CBMs. ACRS generated two maritime framework arrangements. The first was a regional 'Prevention of Incidents at Sea Agreement' (INCSEAS) whilst the second dealt with regional search and rescue operations (SAR).

ACRS has been paralysed by the Israeli–Egyptian stand-off on nuclear weapons in 1995.[11] It did not hold a plenary meeting in 1995 and 1996. This stalemate has been formalized by the April 1997 decision of the Arab League to freeze participation in the Madrid Multilateral Track. The breakthrough in

Israeli–Palestinian negotiations and the opening up of an Israeli-Syrian track in late 1999 may not necessarily revitalise ACRS, but the above-mentioned achievements cannot be undone, and their successful implementation only depends on political decision. This leads to the possibly subversive suggestion, in the context of the Middle East peace process, as to whether – in the light of the continuing sub-regional politico-military stalemate – the Barcelona Process may not represent a more propitious framework for soft security cooperation, thereby yielding to the temptation of a 'friendly take-over' of the ACRS's own achievements.

Sub-Regional CBM-Regimes

There exist a small number of formal and informal sub-regional CBM-arrangements, both in the Middle East and the Eastern Mediterranean. In the Middle East region, Israel and Syria worked out a number of 'red-line' arrangements in the late 1970s. These informal agreements, sponsored by Washington, were made up by agreed geographical constraints on force deployments, including surface-to-air missiles within Lebanon. Syria also accepted geographical limitations on its air and naval activities in Lebanese air space and territorial waters until the Israeli invasion of Lebanon in 1982. Following the partial withdrawal of the IDF in 1985, the 'red-line' system was renewed with some modifications.[12]

In the Eastern Mediterranean, Greece and Turkey have established a CBM regime covering their maritime relations in the Aegean Sea. The 1988 Memorandum of Understanding on Confidence-Building Measures was designed to avoid tensions and escalation in an uneasy relationship over territorial disputes. They also negotiated guidelines for the prevention of incidents in 1988.[13] In the aftermath of the cold war, Turkey worked out a bilateral CBM-system with Bulgaria, Macedonia and Albania. For example, the Sofia Document on Mutually Complementary Confidence-and-Security-Building Measures and Military Contacts refines commitments made under the 1990 Vienna Document. The complementarity is illustrated by the fact that certain measures taken under the Sofia Document are also reported under the OSCE Annual Exchange of Military Information Agreement.[14]

Middle Eastern Post-Conflict Arrangements

A number of states in the Middle East and the Eastern Mediterranean have agreed to CBMs and other constraints in the framework of conflict termination agreements. In the aftermath of the October War of 1973, Egypt, Syria and Israel accepted a number of commitments on the grounds of the cease-fire agreements that included demilitarised zones, hot-lines, limitation of forces areas and inspections by the United Nations. The Camp David Agreement has extended the constraints and CBMs between Israel and Egypt.

They included early warning stations in designated areas, monitoring, surveillance and inspections of military formations and troop movements.

Scholars and practitioners have underrated the value of such CBM regimes for regional security cooperation for a long time. Indeed, little attention was paid to them until the ACRS negotiation process finally attempted to benefit from the lessons learned from the Sinai arrangements: In 1993, for instance, the ACRS Working Group visited the Sinai, 'where verification measures carried out pursuant to the 1979 Israel-Egypt peace agreement were observed'.[15] Furthermore, during the Barcelona deliberations, a number of officials made repeated reference to the 'merits of the CSBMs incorporated into the Egyptian–Israeli Peace Treaty of 1979 and the agreements of disengagement of forces that preceded it'.[16]

The Nuclear Weapons Conundrum as an Obstacle to EMP Security Co-operation

The regression of the Middle Eastern Peace Process in spring 1997 highlighted the clear limits of the EMP in the area of co-operative security. In more practical terms, the issue of weapons of mass destruction and the 'peace first' condition advanced by a number of states in the Near East before progress could be made in this direction has prevented any serious effort to engage the Partners in a process that could lead to CBMs and arms control. The 'peace first' condition may now be losing its relevance if there is progress in Israeli–Palestinian negotiations and the Israeli–Syrian track in the wider peace process really opens up.

Yet Israel's ambiguous nuclear policy continues to impose serious constraints to militarily significant security co-operation. The presence of operational nuclear warheads in Israel complicates the efforts to promote regional co-operative security measures. Israel argues that its 'ambiguous' nuclear policy is justified as a deterrence against both large-scale conventional and weapons of mass destruction (WMD) attacks.[17] However, Israel's nuclear capabilities are taken as a pretext by Arab states and Iran to pursue their own programmes of weapons of mass destruction. Egypt refuses to sign the Chemical Weapons Convention as long as Israel stays away from the NPT. According to a Western European Union (WEU) report, an impressive number of Euro-Mediterranean states are involved actively in chemical weapons programmes, as well as in continuous efforts to increase the range of their delivery systems.[18]

The linkage between WMD and conventional armament has surfaced in several multilateral forums. The Arab–Israeli dispute over nuclear weapons has stalemated the ACRS process, the only regional effort to work out military CBMs and conflict prevention mechanisms. In addition, the linkage dogma has stymied efforts to infuse more transparency into the armament control arena in the Mediterranean. Egypt, for instance, attempted to broaden the scope of the Register on Conventional Arms to include weapons of mass destruction, and deliberately withheld its data to force the issue.[19] A similar fate overtook the UN Conference on Disarmament. This has failed, since 1997, to establish the *Ad Hoc Committee on Transparency in Armaments*, due to disagreements over linkage questions. Even efforts to ban land mines risk becoming victim of the dispute over nuclear weapons.

Gateways to Arms Limitation and CSBMs

As the above discussion has shown, the crisis in the Middle East and the issue of weapons of mass destruction has caught up with the Barcelona Process. Given the number of obstacles to effective security co-operation, the Euro-Med Partnership needs to pursue its stated objective of peace and security by a gradualist approach. There area number of steps, mostly drawn from the OSCE and ACRS experience, that could establish during the immediate future a more propitious basis for creating a common security regime based on notions such as defence sufficiency, minimal defence, and differentiation of circles of participation and sequencing. The foremost objective would be to foster a culture of dialogue and co-operation in the politico-military sector. This can be accompanied by transparency measures, low-cost military CBMs and region-specific refinements of existing global agreements, such as the Register on Conventional Arms and the Inhumane Weapons Convention.

Creating a Culture of Interaction and Dialogue

Given the diversity of the Mediterranean region, the Euro-Mediterranean process should make sure that participants acquire a common understanding about the key concepts of security co-operation, such as confidence-building, sufficiency, defence restructuring, conflict prevention and risk reduction. In this context, presentations of various perspectives on arms control, as prescribed by the Action Plan, would be a most useful exercise. Such activities would involve the identification of national points of contacts for CBM or arms control activities. Semi-formal military contacts are key to this for they can in future be extended to include *ad hoc* invitations to visit military bases or manoeuvres. These activities represent low-cost CBMs with a high potential of long-term payoffs, as they contribute to the deconstruction of stereotype images of 'the enemy' that still exist in the Mediterranean region.

The objective of creating a culture of cooperation should also target groups outside military establishments. It is important that the politico-military debate in the Mediterranean region is not confined to a handful of officials in the relevant defence and foreign affairs ministries. Vital questions of security co-operation in the Euro-Mediterranean framework should stimulate research, curriculum development, and public debate in civil society and university circles. In this sense, the launching of the EuroMeSCo initiative in 1996 represented a necessary but still not sufficient initiative in broadening the arms control and security community in the Mediterranean region.[20]

Towards a Common Transparency Policy

Transparency is a prerequisite for security building in the Euro-Mediterranean region, as past experience demonstrates. The arms control literature has clearly established a direct link between CBMs and threat perception, for more openness and less secrecy help to remove the cliché of enemy images and other misperceptions and thereby reduce the risk of surprise military attack and unintended conflict. In the Euro-Mediterranean context, in particular, it is important to remove the veil of secrecy that still surrounds military establishments. 'Seminar diplomacy' of the kind discussed above is a suitable instrument that should include non-intrusive items on its agenda, such as identifying national defence priorities, military doctrines, defence concepts, and possibly military budget priorities. Given the salience of internal security in many countries of the Mediterranean region, transparency could be increased by the exchange of information on paramilitary forces, border police and organizations designed and structured to perform security functions during peacetime.

Analysis and discussion of national threat perceptions of Mediterranean countries has been carried out in various forums outside the Barcelona Process.[21] The Euro-Mediterranean setting would provide the advantage that the result of such exercises could feed directly into negotiations under the Politico-Security Chapter of the Process. The creation of a communication network represents a first institutional step in a common transparency policy. The Barcelona Process can draw from the achievements of the OSCE and ACRS. The Vienna Documents of the OSCE addressed the information costs of the parties with a number of measures.[22] Furthermore, focal points of contact have already been established within the ministries of the partner-states in a communications network and the next step would be to agree on a common list of items to be communicated to each other. Drawing from ACRS experience, the Euro-Mediterranean communication network could be linked to a number of regional centres that represent sub-regional focal points.

Furthermore, to promote effective information flows, it would make sense to create a 'Euro-Med Defence Internet Forum', similarly to the Internet Forum for Euro-Med Diplomats that was officially launched at the Malta ministerial meeting in 1997.[23] A Defence Internet Forum should also be linked to a future network of National Defence Academies. It could contain categories of information such as official national defence documents, unclassified military publications and training manuals, calendars and agendas for national defence-related meetings and activities, as well as links to security institutions, such as the United Nations Department of Peace-Keeping Operations (DPKO) or the OSCE.

Arms Register

The UN Register of Conventional Armaments is an instrument intended to promote transparency in the secretive arena of the arms trade. The idea of a Register took on new urgency in the immediate aftermath of the Gulf War, when it became clear how much military technology and equipment Iraq had secretly procured for the purpose of creating weapons of mass destruction and their delivery systems. The objective of the Register is to provide an early warning mechanism by exposing excessive and potentially destabilising arms build-ups. It requires the states concerned to provide data on arms imports and exports for the preceding year in seven heavy weapons categories.[24] The Register is, however, not a binding instrument on the international community, which is why thus far only about half of the membership of the United Nations has provided the required data to the international body.

The compliance record of Mediterranean states is particularly weak. In 1995, for instance, according to the Arms Control Reporter, more than half of the states of the Mediterranean region did not return any information on their arms exports or imports. They included Algeria, Cyprus, Egypt, Greece, Jordan, Libya, Morocco, Syria and Tunisia.[25] The lack of compliance with the Register is particularly disturbing for those countries in the Middle East and North Africa that were listed as importers by arms exporting states. A number of Mediterranean states also abstained from the United Nations General Assembly Resolution 50/70D that called on states to 'provide data for the Register of Conventional Arms in their arms imports and exports and on their military holdings and procurements'. A major reason for such non-compliance with the Register Arab states is its insistence on extending the Register to include items related to weapons of mass destruction.

The promotion of transparency through the Register of Conventional Arms must be understood in the context of the *United Nations system of standardized reporting of military expenditures*. The First Committee of the United Nations General Assembly sponsored a text on 8 November 1995, encouraging all Mediterranean states to participate in both United Nations systems. The standardized reporting of military expenditures had originally been introduced by the United Nations in 1980 and has since been adopted as the official reference standard by the OSCE. The use of this standardized reporting scheme would allow the Euro-Mediterranean states to publish military budget data annually, for instance. This would represent a more solid basis for military co-operation than the sporadic publications of military budgets by some countries and it could also provide an authoritative source of information on this topic, complementing the compilations made by non-governmental organisations such as SIPRI, the IISS, the Jaffee Center or the Al-Ahram Center for Strategic Studies.

Restraints on Inhumane Weapons

The Barcelona Declaration also called for participant states to adhere to the Inhumane Weapons Convention (CCW).[26] This Convention is an important instrument which implements the arms control objective of reducing the scope of violence and suffering after war breaks out, which was discussed earlier. The Convention restricts or prohibits the use of several conventional weapons whose efforts are excessively violent or which do not discriminate between legitimate and illegitimate – especially civilian – targets. It bans or restricts the use of items such as mines, boobytraps, incendiary weapons, and blinding laser weapons.

In recent years, there has been an international drive to reduce or eliminate the large land mine and anti-personnel mine inventories of many national armed forces and to clear the mines that infest large areas of war-torn countries. The Euro-Mediterranean process has, to a large extent, ignored the international activities and lobby initiatives targeting the possession of mines, their production and sale. This has not been so true of national initiatives, however. In the light of the 1995 Inhumane Weapons Review Conference focussing on the mines issue, a number of Mediterranean states have made unilateral statements pertaining to *land mines*.[27] With regard to *anti-personnel mines* (APMs), several Mediterranean states have joined the ranks of 33 states that formally call for a complete ban on APMs.[28]

There have also been attempts to place the issue on the Barcelona agenda. During the Senior Official meetings before the Malta Ministerial Meeting, Egypt suggested that the clearing of land mines should be included in the Action Plan. This initiative that was tabled with the objective of gaining access to EU funds for mine clearing activities in the Egyptian desert, where deployed mines date back to the Second World War. The EU reaction to this initiative was, regrettably, lukewarm at best, as its mine clearing programme has regional priorities other than the Euro-Mediterranean area.

Global Arms Control Instruments

The Barcelona Declaration and the Action Plan refer to the importance of global arms control arrangements for the Mediterranean region. The Barcelona Declaration refers to 'arms control and disarmament agreements such as the NPT, CWC, BWC, CTBT, and/or regional arrangements, such as weapons free zones ... '.[29] They represent an important aspect of regional security co-operation for the Barcelona Process, for they provide a means of exchange, in regional forums, of 'the presentation of various perspectives on arms control', as suggested by the Action Plan. Furthermore, the growing number of global instruments of disarmament increases the necessity for regional action by promoting regional arms workshops or training sessions. Malta, for instance, hosted a CWC training seminar in June 1996 with the objective of preparing national authorities for the technical side of the CWC implementation. Euro-Mediterranean countries, such as Cyprus, France, Greece, Italy, Jordan, Malta, Morocco, Spain and Turkey attended the meeting.

Preparing the Toolbox

In light of the impossibility of penetrating into the realm of hard security co-operation through the Barcelona Process, the EMP partners are nevertheless able to prepare a number of tools that will be necessary for the construction of a future Euro-Mediterranean security regime. Such a Euro-Mediterranean 'toolbox' would contain agreed concepts and principles, negotiation mandates and codes of conduct. The Cairo Declaration of the ACRS conceptual basket could serve as a source of inspiration, together with the codes of conduct worked out within the framework of the OSCE. The preparing of such a toolbox would also represent, *ipso facto*, a confidence-building effort within the EMP. It is, however, evident that the political climate in the Middle East will have to change before these tools can be used effectively.

Conceptual Clarification

The 1995 Barcelona Declaration and the 1997 Malta Action Plan, together with the 1999 Stuttgart Draft Charter on Peace and Security, introduced a number of concepts and principles pertaining to confidence-building or arms control, without, however, elaborating further on the modalities involved. This needs to be rectified and exchanges of views on significance and content of concepts such as *national security, legitimate security concerns, defence sufficiency* and *military capacity beyond legitimate defence requirements* should be included in Euro-Mediterranean dialogue programmes.

Codes of Conduct

The development of such codes of conduct could be transformed into important *standard-setting instruments* of the Euro-Mediterranean toolbox, for they would provide previously agreed principles and commitments with an operational dimension. Moreover, they would reaffirm earlier commitments and put them into an interactive operational relationship with each other. The advantage of such codes of conduct is twofold. First, their drafts could be confined to specific categories of security co-operation, thus providing a way around the linkage dilemma. Secondly, the drafts could serve as an important source of reference for future arrangements – for example, the language of the Code of Conduct on Politico-Military Aspects of Security, worked out by the Forum for Security Co-operation, has been largely integrated into the 1996 Framework for Arms Control and similar action could be taken in the Euro-Mediterranean context. There are a number of codes of conducts that could be developed within the Euro-Mediterranean framework. They include:

- *Code of conduct in the politico-military field.* Such a code could develop the principles agreed upon in the Barcelona Declaration, the Action Plan or the Mediterranean Charter. The code would have to address the link between CBM and arms control regimes as well as the link between CBMs and conflict prevention. Such a code could also provide a basis for the common elaboration of stabilisation measures in sub-regions with latent or overt conflicts. Finally, this code could define ground rules for the institutional environment in the Mediterranean that will inevitably emerge if the Barcelona Process were to make progress in the security field.

- *Code of conduct or principles governing conventional arms transfers.* Such a code could draw from the United Nations resolutions surrounding the establishment of the Register on Transfer of Conventional Armaments and the OSCE 1993 Principles Governing Conventional Arms Transfers. It could focus on the restrictions of transfers that tend to: (1) prolong or aggravate existing armed conflicts; (2) destabilise a regional military balance, and (3) be used for the purpose of repression or support of terrorism. Furthermore, no transfers of arms should be endorsed to any countries that do not participate in the United Nations Register.

- *Code of conduct in military–civilian relations.* This code is, by and large, a neglected dimension of the EMP. The envisaged political liberalisation in Mediterranean countries and their transition towards democracy should be reflected in efforts to increase the *droit de regard* of governments and parliaments into the military domain. A number of measures were presented to Mediterranean states on the occasion of the Special Seminar on the OSCE Experience in the Field of Confidence-Building that was held in Cairo in September 1995. Democratic political control over the armed forces was portrayed at the meeting as an indispensable element of security. Items that should be discussed in Euro-Mediterranean meetings could then include civilian control or oversight over military procurement policies and defence expenditures, legal and institutional instruments for democratic control over armed forces and political control over armed forces in times of crises.

Structural Arrangements

The toolbox approach for arms control and CSBMs would also require some structural steps. First, a focal point – an institution - is needed to administer and logistically support activities such as the following, which would be an intrinsic part of the toolbox:

- Information exchange;
- Verification activities; and
- Regular assessment meetings or implementation review meetings.

The locus of such a focal point institution could be either in the European Commission or in a new monitoring centre created specifically for the Barcelona Process security chapter. Such a centre could also coordinate future negotiations on arms control and CBMs. The centre could also assume other responsibilities within the Barcelona Process, including the following tasks:

- Setting the agenda for arms control-related negotiations or talks on mandates, codes of conduct and agreements;

- Updating a database on the status of adherence to various international disarmament instruments. This work is being currently carried out by the Council of the European Union, which has submitted questionnaires to the Senior Officials Committee of the Barcelona Process.

- Co-ordination with other regional centres dealing with CBMs and arms control. Liaison, coordination and exchange should be assured between the Barcelona Security and Political Committee, the Steering Committee of the Madrid Multilateral Peace Process and the OSCE Conflict Prevention Centre in Vienna.

- The convening of regional experts meetings and training courses in the area of arms control and CSBMs.

In the longer term, the institutional structure of the EMP, which will have to be developed, will have to consolidate the various autonomous institutions and initiatives that emerge in the context of co-operative security. Ideally, the arms control and CSBM structure should eventually be linked to centres dealing with conflict prevention, risk reduction and crisis management.

Conclusions

The results of the various ministerial meetings within the Barcelona Process have shown that the Euro-Mediterranean region is not yet ready for full-scale arms control or military CSBMs. The escalation of violence among EMP partners in the Middle East and the conditionality of some Arab states, in demanding success in the Middle East peace process as a precondition of agreement, jeopardises even the development of very modest security schemes within the Barcelona Process. Furthermore, progress towards military security cooperation will be slow as long as Israel is not prepared to take some tangible steps towards joining the NPT and as long as Arab states see an intrinsic link between conventional armament and nuclear armament, both in terms of security and arms control.

The encouraging aspect of the Malta ministerial meeting, despite the generalised gloom over the Middle East peace process, was the determination of all parties to continue a regular dialogue in the field of security in parallel to economic and cultural co-operation. This study has attempted to show that the Barcelona Process can pursue – along the lines of the Malta and Stuttgart communiqués – security co-operation in select niches that, over the longer term, may lead to the creation of a Mediterranean-specific security regime. First, a culture of co-operation and dialogue needs to be established, followed by a common transparency policy that would reduce the current high level of information costs. Second, the EMP partners should capitalise on existing commitments in the field of arms control and disarmament and pursue low-cost CBMs, such as declaratory measures, non-intrusive military CBMs and region-specific refinements of existing global agreements.

The prospect of entering into an operational phase of Euro-Mediterranean security co-operation will require the general acceptance by the states involved that there already exists an important *acquis* of global and sub-regional commitments in the CBM, arms control and disarmament areas, on which they can build. From this point of view, the Euro-Mediterranean process can take an important step forward by providing these existing commitments with a Mediterranean-specific agenda and operational codes, while retaining the principles of *non-hierarchy*, *differentiation of circles of participation* and *sequencing*. Whilst waiting for the political landscape to become more harmonious in the region, the EMP partners can begin to prepare a 'toolbox' of instruments required for future arms control and military CSBM negotiations. Such initiatives are important, even if they do not promise to yield instant security payoffs. They will at least satisfy Hedley Bull's arms control objective of upholding the moral obligation to combat the militarisation of society.

NOTES

1. Hedley Bull, 'Arms Control and World Order', *International Security*, 1/1, Summer 1976.
2. R. Jervis, 'Arms Control, Stability, and Causes of War', *Political Science Quarterly*, 108/2, 1993, p.239.
3. G. Kemp, 'Military Technology and Conflict', in C. Crocker and F.A. Hampson (eds.), *Managing Global Chaos*, Washington, DC: USIP, 1996, pp.129–40.
4. E. Adler, 'Arms Control, Disarmament, and National Securit', in E. Adler (ed.), *The International Practice of Arms Control*, Baltimore, MD and London: The Johns Hopkins University Press, 1992.
5. See, for instance, M. Krepon, D. McCoy and M. Rudolph (eds.), *A Handbook of Confidence-Building Measures for Regional Security*, Washington, DC: The Henry L. Stimson Center, Sept. 1993; or M.-F. Desjardins, *Rethinking Confidence-Building Measures*, Adelphi Paper, 307, London: IISS/Oxford University Press, 1996.
6. The first seminar was held in Cairo (1995), the second in Tel Aviv (1996). Recent OSCE initiatives also involved Mediterranean Partners in fact-finding missions in the OSCE area.
7. Tanks, artillery, armoured combat vehicles, combat helicopters and attack aircraft.
8. It includes administrative issues, calendars, working group papers, general information on CBMs and arms control.
9. They include: the organization of seminars on arms control and regional security; the encouragement of educating and training on issues related to the peace process and; the support of issues relating to arms control and regional security arrangements.
10. 'The creation in the Middle East of a region free from hostile alliances and coalitions'; and 'the creation of a Middle East free from weapons of mass destruction, both conventional and non-conventional, in the context of a comprehensive, lasting and stable peace, characterized by the renunciation of the use of force, and by reconciliation and good will'.
11. Peter Jones, 'Arms Control in the Middle East. Some Reflections on ACRS', *Security Dialogue*, 28/1, 1997, pp.57–70.
12. Y. Evron, 'Confidence-and Security-Building Measures in the Arab-Israeli Context', in E. Inbar and S. Sandler (eds.), *Middle Eastern Security*, London: Frank Cass, 1995, pp.156f.
13. S. Miller, 'CBMs in the Maritime Area', in S. Feldman (ed.), *Confidence Building and Verification: Prospects in the Middle East*, Tel Aviv: Jaffee Center for Strategic Studies, 1994, p. 79.
14. A visit by Bulgarian officers of a Turkish mechanized infantry regiment in Suloglu was also reported to the OSCE under 'Evaluation visits'.
15. S. Feldman, 'The Middle East Arms Control Agenda: 1994-1995', *International Spectator*, 29/3, July–Sept. 1994, p.71.
16. Paper of H.E. Mr. Mohamed Fathy El Shazli, Assistant Minister for European Affairs, presented at the Euro-Med Information and Training Session for Diplomats (II), Malta, 16 March 1997.
17. Statement of the Foreign Minister of Israel, Shimon Peres, at the Signing Ceremony of Chemical Weapons Convention, Paris, 13 Jan. 1993.
18. The Report mentions Israel possessing a nuclear force 'while others possess very significant chemical, biological and missile capabilities'. It specifically refers to the 'continuing chemical weapons programmes of Syria and Libya', Assembly of the Western European Union, *Parliamentary Co-operation in the Mediterranean*, Document 1485, 6 Nov. 1995, Appendix.
19. *Arms Control Reporter*, 11/96.
20. EuroMesco is an association of foreign policy institutes in the Euro-Mediterranean area. EuroMesco has been adopted as a CSBM under the Inventory of CSBMs of the Barcelona Process.
21. Threat perception exercises have been held in the informal framework of UNIDIR and the more official setting of the OSCE Contact Group during meetings about the Security Model

in Vienna. For the results of the UNIDIR meetings, see *National Threat Perceptions in the Middle East*, Research Papers, No.37, UNIDIR, United Nations, Geneva and New York, Sept. 1995.

22. Creation of a CSCE communication network; an annual exchange of military information on forces, equipment, and budgets; and evaluation visits allowing for the verification of the exchanged data.

23. The Euro-Med Internet Forum grew out of the Euro-Med Information and Training Sessions organized by the Mediterranean Academy of Diplomatic Studies, Malta. The address of the Euro-Med Internet Forum is: http://www.diplomacy.edu/euromed/euromed.htm

24. Battle tanks, combat helicopters, large-calibre artillery, combat aircraft, warships, and missiles and missile launchers.

25. *Arms Control Reporter*, 2/97.

26. CCW stands for *the Convention on prohibition or restriction on the use of certain conventional weapons which may be deemed to be excessively injurious or to have indiscriminate effects.* The Mediterranean adherence record to the CCW is marked by the absence of most Arab states: As of 31 December 1996, the following Euro-Med states were not party to the CCW: Algeria, Egypt (signed), Lebanon, Morocco (signed), Portugal (signed), Syria, Turkey (signed).

27. Greece declared an indefinite export moratorium; Israel declared a two-year export moratorium; Italy declared an export moratorium, which would remain in effect until the international system devised a way to control the export of land mines; Jordan declared it did not produce or export land mines; Malta declared it did not produce or export land mines; Spain declared a one-year export moratorium; Turkey instituted a renewable three-year moratorium on the export and transfer of land mines.

28. France – CCW Review Conference, 3 May 19966; Italy – Statement by Foreign Minister at 51st UN General Assembly, 26 Sept. 1966; Malta – CCW Review Conference, 2 May 966; Portugal – CCW Review Conference, 3 May 1996.

29. All Euro-Mediterranean states are parties to the NPT except: Israel, to the BWC except: Algeria, Egypt (signed), Israel, Morocco (signed), Syria (signed), Tunisia (signed), to the CWC: except Cyprus (signed) Egypt, Israel, (signed), Jordan, Lebanon, Luxembourg (signed), Malta (signed), Syria, Tunisia (signed), Turkey (signed). Euro-Mediterranean states that have not yet signed the CTBT are Lebanon and Syria.

Conclusion

11

Challenges and Prospects

ROBERTO ALIBONI and ABDEL MONEM SAID ALY

The contributions in this volume deal with a set of political, economic and security trends which affect the implementation of the Euro-Mediterranean Partnership (EMP), established in November 1995 by the Barcelona Declaration. Meanwhile, what about the evolution of the Partnership itself and its prospects?

As this volume is being published, four and a half years have elapsed since the establishment of the EMP. The balance sheet is less positive than could be expected at the time the Barcelona Declaration was signed, particularly from the point of view of the European Union (EU). In fact, even though the EU's Mediterranean partners may complain about asymmetries, shortcomings and delays in the implementation of the Partnership, both the economic basket and the special political relationship instituted by the EMP – in which Southern Mediterranean countries were mainly interested – are working. On the other hand, benefits from the European investment in a Euro-Mediterranean security relationship -with its expected feedback in terms of strengthening the Union's Common Foreign and Security Policy (CFSP) – are tardy, to say the least. As evidence of this is the fact that, after almost four years, negotiations on the Euro-Med Charter for Peace and Stability – an agreement that aims to make the EMP more effective in broad security terms – has made very little progress and looks very vague in terms of its potential contents.[1]

An overall evaluation of the Partnership, however, must take into consideration the fact that it has survived a number of very difficult political issues, thus providing evidence that it is considered by both Israel and Arab members – although much less so by Turkey – as a very positive element in their increasingly important relationship with Europe. Furthermore, in 1999 a set of factors affecting security issues, such as the new EU–CFSP structure and the government in Israel, changed. Such changes may produce significant changes in the Euro-Med Partnership.

To provide an evaluation of Euro-Med Partnership achievements to date and to provide some indication of its future, we will consider two main points:

(a) the international context in which the Partnership has developed, the challenges it is facing and changes under way;

(b) the future of EU policy in the Middle East.

Four Years of EMP: Developments and Challenges

As noted above, the EMP can only be properly evaluated in terms of the developments and challenges that occurred in the years since its inception, together with the possible impact of recent changes. Developments and challenges came from both the international context and EMP's own internal development. The most important challenges were related to (a) weak institutional aspects in the EU integration process; (b) the weakness of trans-Atlantic co-ordination and common understanding in dealing with the regions to the south of Europe; (c) the more rapid Western and European co-operation with Eastern Europe compared to the Mediterranean and the Middle East; (d) hesitations in developing horizontal and multilateral ties in the field of economic co-operation; and (e) mutual mistrust with respect to political reform in Southern Mediterranean countries, in particular over human rights and democratization.[2]

Up to mid-1999, when the Treaty of Amsterdam, which provided for reform of the CFSP – unsatisfactory although it may be – was finally implemented, the EU acted in the EMP on the basis of the old CFSP framework. In broad terms, this prevented the EU from acting cohesively and decisively in bringing its weight to bear within the EMP. CFSP weakness has played an important role in shaping reductive Southern Mediterranean perceptions of the EU as well as of the EMP role in the Middle East Peace Process. It also played a negative role in preventing more structured security co-operation from taking place within the EMP. Despite Arab mistrust towards NATO, it appeared at times that Arab EMP Partners considered NATO as a more credible security partner than the EU, should formal security co-operation be established. Algeria, for instance, overtly came to this conclusion. In this respect, the ambivalent attitude of EU member states towards, the Western European Union (WEU), their security and defence structure, was an important factor. Ultimately, while NATO made some progress in its approaches towards its partners in the NATO Mediterranean dialogue, WEU members prevented the WEU from acting effectively so that no progress was possible, both in the WEU Mediterranean Dialogue and in the EMP.

The enduring weakness of the CFSP has not reduced the EU's ambition of playing a more visible political role in the Mediterranean and the Middle East although the absence of such a political status has frequently been pointed out by the EU's southern partners. Many Southern Mediterranean analysts, such as those contributing to this book, stress this weakness as a cause of the EPM's poor performance in the implementation of the proposed 'area of peace and stability'. In conclusion, there is no doubt that, quite apart from other factors in the Barcelona Declaration, the difficulties of the EMP in achieving an understanding on security policies and security co-operation have been generated to a significant extent by the state of the CFSP within the Union.

Another major factor which has had a negative effect on the Partnership has been the absence of trans-Atlantic co-ordination and understanding with respect to the Mediterranean and the Middle East. In a sense, this lack of co-ordination is an aspect of the weak status of Europe's CFSP. In the 1990s, many Europeans maintained that the US did its best to prevent a European security and defence identity from emerging. However, others claim that European governments, not the Americans, were responsible for failing to enforce the CFSP. Whatever the truth, EU–US synergy in the region, explicitly mentioned in the first common goal of the December 1995 'New Trans-Atlantic Agenda',[3] has not worked. The reshaping of NATO's command structure proved very divisive in the Mediterranean. The inability of the Alliance to reach a compromise on this structure prevented the anticipated re-integration of France into NATO's military structure, a factor that would, in general, have been very positive for Europe and the US, in order to conduct a more consistent and effective common policy in the region south of the Mediterranean.

Beside the issue of NATO reforms, there were other differences between EU and the US over the Mediterranean and the Middle East in the 1990s. One such difference involved the status of Turkey with respect to the EU. Other important differences related to policies towards the so-called 'rogue states' – Libya, Iraq and Iran. In general, the US would have preferred to see Europeans linking the Mediterranean area to the Middle East and the Gulf more explicitly and taking more responsibility in the latter arena. All these differences are reflected in the fact that, while the Europeans felt committed to the 'Mediterranean', the Americans – with some exceptions[4] – used to talk more about the 'Greater Middle East'.[5]

The impact of trans-Atlantic relations on the EMP can be presented in a broader context. In fact, the EMP has not only been affected by trans-Atlantic differences over the Mediterranean and the Middle East but also by the fact that, in Eastern Europe, NATO and the EU have acted harmoniously and constructively. Both the North Atlantic Co-operation Council and the Partnership for Peace initiatives have developed well. The same is true for the European Association Agreements signed between the Union and Central and Eastern European countries. Despite differences and recurring tensions with the Russian Federation, the Western allies pursued with determination their respective enlargement policies towards Eastern Europe in the 1990s. The East-South gap, which was to be narrowed by the EU decision to proceed with the Euro-Mediterranean Partnership in 1995, has thus gradually re-emerged. Despite these developments, it continues to be the case that the Euro-Med Partnership ensures constructive political relations between the EU and Southern Mediterranean countries. The Euro-Mediterranean relationship cannot work in isolation, however. Persisting trans-Atlantic differences over the Mediterranean and the Middle East, as well as the re-emerging gap between processes of integration and stabilization north and south of the Mediterranean have clearly exposed the danger of the EMP becoming weak and irrelevant.

Such risks have, of course, affected the political and security dimension more profoundly than the commercial and economic aspect of the Partnership. Although economic, commercial and financial relations developed more quickly and substantively than the 'area of peace and stability' and the 'human-social' dimension envisaged by the third 'pillar' of the Barcelona Declaration, in the first four years of the EMP some deficiencies in the field of economic co-operation cleared emerged. Despite greater interest in the economic side of the Partnership, the attitude of the EU's Southern Partners with respect to the EMP economic agenda has become 'unilateral'. Southern Partner interest in developing South–South relations remained very limited, to say the least. Conversely, there is no doubt that, first and foremost, they sought to develop their own individual relations with the EU.[6] On the other hand, a trend towards politically-based sub-regional coalitions emerged which may prove detrimental to the kind of overall regional economic co-operation the EMP would like to pursue. The rapprochement between Turkey and Israel and the renewed Arab engagement to pursue a common Arab trade area, primarily a political rather than an economic perspective, may weaken the outlook for region-wide economic co-operation.

This suggests that it could be anticipated that the development of horizontal ties among Southern countries would be very slow and uneven. On the other hand, the Euro-Mediterranean free trade area will only succeed if there are some significant developments in South–South commercial and economic relations. Within the region, particularly amongst Arab states, the geo-economic logic of the EMP is really valued and the political use that governments can make of regional economic perspectives tends to be over-estimated.

Such 'realism' can be understood, however. As a consequence of the stagnation of the peace process during the years of the Netanyahu government, politics and national security have reasserted their stark pressures on regional governments. This development hindered international co-operation, let alone security co-operation. From this point of view, the downgrading of the Middle East peace process has been the most important specific factor determining the poor performance of the Partnership in trying to develop co-operative security in Euro-Mediterranean relations.

It must also be stressed that co-operation with respect to human rights and democratization was another issue where there was no substantive progress within the EMP. Furthermore, regional security, human rights, the rule of law, and democratization were further dimensions in which the EU intended to make political investments in establishing the Partnership but was disappointed. Progress here was prevented by a number of circumstantial and structural factors. One of these was the return to 'realism' triggered by the standstill in the Middle East peace process which is discussed below. Other factors included the extremely violent internal conflict in Algeria, which broke out in 1992. This conflict helped to make the implementation of the EMP's 'human dimension' and its democratization agenda very problematic, both with respect to Algeria as well as to the EMP as a whole. In fact, the common policies envisaged by the Euro-Med Partnership to monitor and guarantee human rights, the rule of law and democracy amongst its members could not have operated in a situation of extreme and open violence like that prevailing in Algeria.

Political conditionality – the cancellation or suspension of economic aid to compel Partners to comply with EU notions of human rights – could not be enforced, for example. It was evident that this instrument was quite irrelevant to the ongoing situation in Algeria. Not would only any EU request for the respect of human rights have fallen upon deaf ears, but the application of conditionality could have resulted in increased instability. Attempts at enforcing political conditionality would, therefore, have resulted in another case of ineffective international sanctions.

Most Southern Partners consider political reforms, particularly human rights, as a highly destabilizing structural factor. The window of opportunity for political reforms which opened up at the beginning of the 1990s closed very quickly in response to the upsurge of political Islam and domestic violence. Today, all Southern Mediterranean regimes tend to consider EU insistence on the achievement of political reforms as an interference, exacerbated by European domestic xenophobia, as well as European willingness to provide asylum to individuals and organizations they see as terrorist. Cultural relativism amongst Southern Mediterranean governments also increased in the 1990's, although this was less a cultural than a political concern, for they feared that more globalization would prove to be even more destabilizing. These factors, as a result, have prevented the EMP from developing a common discourse and action over human rights and democratization, an area which the EU had expected to make an important contribution to security, stability and co-operation.

New Factors

A set of new factors emerged in 1999, which may have a considerable impact on future developments. In general, this impact should prove to be positive, as is the case with institutional reforms in the EU. Other factors may prove to be more ambivalent, however, as is the case, for instance, with the consequences of NATO's new strategic doctrine as outlined in the April 1999 North Atlantic Council anniversary meeting.[7]

Developments concerning Serbia and NATO's military campaign in Kosovo have accelerated decisions by Western allies to upgrade the European Military and Security Identity (ESDI) by allowing for its development within NATO. In Washington, ESDI has been accepted more clearly and firmly than expected – despite Turkey's opposition. At the same time, the British government, by changing its long-standing opposition to the idea, has given impetus to the creation of an effective joint European military capacity. This in turn has allowed for the incorporation of the Western European Union (WEU) into the EU, thus paving the way for the setting up of a new common European dimension of security and defence. How this new dimension will be institutionally and military structured is still to be decided. In any case, these developments will make US and EU policies towards the Mediterranean and the Middle East more convergent than they have been in the 1990s and will therefore reduce contemporary East–South gaps and imbalances. This should be beneficial for the EMP.

Another development that may prove beneficial to the EMP is CFSP reform, finally introduced in 1999 The establishment of the High Representative of the CFSP – with its new instruments for early warning and policy planning – as well as improved co-ordination between the Commission and national governments, reflected in the composition of the new troika, should make the CFSP more cohesive. As a more cohesive entity, CFSP should make, in turn, the EU role in the EMP more credible and effective, for it should amplify the EU's authority and speed up decision-making within the EMP.

Unfortunately, this overall strengthening of European and Western instruments is not necessarily welcome to the Southern, particularly the Arab, side of the Partnership, for the Kosovo campaign and the outlines of the new NATO strategic approach that have emerged suggest to the South a less co-operative and more unilateral and intrusive Western and European policy, rather than one based on co-operation.

In reality, the EMP, whatever its shortcomings, was established as a co-operative venture, but their vision of its security component corresponds to the security picture outlined in the new NATO strategic doctrine approved in Washington. Just to give one example: migration is expected to yield new forms of trans-Mediterranean co-operation in the EMP, but is identified in the new NATO strategic concept as a threat which may lead to intervention. Furthermore, whilst human rights differences are being debated in the EMP with a view to consensus and co-operative action, in the NATO concept the same differences of opinion may result in interference and military intervention. The question, therefore, is what policy will the EU adopt in seeking policy convergence with NATO, will it be closer to the declared co-operative values and aims of the EMP or to NATO's interventionist guidelines and objectives.

In fact, the military restructuring currently taking place in NATO has not yet established mechanisms for trans-Atlantic political co-operation and decision-making. While NATO cannot act as the political focus of trans-Atlantic co-operation, there is as yet no such alternative focal point. As things stand, the question is what political purposes will the more flexible and potentially separate military powers of the US and the EU that are expected to emerge pursue? What kind of co-operation, both in security and in other fields, will the EMP pursue, if military policies and instruments are more closely linked to NATO? These questions continue to be particularly relevant to the issues which have divided the US and the EU in the 1990s in the Mediterranean and the Middle East – rogue states, Turkey, Palestine and other aspects of the Middle East Peace Process. These are all political issues which cannot be solved by a stronger and more flexible military organization.

With regard to the Middle East Peace Process, the election of a Labour-based government in 1999, under Ehud Barak as premier, has revived the peace process, which the Netanyahu government had effectively closed down. This good news none the less raises questions for the EU and the EMP. In the context of trans-Atlantic *rapprochement* and a successful peace process, what would the role of the EMP be and how sensible was the contemporary separation between the EU's Mediterranean and wider Middle Eastern policies? Perhaps the EU's policies would have to be revised even before EMP objectives were reviewed.

In fact the Middle East Peace Process is playing a more decisive role than envisaged in the Barcelona Declaration for the EMP for the Declaration excludes EMP interference in the Middle East Peace Process. Yet, at the 1997 Malta ministerial meeting, the EMP Partners accepted that the attainment of a just and lasting peace in the Middle East was crucial to the notion of security within the EMP. For this reason, the EU's role towards the Middle East process will not only be important in the context of future developments, but is extremely important in the present situation as well.

The Middle East Challenge

European initiatives in the Middle East have taken place in three directions. First, despite its observer status at the Madrid Middle East Peace Conference and after customary diplomatic contacts in the Middle East by the European Presidency, the EU appointed Ambassador Miguel Angel Moratinos as a special representative to the Middle East peace process. His mission is to communicate with all the parties concerned with the Arab–Israeli peace process; to monitor the peace negotiations among the parties and to contribute to its success through mediation; to communicate to the parties the necessity of respecting fundamental principles of democracy and human rights as a contribution to the implementation of agreements; to monitor actions by the parties that may damage the permanent status negotiations; and to report to the European Commission.

Second, the EU supported the multilateral component of the peace process and sponsored the Regional Economic Development Working Group (REDWG), which carried the burden of integrating the Middle East economies into the global economy. The EU was also active in the MENA economic conferences in Morocco, Jordan, Egypt, and Qatar and, beside funding and supporting many of these activities, the EU has been the largest financial sponsor of the Palestinian National Authority, with a contribution that amounted to $650 million (1994–99) in addition to emergency funding for Palestinian needs that resulted from the repeated Israeli closures of the occupied territories since 1996.

Third, the EU launched the far-reaching Euro-Mediterranean Partnership Initiative, focusing on the three areas of co-operation discussed above: (a) political and security co-operation in the areas of arms control, regional security, terrorism, organized crime, and drugs; (b) economic co-operation through the Mediterranean free trade area by the year 2010, and a favourable climate for investment, technology transfer, and environment protection; (c) co-operation in the areas of cultural and social development to enhance democracy, civil society and respect for human rights. The EU committed Euro 4,685 million for the EMP during the 1995–99 period and plans new funding for the future. The EU initiative effectively complemented other Middle East initiatives, by bringing Syria and Lebanon into the process of transformation of the Middle East and adding new areas for co-operation, such as the fight against terrorism, crime, and drugs, alongside trade issues as well as political and social development. However, despite this growing European commitment in the Mediterranean, European influence on the Arab–Israeli peace process and the Middle East is still inadequate. Europe's initiative to transform the Middle Eastern vision from geo-politics to geo-economics has not escaped the fate that also awaited American sponsored initiatives for regional transformation.

This factor, in turn, calls for a serious re-examination of the peace process itself, for the consequent deadlock has handicapped the smooth evolution of EMP as well. The deficiencies of the peace process can be summed up as follows.

First, the philosophy of the process is based on gradualism and the mutual acceptance of the Palestinian and Israeli peoples to coexist with each other. Although this approach has merit and has enjoyed support, it has also given those who oppose the process on religious or historical grounds the opportunity to sabotage it at very little cost. This in turn raises serious questions among the majority about the intentions of their opponents. This has been even more the case when timetables set for the evolution of the process have not been respected. This defect has been exacerbated by the fact that the Israeli leadership was strongly opposed to the entire process until the elections in Israel in 1998. In fact, several members in the Israeli government continue to express their opposition to this day. The end result is agreements that are not properly implemented, or procrastination over fulfilling agreements, as well as concessions to settlers and Jewish religious extremists when agreements are implemented, if only in part. It is compounded further by the fact that the final status of the negotiations on the Palestinian question is not defined, so that there is no guide to the way forward for negotiations and opponents can thus seek to insert their own objectives. Such a result guarantees the continuation of the conflict.

The second defect is related to the frame of reference of the entire process, which is often ignored in the detailed negotiations. The international community had envisioned a two-state solution to the Israeli-Palestinian dispute ever since the Partition resolution of 1947. In fact, the Israeli declaration of independence was based clearly on that resolution, which remains the only document in which Israel borders are defined. Security Council Resolution 242 is clearly based on the formula of exchanging land for peace. Israel will withdraw from the territories it occupied in 1967 in exchange for peace, thus allowing the Palestinians the right of self determination. Israel implicitly accepted such a principle when it recognised the PLO as the sole representative of the Palestinian people. However, during the subsequent, prolonged negotiations, Israel more often than not, has ignored this frame of reference and has acted as if the West Bank, Gaza and the Golan were disputed areas which it has the right to settle and annex on the grounds of security, religion or for economic reasons. Israeli settlement policy has ran counter to all legal and moral principles recognized by the community of nations, has increased the influence of Jewish extremists in Israeli society and has fanned Islamic fundamentalism in Palestinian society.

The third defect reflects the structural imbalance of power that surrounds the negotiations. Israel has secured a position of superiority in conventional and non-conventional weapons to ensure peace in the Middle East through fear of its massive military power. To a degree, Israeli violence and the settlement policy were a reflection of the Israeli notion of an armed peace under its own control, which is a nightmare for Arab, in particular Palestinian, expectations of national security. In interview after interview, the former Israeli prime minister defined Israeli peace with Arab countries, including Egypt, in terms of deterrence, power politics and Israeli military superiority, completely ignoring the notion of withdrawal from Arab territories as the basis for peace. Sometimes he appeared to be reversing the land-for-peace formula in order to gain the land for Israel in exchange for giving peace to the Arab countries. This approach weakened the peace process; for the international community, despite its awareness of this strategic imbalance, has let Israel indulge in major violations of agreements that no other party could have achieved, at the price of concessions from the Palestinians that they could not afford without enhancing fundamentalist opposition. In fact, the international community has been ready to accept the perpetuation of this imbalance by ignoring Israel's nuclear proliferation and its refusal to adhere to the Non Proliferation Treaty (NPT). The current Israeli leadership has not yet done anything to counter these experiences.

The fourth defect is a direct result of the obsession of current regional leaderships and elites with geo-politics rather than with geo-economics. For them, history is always defined in terms of the past, not in terms of the future. There is no parallel in the Middle East to the founding fathers of the European Community. Even when Shimon Peres, the former prime minister of Israel, called for a New Middle East, his ideas were mocked both in Arab countries and in Israel, particularly by current Israeli leadership. Consequently, the geo-economic components of the peace process, in terms of the multilateral negotiations or the economic agenda of the EMP, were seen as a concession from Arab countries, as a test of will for Israel, and an aspect of crisis management for other countries. The end result has been a lack of strategic understanding among regional leaderships about the regional future; and the absence of active support for Mediterranean Partnership or for a Middle Eastern community.

The fifth defect has been that the peace process was always a government-to-government process from which popular aspirations were excluded. Even when normalization of relations was envisioned, it was expressed in terms of the economic gains that would inspire Arabs and Israelis to accept each other. However, both peoples are not merely economic entities that look for gains in the open market of global capitalism. Nor are they indulging only in the pursuit of happiness, overlooking the historical and cultural complexes that control their lives. Indeed, it was extremely difficult for Israelis to overlook the historical legacy of the struggle against the many Gentiles who had crushed their dignity over centuries. And, as the present is a mere extension of the past, it was easy to see in the Arabs the extension of that powerful enemy now determined to push them to the sea. It was even more difficult for the Arabs to overlook the historical legacy of colonialism, in which small number of colonial soldiers dominated their lives for centuries by the sheer use of military power and technological prowess. Israel neatly conformed to this experience of the past with its military and technological superiority and its close association with the West. An Arab will easily recognize the question that was asked by an Algerian Sheikh when he was told that the French colonial troops had actually come to Algeria to spread Western civilization and modernity. The Sheikh asked: 'But why have they brought all this gunpowder?' Hearing talk of peace with Israel today, an Arab would ask the same question, only replacing gunpowder by nuclear weapons. These historical memories cannot be dealt with by the peace process alone; nor can they be resolved just by economic normalization. It requires people-to-people contacts that allow for understanding historical complexes, cultural patterns, and human and societal limits.

The sixth defect arises from America's paradoxical role in the negotiations. On the one hand, the US has been the major mediator in the Arab–Israeli conflict from October 1973 onwards. It was the country that supervised the Egyptian–Israeli peace treaty in 1979. It was the country that designed and encouraged the Madrid peace process along its bilateral and multilateral tracks, and in 1994 it oversaw another peace treaty between Israel and Jordan. Even when the Oslo Accords were drawn up in Norway, the US took over the entire process. In fact, the US has guarded its position as the sole mediator in the process jealously and looked suspiciously at any other mediation initiatives from Europe, the USSR, or more recently Russia, either as a complicating factor in its efforts or as outright subversion.

On the other hand, the US, because of its domestic politics, is not an impartial third party to the conflict. The influence of the American Jewish community in domestic politics is far-reaching and affects the foreign policy agenda. Hence, more often than not, American national interests are defined in terms of Israeli interests. This, in turn, handicaps American mediation to such an extent that, at times, mediation between the American administration and the American Jewish community seems to be as necessary as between the US and Israel. Furthermore, the US is a global power and, after the cold war, is the only remaining superpower with world-wide responsibilities and interests. Consequently, the time and interest that the US administration can devote to the Middle East peace process is not limitless. This factor is also complicated by the American presidential and congressional election cycles which create mediation vacuums at critical moments in the negotiations.

Although the lack of progress in the Arab–Israeli peace process was a major reason for the retardation of the European initiative in the

Mediterranean, other reasons also exist. First, despite the expanding process of European integration, the EU is not a state that is capable of defining interests and formulating a coherent foreign policy. EU policy towards the Arab-Israeli peace process has therefore been based on the lowest common denominator of mutual interest among European states. From an Arab point of view, although EU declarations on the principles of an Arab-Israeli settlement are satisfactory; the ever-closer relationship between the EU and Israel calls the credibility of these declarations into question. Furthermore, EU member states have not spoken with one voice when major issues, such as Israeli settlement policy, have been discussed at the UN General Assembly. This, in turn, has placed serious limitations on Ambassador Moratinos' mission in the Middle East. In fact, he has to ensure that his initiatives are not only acceptable to the major parties to the Middle East conflict but also to major European powers.

Second, the EU attempt to complement US moves in the Middle East has led to an abdication of European responsibilities and interests. In many ways European efforts were also involuntarily affected by US domestic constraints. These tend to force Washington to adjust its politics to the wishes of the Jewish lobby and hence to the Israeli government. Under his mandate to track the US, as the European version of Dennis Ross, as Ambassador Moratinos would usually describe himself, he could not depart significantly from the American vision of peace in the Middle East.

Third, European initiatives have emphasised geo-economic concerns much more than geo-political agendas in the Middle East. In a region that is still in the process of transformation, such approaches cannot be sufficient. Neither Israelis nor Arabs can sacrifice their geo-political agendas on the altar of economic gains. In fact European efforts should seek to facilitate the peace process and should not be a substitute for it.

Re-tuning Euro-Med Relations

The challenges just described are not helping the EMP to develop as easily and quickly as it was commonly expected when the Partnership was designed. Nonetheless the outlook of the Partnership – and, more broadly speaking, of Euro-Mediterranean relations – remains positive, provided that the Partners are ready to make difficult choices and hard decisions. The cost of such developments should be judged against the cost of a possible deterioration in relations as a result of the collapse of the Arab–Israeli peace process, possible crises in the Gulf, and the spread of instability as in Algeria or Turkey. The EU is faced with a strategic choice in the Middle East between benevolent indifference and constructive response to Middle Eastern concerns. Its response will condition the success of its Mediterranean policy and the EMP.

The case for benevolent indifference can be supported by the fact that Europe itself is undergoing a transformation. In the last few years, the foreign policies of European countries and of the EU have been concentrating on four areas:

(a) the consolidation of European integration;

(b) the consolidation of the world capitalist system through trans-Atlantic and WTO links towards full globalization;

(c) neutralizing the possibilities of international destabilization after the collapse of the Soviet Union, and attempting to integrate the former Soviet bloc into the world order by expanding NATO and integrating Eastern European countries into the EU;

(d) preventing regional crises from disturbing global development as in Bosnia, Kosovo, the Arab–Israeli conflict and conflicts in the Gulf.

European attitudes towards the Middle East have placed the Arab–Israeli crisis in the global context. All-in-all, European policies have been successful in helping to ensure Israel's security and acceptance in the area and in ensuring gulf security, as well as continued oil flows from the Gulf to the West, and to Europe in particular. The Middle East, given its level of development, does not offer a tempting market except in arms supplies. As oil prices fluctuate and as the West has learned to deal with the consequences of the energy crises of the 1970s, the Middle East has become less important. Arms supplies, however, particularly from the US, France and the UK, have been flowing to the area in large amounts over the past two decades, despite the hyperbole over regional security and disarmament.

The case for a constructive response should, however, be more encouraging. First, Western dependence on Arab and Middle Eastern oil will continue well to the twenty-first century. A recent study by a Houston-based consulting firm[8] indicates that world oil demand is expected to rise in the future. In East and South Asia alone, demand is projected to grow by 3.5 per cent per year through 2000 before levelling off to around two per cent annually in the 15 years to 2015. The study expects the Middle East to provide 80 per cent of this incremental demand, or about 8.5 million b/d in the next 20 years over and above what it is providing today. The US Department of Defence also issued a report in May 1995[9] outlining the enduring American strategic interests in the Middle East. The study points out that the world will become even more dependent on Gulf oil in the early twenty-first century than it is today.

Second, the Middle East is undergoing a painful process of transformation that breeds violence and disintegration. No matter what the reasons for this state of affairs are, the West, particularly Europe, will not avoid the consequences, for fundamentalist and nationalist violence of all sorts will not be confined to the Middle East region alone. The case of Algeria is merely a prelude for what may come. Because of the region's proximity to Europe geographically as well as historically, events in the Middle East have always had a spill-over effect in the North of the Mediterranean.

Third, the Middle East has the potential to become a viable economic partner to Europe although it is not so today. It was in the past during the oil boom days and it could be even more so in the future. With major economic reforms – some already under way – the Middle East market may become more attractive.

If Europe wishes a constructive response to the Middle East, it will have to take a more daring and active role than it is taking today. It is to be expected however, that Europe will be able to become more pro-active as its own integration process moves towards completion. Yet, even now Europe could do more for the resolution of the Arab–Israeli conflict, for example. Any such initiatives, however, should meet the following requirements:

(a) it should contribute to basic European interests in the region;

(b) it should be accepted by the parties concerned in the region and beyond;

(c) it should be in harmony with the basic global transformations in the post-cold war era; and

(d) Europe should bear the costs implicit in such a role because in politics, as in life, there is no free lunch. Any effective European role will require trade-offs and there will be a price to pay.

The general guidelines for European action are twofold in nature:

(a) Europe should add substance to its positions towards both Arabs and Israelis. European declarations should be supported not only by rewards for major agreement but also by a gradual process of penalty in the case of non-compliance. Europe has the economic leverage to do this;

(b) Europe should reach a strategic understanding with the US regarding the Middle East as it did over Eastern Europe and the former Soviet bloc. To arrive at this strategic understanding, the EU should open dialogue with Congress and with the American Jewish community. The purpose of this strategic understanding should be to ensure the implementation of agreements mediated and approved by both Europe and the US.

Fortunately, there are no major disagreements between Europe and the US over the issue of peace in the Middle East. However, the limitations in America's active role in the region, as outlined above, provide an opportunity for more concerted efforts to harmonize policies towards the Middle East and the Mediterranean which are now hampered by the Arab–Israeli peace process. One possible way forward would be to conduct a Dayton-type conference to enforce not only the agreements on the Palestinian–Israeli track of the peace process, and to resume all the other bilateral and multilateral tracks; but also seek to create a general strategic understanding on other major issues of strategic importance in the south of the Mediterranean.

Reviving the EMP requires less the improvement of the EMP itself than a stronger and more effective European policy towards a resolution of the Arab–Israeli conflict and streamlining Western policies towards the Middle East. International and regional issues have caused numerous major difficulties in the implementation of the co-operative initiatives envisaged by the EMP, particularly in the context of the Arab–Israeli conflict. The EMP is a significant opportunity for both the EU and the Southern Mediterranean countries but it can only yield its fruits if the EU is enabled by its member states to reinforce its Middle Eastern policies and develop as a responsible actor in both international and regional arenas.

NOTES

1. Roberto Aliboni, *The Charter for Peace and Stability in the Mediterranean*, presentation to the Informal EuroMeSCo-Senior Officials Seminar on 'Euro-Mediterranean Security Dialogue' organized by the German Ministry of Foreign Affairs, Bonn, 19–20 March 1999 (mimeographed).
2. See George Joffé (ed.), *Perspectives on Development: The Euro-Mediterranean Partnership*, London and Portland, OR: Frank Cass, 1999.
3. H.G Krenzler and A. Schomaker, 'A New Transatlantic Agenda', *European Foreign Affairs Review*, 1/1, July 1996, pp.9–28.
4. Ian O. Lesser, *Southern Europe and the Maghreb: U.S. Interests and Policy Perspectives*, P-7968, Rand, Santa Monica, CA: 1996.
5. Robert D. Blackwill and Michael Stürmer (eds.), *Allies Divided: Transatlantic Policies for the Greater Middle East*, Cambridge, MA and London: MIT Press, 1997; D.C. Gompert and F. Stephen Larrabee (eds.), *America and Europe: A Partnership for a New Era*, Cambridge: Cambridge University Press, 1997.
6. George Joffé, *The Euro-Mediterranean Partnership: Two Years After Barcelona*, The Royal Institute of International Affairs, The Middle East Programme, Briefing No.44, May 1998. For more general comments on the economic relationship, see George Joffé (ed.), *Perspectives on Development: The Euro-Mediterranean Partnership*, London and Portland, OR: Frank Cass, 1999.
7. The Rand Corporation proposed a NATO policy agenda for the Mediterranean in February 1999. Rand is an important American contributor to the debate on the role of the Mediterranean in trans-Atlantic relations. See Gompert and Stephen Larrabee (eds.), op. cit. A set of European points of view are collected in a report issued by the Centre for Strategic

and International Studies (CSIS) in Washington, which includes the proceedings of an international conference on 'Transatlantic Approaches to the Mediterranean: Impact of the New NATO on North-South Perspectives', organized by the CSIS and the Instituto de Estudos Estratégicos e Internacionais (IEEI) in Washington, DC, 7–8 May 1999.

8. Purvin and Gertz Inc., as quoted in 'The World Refining Industry to 2015: The Increasing Importance for Far East Markets', *Middle East Economic Survey*, 31 July 1995.

9. US Department of Defense, *US Security Strategy for the Middle East*, Washington, DC: US Department of Defense, 1995.

Notes on Contributors

Álvaro de Vasconcelos is the Director of the Instituto de Estudos Estratégicos e Internacionais in Lisbon.

George Joffé is a senior research fellow at the School of Oriental and African Studies and a visiting fellow at the Centre for International Studies at the London School of Economics and Political Science.

Azzam Mahjoub is Professor of Economics at the University of Tunis.

Hafedh Zaafrane is a consultant and is also at the University of Tunis.

May Chartouni-Dubarry is responsible for Middle East research at the Institut Françai des Relations Internationales.

Mustafa Hamarneh is the Director of the Center for Strategic Studies and associate professor at the University of Jordan.

Gema Martin-Muñoz is Professor of Arab Studies at the Universidad Autónoma de Madrid.

Mohamed El-Sayed Selim is at the University of Cairo.

Mark Heller is at the Jaffee Centre in Tel Aviv.

Pascal Boniface is Director of the Institut de Relations Internationales et Stratégiques in the Université de Paris.

Fred Tanner is the Deputy-Director of the Geneva Centre for Security Policy.

Roberto Aliboni is the director of studies at the Istituto Affari Internazionali in Rome.

Abdel Monem Said Aly is the Director of the Al-Ahram Institute of Security Studies in Cairo.

Index

ACDA (US Arms Control and Disarmament Agency) 175
ACRS 136, 138, 166, 194–5, 197–8, 201 visit to Sinai 196
Ad Hoc Committee on Transparency in Armaments 197
al-'Adl wa'l-Islah (Justice et Charité) 105–6
Africa 37, 154
Al-Ahram Center for Strategic Studies 200
Ahmed, Aït 115, 123
AIS (*Armeé Islamique du Salut*) 117, 120, 125–6
Alaoui, Abdelqader M'Daghri 111
Albania 195
Algeria 44, 62, 97, 199, 220
 Berber community 115–16
 BP gas and oil 34, 43, 45
 civil war 101
 clan interests 121
 coup d'état (1992) 122
 crisis 40, 67, 86, 113
 debt 27, 118–19
 elections (1997) 97
 FDI 37–9
 free trade problems 20, 22
 health issues 119, 121
 human rights 126
 Islamism 65–6, 72, 114, 117, 122
 law of 'Civil Concord' 124–5, 130n.37
 military regime 115
 NATO and 210
 NPT 178
 nuclear research reactor 133, 178
 oil-rich 118
 political reform and violence 114–19, 213, 222
 presidential election (1999) 119–22
  candidates 122–4
 press, the 119, 129n.31
 privatization 118–19
 Sant' Egidio Accord 114–15
 sovereignty over gas and oil 37
 unemployment 119
Algerian 'revolutionary family' 116
Ali, Ben 113
al-Amaoui, Noubir 102
Amman, regional security centre 194
al-Ansar bulletin of GIA 117

Arab League, Madrid Multilateral Track 194
Arab world
 authoritarianism 54–5
 culturalist approach 55–6
 ingredients of 56–7
 strong state against weak society 57–9
 chemical weapons disarmement treaty 182
 common trade area 212
 developmental debate 78
 elections 60
 fragmented 184
 Islamist protest 65
 legacy of colonialism 219
 middle classes and democracy 58
 military defeat (1967) 57
 NPT 175
 nuclear weapons 143, 174
 removal of biological/chemical weapons 139–41
 role of United States 72–3
 WMD 196
Arab-Islamic societies, democracy and 55
Arab–Israeli conflict 3, 79, 82, 91, 152, 221–3
 Moroccan attitude 101
 nuclear deterrence 144
Arab–Israeli disequilibrium, WMD and 146, 148, 154, 183
Arab–Israeli dispute over nuclear weapons, ACRS and 196
Arab–Israeli peace process 143, 216, 218–20, 223
Arabian Gulf 136, 148
Arafat, Yasser 62, 88
area of shared prosperity (ASP) 10, 11–13
Argentina 175
Armed Forces Committee of the Chamber of Representatives in Congress 177
arms control
 implications for EMP policy 163–6
 Israeli perspectives on WMD 162–3
 national security and 159
 varieties of 159–62
Arms Control and Regional Security Working Group *see* ACRS
Asad, President 64, 69
Asian financial collapse (1997) 34
Aspin, Les 151

Atomic Energy Commission's Military
Applications Directorate (France) 179
authoritarianism 54–7, 59, 64
Azoulay, André, 102, 110
Azziman, Omar 111

Baghdad Pact (1950s) 86
Bahrain 38–9
Baker, James 98
Balkans 135, 150, 193
ballistic missiles 180–81, 184
Barak government, Israel (1999) 189, 215
Barcelona Declaration 5, 9, 11, 17, 209, 212
    arms control in Mediterranean 200–1
    debt question 11
    Euro-Mediterranean dialogue 96
    Euro-Mediterranean FTZ proposals 15
    free trade adjustment (FTA) 12
    human rights 69
    Inhuman Weapons Convention (CCW)
        200, 206n.26
    Israel and 173
    problems over WMD 135
    regional security 134
    WMD, non-proliferation emphasis 143,
        148, 154
    'zone of peace and stability' 189, 211
Barcelona Process 3, 9–11, 49, 168
    difficulties 4
    FTZ and 16
    FTZ and industrial free trade 30–31
    good governance 47
    investor confidence and 44–5
    Middle East 54, 197
    Morocco and free trade 102
    political change 44
    Politico-Security Chapter 198
    security 3, 195
    Senior Officials Committee 203
Basri, Driss 102–3, 111
Belarus 137
Benjedid, Chadli 115, 122
Benkirane, Abdelillah 106
Berlin wall collapse 172, 183
'best practice' 48
Betchine, Mohammed 119
bilateral free trade zones 11
Biological Weapons Convention *see* BWC
Bosnia 221
Bourguiba, Habib 112
Bouteflika, Abdelaziz 123–6
Brazil 175
Brejnev, Leonid 186
Britain 86, 138
    arms to Middle East 221
    Jewish entity, Palestinian society and 79

'know-how' fund for Eastern Europe 47
NPT and 152
nuclear weapons 141, 144–5, 169, 170–71,
    175
British Labour Party, nuclear weapons and
    170–71
Brtish Petroleum, Algerian gas industry 34
Bulgaria 195
Bull, Hedley, objectives of arms control 190,
    204
Bush, President 138, 174
BWC 134, 149–50, 200

Cailleteau, François 183–4
Cairo Declaration of ACRS 201–2
Camp David Agreement, CBMs between
    Israel and Egypt 195–6
Canadian company, waste dumping in
    Western Sahara 46
capitalism 77–8, 101
CBMs 151, 154–5, 161, 175–6, 197, 203
    joint strategic observatory 186–7
    maritime 194
    Mediterranean region 189–90, 201
    regimes 191
        sub-regional 195–6
    threat perception and 198
CDT (*Confedération Démocratique du
    Travail*) 102–3, 107
Central Asia 148, 150
Central Europe, CFE and 193
Centre parties (Morocco) 105, 107–10
CFE 191, 194
CFE Treaty, OSCE and 193
Chamber of Representatives (Morocco) 100,
    105, 109
Chemical Weapons Convention *see* CWC
Chile 35, 44
China 34, 141, 148, 177–8
Chirac, President 169
citizenship 30
civil society 58, 64–5, 80–88, 88, 91
Claes, Willy 184
Clinton, President 139
code of conduct in military–civilian relations
    202
Code of Conduct on Politico-Military
    Aspects of Security 202
code of conduct in politico-military field 202
code of conduct or principles governing
    conventional arms transfers 202
Cohen, Avner 139, 144
Cold War 79, 80, 91, 96, 174, 183
    American–Soviet agreement 137
    CFE 191
    East–West debates during 160, 172

end of 190
superpowers and WMD 145
colonialism 77–8, 219
Common Foreign and Security Policy
(CFSP) 209–11, 214
communism 53, 89
comparative advantage 4, 33–5, 46, 48
compensation 36, 42, 47
Comprehensive Test Ban Treaty *see* CTBT
Conférence de l'Entente (Algiers 1996) 114
conference on security and co-operation in
the Middle East (CSCME) 194
'confidence-and-security-building measures'
see CSBMs
confidence-building measures *see* CBMs
Conventional Forces in Europe *see* CFE
co-operative security 159–61, 197–8
corruption 43, 68, 121, 125
crisis instability 159
critical space, society and the state 77, 84,
88, 92n.1
cross-Mediterranean cooperation 3, 5
CSBMs 161, 164, 166, 192–4
Egyptian–Israeli Peace Treaty 196
gateways to arms limitation 197, 203
arms register 199–200
global arms control instruments 200–21
interaction and dialogue 197–8
restraints on inhuman weapons 200
transparency policy 198–9
CSEM 9
access to European market 18
constraints 27–8
convergence (1975–85) 25
DFI and 26
economic conditionality 14
Euro-Mediterranean arena and 30
external debt recycling 28
fall in GNP per capita index 25
FTA 15
FTZ and 13–14, 15–16, 20–22
CTBT 134, 169, 200
Cuba Sanctions Act 42
cultural development 11, 72
cultural and religious rights 5
customs tariff regimes 45
CWC 134, 142, 150, 196, 200–201
Cyprus 182, 193, 199, 201

Dayton-type conference 223
'de-politicization' of society 56–7, 72
debt or debt swaps, human resource
promotion 27–31
declaratory arms control 160–61, 163–4, 204
democracy 5, 16, 44, 54, 216
civil society 53, 58, 78, 88

Islam and 122
middle classes 58
migrant experience 30
variable geometry 60–61
democratic deficits 3, 96
democratization 46, 53, 72–3, 79, 92, 210,
213
Jordan 60–1, 63–4
Palestine 61
demographic growth, reduction 28
deterrence 144, 159, 169, 186, 196, 218
developing countries 36, 40–42, 46, 77,
180–81, 184
direct foreign investment (DFI) 13–14, 19,
25–6, 36, 38–9
Dlimi, General, *coup d'état* (1983) 100
domestic savings 13
drugs and crime 43–4

East Asia/Pacific, foreign investment 36
Eastern Europe 37, 47, 54, 78, 210–12
economic liberalization 35, 38, 44, 58, 64, 96
economic *rapprochement*, free movement of
capital and labour 29
Egypt 20, 22, 41, 53, 62, 66, 199
ballistic missles 180
chemical weapons 133–4, 196
debt 27
democratic principles 61
FDI 37–9
Islamism 65–6, 67
land mines 200
laws of 49
liberalization 62–3, 68
MENA economic conference 216
multi-party elections 63
NPT 174
Pelindaba Treaty 154
Register on Conventional Arms 197
spending on education 28
Treaty of Paris (1993) 182
US 56, 72
WMD in Arab–Israeli context 140, 144
Egypt, Syria and Israel, agreements after
October War (1973) 195
Egyptian–Israeli Peace Treaty (1979) 196,
219
emigration 24, 27–9
EMP 3–5, 10, 96, 133, 167–8, 189
agreement with EU 17–18, 45
application of arms control or CSBMs
191–3
CBMs 204
control of WMD 138, 148, 165
Arab–Israeli context 138–41
European context 141

CSBMs and 164, 190
developments and challenges 210–15
DFI and 26
forums for WMD 134, 136
good governance 44, 46
highly diversified entity 135
impact on Middle East transition 69–70
  ambiguity, unpredictability and
    reversibility 70–71
  democratic pact 71
  external variable 72–3
  issues in Islamic protest 71–2
  significance of cultural argument 72
land mines 200
liberal vision 31
non-proliferation 147
policy framework for control of WMD
  141–2
  conceptual dimensions 142–9
prospects 209, 220, 223
security co-operation
  nuclear weapons as obstacle 196–7
  'soft security' 158, 189, 195
strategic disequilibrium 137
tools for security regime 201
  codes of conduct 201–3
  structural arrangements 203
trans-Mediterranean co-operation 213
WMD 150, 154, 163–4, 176
employment opportunities 29
environmental and ecological issues 45–6, 48
Ettahadi Party (Algeria) 121
EU
  agricultural products 18
  Algeria 112
  Arab–Israeli peace process and 220
  co-operation with Mediterranean region
    96, 151
  EMP and 209, 216–17
  Euro-Mediterranean issue 24
  foreign policy in Europe 221
  FTZ partnership 20
  good governance 47
  guarantees to non-Europeans 153
  Mediterranean products 18
  NATO 133, 138
  nuclear weapons 168
  official development aid 38, 40, 47–8,
    49n.7
  peace agreements and WMD 153, 155
  role in control of WMD 151–2, 155
  south Mediterranian countries 4–5
  stockpiles of WMD in Europe 152
EU markets, quotas 31
EU–Maghreb relations 102
Euro-Med Charter for Peace and Stability 209

'Euro-Med Defence Internet Forum' 198,
  206n.23
Euro-Mediterranean agenda for action 151–4,
  197
Euro-Mediterranean conference (27–28
  November 1995) 9
Euro-Mediterranean FTZ 11, 13, 212
Euro-Mediterranean fund, human resources
  28–9
Euro-Mediterranean Partnership *see* EMP
Euro-Mediterranean region 17, 213
  arms control and military CSBMs 204
  CBMs 189
  chemical weapons programmes 196
  codes of conduct 201–2
  CSBMs 192–3
  dialogue 54
  free of WMD 164
  human resources 23
  transparency 197–9
EuroMeSCo 4, 198Europe 4, 44, 150, 152,
  180
  CSBMs and arms control regimes 193–4
  differentiated security regime 194
  fundamentalist and nationalist violence
    222
  guidelines for action 222–3
Europe and CSEM region, income gap 24
Europe/Central Asia, foreign investment 36
European Association Agreements 211
European Commission 4
European Investment Bank, soft loan
  facilities 11
European markets, economic dumping 46
European Military and Security Identity
  (ESDI) 214
European society, fundamental values 30

family planning policies 29
Far East 37–8
fatwas of GIA 117
Federation of Professional Associations
  (Jordan) 85
Feldman, Shai 144
FFD (*Front des Forces Démocratiques*) 106,
  111
FFS (*Front des Forces Socialistes*) 115–16
Filili, Abdellatif 111
financial co-operation, political conditionality
  14–15
financial and political transparency 15, 49
First World War 79, 160
FIS (*Front Islamique du Salut*) 114–17,
  120–25
FLN (Algerian party) 115–16
foreign distrust, political interference 33

former Soviet Union 37, 137
Forum for Security Co-operation 202
Framework for Arms Control (1996) 202
France 79, 86, 138
  Algeria and Morocco 184
  arms control plan 138–9
  arms to Middle East 221
  CWC and 201
  NPT and 152, 169
  nuclear weapons 141, 145, 168–9, 170,
    171–2, 175
  terrorism (1998) 181
  White Paper on Defence (1994) 170, 172
free trade 16, 20–22, 24
free trade adjustment (FTA) 12–13, 15–17,
  19–23, 47
Free Trade Zone *see* FTZ
FTZ 3–5
  economic activity and public finance 18
  foreign investment and 14
  inter-cultural *rapprochement* 189
  liberalization and 17–18
  market economy principles 16–17
  migration flows and 23
  objectives for shared prosperity 11–12
  principles for implementation 12
  questions about 15–16
FTZ adjustment, economic consequences and
  social impacts 17–19
FTZ and economic convergence, migratory
  pressure 24–6
fundamental freedoms 10, 15

Gates, Robert 177
Gaza 61, 80, 217
Geneva protocol (1923) on chemical
  weapons 182
German experiment, vocational training to
  Portuguese 30
GIA (*Groupe Islamique Armé*) 117, 120
globalization 30, 213, 221
GNP 24–5
Golan 217
good governance 4, 46, 49
governments, rent-seekers 34
Greece 24–6, 37, 193, 195, 199, 201
Green Party-Socialist Party declaration
  (1997) 171
Gulf oil 221
Gulf states 56, 164, 194, 211, 220
Gulf War 57, 64, 79, 84, 100–101, 163,
  172–3, 178–9, 185–6, 199
  ground-to ground missiles 181
Gur, General 144 *Ha'aretz* (Israeli daily) 175

The Hague, temporary communication

  network 194
Hamas 69, 89, 116–17
Hanoun, Louisa 114
Hashemites, Muslim Brotherhood and 89–90
Hassan II, King 97, 100, 103, 112
Hassan II University, student demonstrations
  (1997) 105
Hassner, Pierre 179
Hersh, Seymour 173
High State Council (Algeria) 114
Hizbullah 69
HMI (*Harakat li'l-Mujtama'is Silm*) 115–16
Holum, John (director of ACDA) 175
Houston-based consulting firm study of oil
  demand 221
human resource promotion, debt or debt
  swaps 27–31
human rights 3, 5, 10, 15–16, 58–9, 216
  Algeria 126
  Southern Mediterranean 45, 213
Huntington, Samuel, predictions for unrest
  185–6
Hurd, Douglas 141
Hussein, King, elections (1989) 64, 66–7, 85
Hussein, Saddam, WMD and UN 146,
  178–9, 185–6
Hyde-Price, Adrian 143
hydrocarbons, investments 36, 41, 45, 121

IAEA 133, 139, 174, 176–8
Ibrahimi, Taleb 123
identity 30
IISS 200
Ikhwan al-Muslimin (Muslim Brotherhood)
  63, 66, 67–9, 75n.34 and 36, 88–90
illiteracy 3
IMF 63, 101, 118, 120–21
immigrant training programmes 29
immigration, citizenship 30
independent legal systems 35–6, 46–9
India 143, 148, 175
India–Pakistan relations, WMD and 145
'indigenization' 34
indirect taxation 19, 22
industrial restructuring, unemployment and
  19
INF Treaty 161
Infitah (opening-up) 63–4
information exchange, ACRS 194
Inhuman Weapons Convention 197
Institut de Relations Internationales et
  Stratégiques (IRIS) 170
Institut des Hautes Etudes de la Défense
  Nationale 181
intellectual property rights 41
International Atomic Energy Agency *see*

IAEA
international migration, Euro-Mediterranean
  23
investment 22, 121, 150
  codes 35, 37–40, 41
  direct foreign 13–14, 19, 25–6, 34, 36,
    38–9
  hydrocarbon 36, 41, 45, 121
  insurance 48
  legal status 36–7, 46
  mining 36, 41
  oil and gas sectors 40
  political dimension 42–4
  private foreign 4
  South Mediterranean region 33
investor
  confidence 34, 47
  distrust 33
  objectives 35–6
  political risk 43
  private, problems of 33
Iran 43, 69
  arms control 140, 164, 167
  ballistic missiles 180
  chemical weapons 182–3
  FDI 38
  Indonesia and 184
  Israel and 192
  nuclear capability 133–4, 145, 176–7
  Treaty of Paris (1993) 182
  WMD 148, 150
Iran–Iraq war (1980–88) 145, 181–8
Iran–Libya Sanctions Act (ILSA) 42
Iraq 62, 64, 145
  1923 War Protocol 176
  arms control 167, 175
  ballistic missiles 180
  chemical weapons 133, 182
  confidence-building 164
  crippled nuclear programme 133
  direct foreign investment 37–9
  international embargo 59
  Jordan's attitude to 84–6, 91
  NPT/IAEA experience of 162–3, 179
  removal of WMD 137
  Treaty of Paris (1993) 182
  UN sanctions 43
  UNSCOM and 176
  WMD 199
Islamism
  challenge to Arab states 71, 73, 122
  Maghreb countries 97
  political transition 64–6
  rise of 53, 55, 60
Israel 11, 22, 64, 79, 86
  ACRS and 194

arms control 167
ballistic missiles 180
closure of occupied territories 216
democratization in Palestine and 90
FDI 34, 37–9
Gaza *intifada* and 80
ground-to-ground missiles against 181–2
invasion of Lebanon (1982) 195
MTCR and 134, 150
'no–first use 141
NPT and 139–40, 154, 173–5, 182, 196,
  204, 218
'nuclear fog' 173, 175, 196
nuclear weapons 173–4, 196
Palestine issue 40
peace process and 72, 138
perspectives on WMD arms control 162–3
'red line' arrangements 195
'security space' 159, 164
Treaty of Paris (1993) 182
use of nuclear weapons (1973) 145
WMD 133, 136, 139–40, 143, 143–5,
  148–9, 217–18
WMDFZ 163
worse-case planning 192
Israel–Egypt peace agreement 196
Israeli–Arab conflict 59
Israeli–Egyptian stand-off on nuclear
  weapons (1995) 194
Israeli–Jordanian Peace Treaty 67, 80, 85,
  194
Israeli–Palestinian negotiations, ACRS and
  195
Israeli–Syrian track, ACRS and 195
Istiqlal 98–9, 103–5, 107–11
Italy 201

Jaffee Center 200
Jericho 61
Jervis, Robert 190
Jordan 20, 22, 53, 79, 199
  after elections (1989) 83–4
  authoritarianism before (1989) 83
  CWC 201
  democratic pact 71
  democratization 61, 63–4
  economic restructuring 91
  election (1993) 90
  failure of statist policies 80
  foreign direct investment 38–9
  Islamism 65, 66, 84–5, 89
  Islamist victory (1989) 88
  kinship pattern in voting 86–7
  liberalization 62, 64, 80, 84–6
  MENA economic conference 216
  multi-party elections 63, 67

Muslim Brotherhood 89
NGOs 80
peace treaty with Israel (1994) 67, 80, 85, 194
Press Association 85–6, 92n.10
US and 72, 91
Juppé, Alain 181

Kazakhstan 137
Kemp, Geoffrey 190
Kennedy, President 186
Khatib, Abdelkrim 103, 106
Korea 78
Kosovo 214, 221
al-Kutla (democratic bloc) parties 98, 103–5, 107–10
Kuwait 38–9, 179, 186

labour abuse concerns 46
labour costs 35
labour legislation 48
labour qualification and mobility 29
Lamari, General Mohammed 120
Latin America 34, 37, 78, 140
Latin America/Caribbean, foreign investment 36
law and governance 44–6
Lebanon 38–9, 53, 58, 79
civil war (1975) 62, 80
democracy 60–1, 62, 84
democratic pact 71
Islamism 65, 66
surface-to-air missiles within 195
Treaty of Paris (1993) 182
voting patterns 87
legal status of institutions 33
legal transparency, political stability 45
Libya
ballistic missiles 180
chemical weapons 133–4, 178, 183
CSBM/ arms control 164, 199
Foreign direct investment 38–9
Israel and 192
Treaty of Paris (1993) 182
UN sanctions 43
London Declaration (1990) 141

Macedonia 195
Madini, Abbasi 120
Madrid Multilateral Peace Process 194, 203, 216, 219
Maghreb 5, 54, 59, 97, 112, 150
Mallaby, Sir Christopher 170
Malta 182, 193, 201
ministerial meeting (1997) 189–90, 192, 198, 200–201, 204

market restrictions 4
Mashreq 5, 54, 59, 77–80, 91
Massachusetts Institute of Technology 145
Mauritania 27, 38–9
MDS (*Mouvement Démocratique Socialiste Tunisia*) 113
MDS (*Mouvement Démocrate-Socialiste Morocco*) 107
MEADS (Medium Extended Air Defence System) project 181
MEDA programmes 4, 11, 14, 47
Mediene, General Toufik 120
Mediterranean Charter guidelines 192, 202
Mediterranean countries,
anti-personnel mines (APMs) 200
arms control and confidence-building 190–91
Arms Control Reporter 199
chemical or biological weapons and 192
liberalization and adjustment 17
security concerns 150
WMD 167
Memorandum of Understanding on Confidence-and-Security Building Measures (1988) 195
MENA economic conferences 216
Mésures d'Adjustement programmes *see* MEDA programmes
Mexico crash (1994) 34
Mezrag, Madani 120
Middle East 201
arms imports 199
BWC and CWC 139–40
challenge 216–20
civil society and democracy 53, 54–5
corruption 43
EMP and 235
European attitudes 220–21
foreign investment 4, 33, 35, 40, 48
instabilities 150
investment codes 37
Israel, dominance of conflict 72
Israel as only nuclear power 146
labour costs 46
NPT, accession of to 138–9
nuclear free zone 174–5, 187n.13
nuclear weapons 134
peace process 34, 154, 163, 204, 216
EMP role 210, 215
hiatus in 189, 192, 196, 213
political transparency 35
power sharing 71
tension over Israel's nuclear capacity 182
zone free of WMD 134, 154
Middle East multilateral track 194–5
Middle East/North Africa, foreign investment 36

Middle Eastern post-conflict arrangements
  195–6
migration 5, 14, 23, 30, 31n.6, 38, 56
Missile Technology Control Regime *see*
  MTCR
Mitterand, President 139, 169, 172–3
MNP (Moroccan centre party) 108–11
modernization 30, 57, 77–8
Monde, Le 173
Moratinos, Ambassador 220
Morocco 20–22, 25, 97, 199
  anti-drugs/anti-smuggling campaign
    (1996) 44
  CWC meeting 201
  debt 27, 100–101
  elections (1997) 97, 99, 105–12
  FDI 37–9
  Islamism 65, 101, 103, 105–6
  the *Makhzen* 100, 102, 110–12, 127n.3
  MENA economic conference 216
  political 'alternance' 104, 107
  regionalization 100
  spending on education 28
  unemployment 101, 127n.6
  virtues and shortcomings of consensus
    97–103
MPDC (*Mouvement Populaire Démocratique
  et Constitutionnel*) 103, 106, 109
MTCR 134, 150, 180
Mubarak, Husni 67
Muhammad VI 98
multi-fibre agreements 21
multilateral co-operative free trade region 6
Multilateral Investment Agreement 41
Multinational Coalition, war between
  civilizations 185
Muslim Brotherhood, Hashemites and 89–90
Mutually Complementary CSBMs and
  Military Documents 195

Nahnah, Mahfoud 117
Nasser 54, 60, 67, 86, 89
National Defence Academies 198
National Democratic Party (NPD) 63
National Movement (Morocco) 99–100
nationalization 34, 36, 40–43, 45, 47
NATO 133, 136, 211, 214–15
  Arab mistrust 210
  expansion 221
  Handbook 141
  Islamic extremism and 184
  reduction of nuclear weapons in Europe
    152
  security guarantees for non-NATO
    members 153
NBC weapons 167

neo-liberal arms control 191
neo-realist arms control 190
Netanyahu government, NPT and 175, 212
'New Trans-Atlantic Agenda' (1995) 211
'no-first use' 141, 160
non-governmental organizations (NGOs) 80,
  91, 200
non-oil investor 34, 45
Non-Proliferation Treaty *see* NPT
non-rent-related operations, investment 36
North Africa 4, 35, 40, 43, 199
  ACRS 194
  EMP and 135
  European gas grid 48
  foreign investment 33–4, 48
  investment codes 37
  labour costs 46
  political transparency 35
  uncertainties 150
  WMD 178
North Atlantic Co-operation Council 211
North Atlantic Council anniversary meeting
  (1999) 214, 223n.7
North Atlantic Treaty Organization *see*
  NATO
North Korea 177
Northern Europe 135
NPT 133–4, 141–2, 149–51, 155, 168, 175,
  200, 206n.20
  Extension and Review Conference (1995)
    173
nuclear, biological and chemical weapons *see*
  NBC weapons
nuclear stockpiles, IAEA and 140
nuclear-free zones of Rarotongo and
  Pelindaba 169

OADP (*Organisation de l'Action
  Démocratique et Populaire*) 99, 104, 110
obsolescing bargain 41, 41–2, 45–6
official development aid 38, 40, 47–8, 49n.7
oil 59, 150, 222
  Algeria and 45, 118
  investment 36, 40
  revenues, effect of 56–7
  shocks (1970s) 41
  world dependence on Gulf 221
Oman 38–9
'openness' 35
operation *Desert Shield* 179
operation *Desert Storm* 179
operational arms control 160–61, 164
Organization of African Unity (OAU) 163
Organization of American States (OAS) 163
Organization for Security and Co-operation
  in Europe *see* OSCE

OSCE 136, 193, 197–9, 201–202
  Annual Exchange of Military Information
    Agreement 195
  Conflict Prevention Centre (Vienna) 203
  Istanbul summit (1999) 193
  Lisbon Document (1996) 194
Oslo Agreement 61–2, 219
over-armament 59

Pakistan 143, 148, 174, 192
Palestine 53, 60–62, 69, 71, 79–80, 84, 87
Palestine Liberation Organization (PLO) 80,
  88, 217
Palestine National Authority 88–9
Palestinian uprising (the *intifada*) 63
Palestinian–Israeli track of the peace process
  223
pan-Euro-Med regime, control of WMD
  149–50
Partnership for Peace initiatives 211
peace 10–11
Pelindaba Treaty 154
Peres, Shimon 173, 175, 218
Perry, William 180
Persian Gulf 177
PND (*al-Wifaq* party) 107–9
Polisario Front 98
political conditionality 14–15
political democracy, capitalism 77
political dialogue, convergence between
  partners 16
political instability 35
political liberalization 44, 55, 59, 62, 69, 77,
  80, 113
  Arab countries and Gulf war 79
  economic liberalization 96
political pluralism 15–17, 56, 60, 191
political risk, oil companies 45
political stability, legal transparency 45
Portugal 24–5, 26, 37, 182
post-cold war 190–91, 193, 222
PPS/PRP (*al–Kutla* party) 109, 111
'Prevention of Incidents at Sea Agreement'
  (INCSEAS) 194
Principles Governing Conventional Arms
  Transfers 202
privatization 33, 37, 118–19
professional training 29
property rights 40–41, 47
PRP (*Parti de Renouveau et du Progrès*) 106
PSD (*Parti Social-Démocratique*) 99, 104,
  106
PT (*Parti des Travailleurs*) 116
public expenditure cutbacks, investment and
  22
purchasing power parity (PPP) 24–5

purposeful attack 159

Qadhafi, Colonel 178
Qatar 38–9, 194, 216

'*rahma*' (clemency) 125
rates-of return 4, 35–6
RCD (*Rassemblement Culturelle
  Démocratique*) 116, 121
'red lines' 61, 64, 195
Regional Communication Network (Cairo)
  194
Regional Economic Development Working
  Group (REDWG) 216
regional search and rescue operations (SAR)
  194
regional structural armament control 191
Register on Transfer of Conventional
  Armaments 202
rent-seeking 34–5
rentier economy 54
repatriation of profits 34–5
restructuring 30, 35, 38, 48, 80, 91, 97
retention of profits 43
risk premium 14
RND (*Rassemblement Nationale
  Démocratique*) 115–16
RNI (*Rassemblement National des
  Independents*) 104–5, 107, 110–11
'rogue states' (Libya, Iraq and Iran) 211, 215
Rome Platform (Sant' Egidio Accord)
  114–15, 122
Ross, Dennis 220
Rufin, Jean-Christophe 183
rule-of-law 3–4, 10–11, 15–16, 36, 43, 48
  Algeria and 118
  EMP 213
  good governance 44
  Morocco and 102
rules of trade, cultural diversity and 15
Russia 175

Sabin, Philip 144
Sadat, Anwar 67
Safty, Adel 144
SALT-I Treaty 162
sanctions 43, 47
'sanctity of contract' 41, 43
Saudi Arabia 37, 38–9
Sayed, Aly Maher El 173
Sayigh, Yazid 143
Second Gulf War 59, 79, 86, 137–8, 145,
  179, 182
Second World War 78, 181, 200
secularism 30, 58
Security Council Resolution 242 217

Segal, Gerald 144
Serbia 214
Shaker, Sharif Zeid ben 85
shared prosperity 10–11
   free trade 10, 11–13
   gamble of economic partnership 24
   peace, stability and security 16
Shari'a law 65, 68, 90
Singapore 75, 78
SIPRI 200
smuggling 43–4
Sofia Document 195
solar energy 48
Somalia 182
South Africa 137
South Asia 34, 36–7, 136
South East Asia 34, 37
South and East Mediterranean *see* CSEM
South Mediterranean 4–5, 54, 209
   democratic change 44
   economic restructuring 4
   foreign investment 37–8
   free trade areas 45
   independent legal systems 47
   intellectual property rights 41
   international conventions 48
   investment 33
   PPP 25
   social impact of FTZ 21
   Value Added Tax 45
South, the 92, 183–4, 193
South–North war risk 181
South–South 4, 179, 181–2, 212
Southern Europe 135
sovereign immunity 42
Soviet Union 78, 151–2, 160, 172, 174, 184, 221
Spain 24, 26, 37, 201
stability 10–11, 36, 43, 79, 91, 113
'stabilization clauses' 42
START II Treaty (1993) 152
status of foreign property rights 40
structural arms control 161, 163
Stuttgart ministerial meeting (1999) 189, 192, 201, 204
Sub-Saharan Africa 36, 184
Sudan 38–9
Suez Canal Company nationalization 86
Suez canal levies 56
Syria 53, 62, 66, 199
   ballistic missiles 180
   chemical weapons 133–4
   coup (1966) 82
   CWC 154
   democracy 60–61
   FDI 38–9

   fragmentation by colonial powers 79, 91
   free trade difficulty 20, 22
   Hama massacre (1982) 69
   Islamism 65, 69, 83, 89
   liberalization 64, 79, 80–82, 87
   Majlis al-Sha'ab 64
   Muslim brotherhood 89
   peace process with Israel 73
   political parties 82–3
   'red line' arrangements 195
   Treaty of Paris (1993) 182
   WMD and 140, 145, 178
Syrian–Lebanese relations 80

Taif national *entente* pact (1989) 62, 66, 75n.27
tariff barriers 11, 45
al-Tawhid wa'l-Tajdid (Unity and Renovation) 103, 105–6
tax holidays 35
technologies 160
Third Wave of capitalism 77
Third World 77–8, 91
Tlatelolco Treaty (Latin America 1967) 140
trade barrier removal 18
   difficulties 20
   impact on public expenditure 22–3
   loss of fiscal earnings 19, 21–2
trade liberalization, economic flexibility 19
trade unions 48, 60
training programmes, movement of labour 21
Trans-Maghreb pipeline 48
TransMed pipeline 48
transparency 15, 35, 45–6, 49, 164, 190, 197–9
   accountability in commercial administrations 35, 44, 47
transport costs 35
Treaty of Amsterdam 210
treaty obligations 42
Treaty of Paris (1993) 182
Tunis, regional security centre 194
Tunisia 112–14, 199
   1996 reforms 97
   debt 27, 44, 77
   FDI 37–9
   free trade difficulties 20, 22
   FTZ and 19–21
   Islamic movement 112–14, 128n.31
   National Pact (1988) 112, 128n.20
   political liberalization 113
   PPP 25
   spending on education 28
   structural adjustment programme (1980s) 23
Turkey 11, 25, 34, 214, 220

arms control 140
CWC meeting 201
FDI 37–9
Greece and CBM regime 195
NATO 136
OSCE 193
rapprochement with Israel 212
transport links 150
Treaty of Paris (1993) 182
Turkish–Greek conflict 152

UC (*Union Constitutionelle*) 105, 107
UGTA (General Union of Algerian Workers)
116
UGTM (*Union Générale des Travailleurs
Marocains*) 102
Ukraine 137
UN Conference on Disarmament 197
UN Department of Peace-Keeping
Operations (DPKO) 199
UN General Assembly 139
Resolution 50/70D 199
UN inspections 195
UN Register on Conventional Arms 197, 199
UN resolutions 202
UN sanctions 43
UN Security Council, Middle East peace
negotiations 138–9
UN Security Council Resolution,
687 (1990) 176
784 (1992) 178
UN Special Commission (UNSCOM) 163,
176
UN World Report on Development, Algeria
and 118
unemployment 3, 19, 27, 119
United Arab Emirates (UAE) 38–9
United Nations system of standardized
reporting of military expenditure 199
United States 34, 44, 91, 170
Arab world and 72–3
arms control proposals 138–9
arms to Middle East 221
compensation and 42
EMP and 164
influence of Jewish community 219–20
legal extra-territoriality 42–3
NPT 175
nuclear ambitions in Arab states 174
nuclear bomb on Japan 143, 145
nuclear weapons 152
role in EMP and WMD 136, 158
Russian nuclear power stations to Tehran
177
Vietnam War 145
US Office of Technology Assessment 133

USFP *Union Socialiste des Forces
Populaires* (Socialist Union of Popular
Forces) 98–9, 101, 103–5, 107–11

Value Added Tax 45
Vanunu, Mordechai 133, 173
Vienna Document (1990) 195, 198, 203

Wafd, the 68
Waltz, Kenneth 143
Warsaw Pact 184
water 59
Weapons of Mass Destruction *see* WMD
Weapons of Mass Destruction Free Zone *see*
WMDFZ
West Bank 64, 80, 88, 217
Western European Union (WEU) 196, 210,
214
Western Sahara conflict 98, 111
Western societies 77, 91, 174
Arab societies and 59
ballistic missiles 180
capitalist evolution and 88
myth of southern threat 183
nuclear weapons and Soviet Union 147
tank armies in East–West negotiations 162
al-Wifaq (l'Entente) 103–5, 107
Wisner, Frank 174
WMD 133
characteristics 135
effect on global and regional security
144–5
elimination by Arabs, Turks and Israelis
153
liberal arguments for control 142–3
North Africa 178
outcomes of conflicts 148–9
'peace first' condition 196
realist arguments about 143–4, 213
regional capabilities 176–8
strategy of equilibrium
concept of linkages 147–8, 155
non-proliferation and 146–7, 155
restricting arms 'transfers' 148
structural dimensions of control 149–50,
155
use of and political regime 145–6
World Bank 35, 45, 48, 63, 91
report on Morocco 98, 101
World Trade Organisation (WTO) 41–2, 46,
48, 221

Yassin, Abdel Salam 105–6
Yemen 38–9, 58, 65
Yusufi, Abderrahman 107, 110

Zeroual, Liamine 119–20, 122

Books of Related Interest

'Europeanization' and the Southern Periphery

Edited by **Kevin Featherstone** and **George Kazamias**

'Europeanization' is a term increasingly used in the social sciences to describe the impact, convergence or response of actors and institutions in relation to the European Union. Its increasing currency is a symptom of the broadening and deepening of the European integration process at the turn of the century. Its usage implies a common understanding, yet it is applied in a variety of different ways. This volume explores the concept in a variety of different settings in order to clarify its meaning.

176 pages 2000
0 7146 5087 0 cloth
0 7146 8128 8 paper

Perspectives on Development
The Euro-Mediterranean Partnership

Edited by **George Joffé**

The Euro-Mediterranean Partnership Initiative, launched by the Barcelona Conference in 1995, is the most ambitious project to date directed at comprehensive prosperity and security in the Mediterranean region. Yet the assumptions on which it is based are untried and untested. This study seeks to analyse what they are and to draw some conclusions as to the potential of the Initiative for success by comparing it with other experiences of regional development.

288 pages 1999
0 7146 4939 2 cloth
0 7146 4499 4 paper

The Euro-Mediterranean Partnership
Political and Economic Perspectives

Edited by **Richard Gillespie**

At the Barcelona Conference in November 1995, the European Union and twelve southern and eastern Mediterranean states established the Euro-Mediterranean Partnership (EMP). The initiative is one of the most ambitious external projects ever undertaken by the European Union.

200 pages 1997
0 7146 4822 1 cloth
0 7146 4370 X paper

FRANK CASS PUBLISHERS
Newbury House, 900 Eastern Avenue, Ilford, Essex, IG2 7HH
Tel: +44 (0)20 8599 8866 Fax: +44 (0)20 8599 0984 E-mail: info@frankcass.com
NORTH AMERICA
5804 NE Hassalo Street, Portland, OR 97213 3644, USA
Tel: 800 944 6190 Fax: 503 280 8832 E-mail: cass@isbs.com
Website: www.frankcass.com

Southern European Welfare States
Between Crisis and Reform
Edited by **Martin Rhodes**

Southern European welfare states – in common with their northern counterparts – are under stress, but they have only recently become the object of in-depth studies, exploring for the first time the particularities of the southern 'type' or 'model' of welfare.

296 pages 1997
0 7146 4788 8 cloth
0 7146 4344 0 paper

The Crisis of Representation in Europe
Edited by **Jack Hayward**

An assessment of the crisis ensuing from the political agenda of European integration. The contributors examine disparities between public opinion and integration into Europe in light of the 1994 European Elections.

226 pages 1995
0 7146 4656 3 cloth
0 7146 4184 7 paper

Federalism, Unification and European Integration
Edited by **Charlie Jeffery** and **Roland Sturm**

Focusing on Germany unity, this book discusses how an established, federal constitutional framework can meet the challenge of achieving German unification and integration.

184 pages 1993
0 7146 4507 9 cloth

The Regional Dimension of the European Union
Towards a Third Level in Europe?
Edited by **Charlie Jeffery**

As a result of such things as changes in EU structural funding rules, increasing importance of regional government and the effects of the Masstricht treaty, this study identifies a growing significance of regional tiers of government in EU politics. This has resulted in what Jeffery calls a shift to the 'Third Level' (regional) of EU government, alongside the first (union) and second (nation-state).

240 pages 1997
0 7146 4748 9 cloth
0 7146 4306 8 paper

FRANK CASS PUBLISHERS
Newbury House, 900 Eastern Avenue, Ilford, Essex, IG2 7HH
Tel: +44 (0)20 8599 8866 Fax: +44 (0)20 8599 0984 E-mail: info@frankcass.com
NORTH AMERICA
5804 NE Hassalo Street, Portland, OR 97213 3644, USA
Tel: 800 944 6190 Fax: 503 280 8832 E-mail: cass@isbs.com
Website: www.frankcass.com